Also by Emma Smith

This Is Shakespeare

Portable Magic

Portable Magic

A History of Books and Their Readers

EMMA SMITH

Alfred A. Knopf

New York

2022

THIS IS A BORZOI BOOK PUBLISHED BY ALFRED A. KNOPF

Copyright © 2022 by Emma Smith

All rights reserved. Published in the United States by Alfred A. Knopf, a division of Penguin Random House LLC, New York, and in Canada by Random House of Canada, a division of Penguin Random House Canada Limited, Toronto. Originally published in Britain by Allen Lane, an imprint of Penguin Random House UK, London, in 2022.

www.aaknopf.com

Knopf, Borzoi Books, and the colophon are registered trademarks of Penguin Random House LLC.

Library of Congress Cataloging-in-Publication data
Names: Smith, Emma (Emma Josephine), author.
Title: Portable magic : a history of books and their readers /
Emma Smith.
Description: First American edition. | New York : Alfred A. Knopf,
[2022] | Includes bibliographical references and index.
Identifiers: LCCN 2022018062 (print) | LCCN 2022018063 (ebook) |
ISBN 9781524749095 (hardcover) | ISBN 9780593081839 (trade
paperback) | ISBN 9781524749101 (ebook)
Subjects: LCSH: Books—History. | Books and reading—History. |
Book industries and trade—History. | Books—Anecdotes. |
Books and reading—Anecdotes.
Classification: LCC Z4.Z9 S63 2022 (print) | LCC Z4.Z9 (ebook) |
DDC 002.09—dc23/eng/20220521
LC record available at https://lccn.loc.gov/2022018062
LC ebook record available at https://lccn.loc.gov/2022018063

Cover design by Linda Huang

Manufactured in the United States of America

First American Edition

For Elizabeth Macfarlane

Contents

Portable Magic

Introduction:
Magic books

There was once a very learned man in the north-country who knew all the languages under the sun, and who was acquainted with all the mysteries of creation. He had one big book bound in black calf and clasped with iron, and with iron corners, and chained to a table which was made fast to the floor; and when he read out of this book, he unlocked it with an iron key, and none but he read from it, for it contained all the secrets of the spiritual world.

This is the opening to the folktale "The Master and His Pupil," first printed in English at the end of the nineteenth century but circulating long before. Even though you probably haven't read it, it may well seem familiar (that's pretty much the definition of a folktale). And when you read the start of the next paragraph—"Now the master had a pupil who was but a foolish lad"—it is probably clear already what will happen. This is a version of the sorcerer's apprentice tale, and the pupil will take his place in a line of hapless book handlers from Victor Frankenstein to Harry Potter. Like them, he will stumble into, read aloud inadvertently from, or otherwise mishandle this magic book, with terrible consequences.

Sure enough, the boy opens the book, which has been left unlocked by the master. As he reads from its red-and-black printed pages, there is a clap of thunder. The room darkens. Before him there appears "a horrible, horrible form, breathing fire and with eyes like burning lamps. It was the demon Beelzebub, whom he had called up to serve him." Asked by this terrifying apparition to set him to a task, the pupil panics. In a strangely domestic moment, he asks the demon to water a potted geranium. The demon complies, but he repeats the action over and over, until the house is awash, "and would have drowned all Yorkshire." The master returns in the nick of time, to speak the countercharm that sends the demon back into the pages of the book.

In the massive compendium of folklore motifs compiled by the American folklorist Stith Thompson in the early twentieth century, this story type is traced across various European languages. Categorized as D, "Magic": subsection 1421.1.3: "magic book summons genie," its exemplars across many centuries range from Icelandic to Lithuanian traditions. Each of these iterations shares an outline. A magical or powerful book is kept under the control of a learned man—a minister, magician, or scholar. While he is temporarily absent, some unskilled person in his household—a child, servant, or friend—finds the book and accidentally summons a devil.

The story captures a widespread fear that books are

powerful and dangerous in the wrong hands. What makes the master the master, and the pupil the pupil, is their ept or inept use of the book: it is the object that secures their relative positions. It is an active agent of social differentiation, conferring status upon its handler. This is absolutely not a parable of books as democratic objects, available to all. Once the pupil can manipulate the book of knowledge effectively, he will become the master. But this is exactly what makes the book a potential disruptor of social hierarchies.

Anxieties about books' disruptive power had begun to intensify in the sixteenth century: in one early version of the story, performed for a culture newly enamored of the products of mechanical printing, an intellectually restless scholar uses them as go-betweens in his conversation with devils, swapping infernal knowledge for an immortal soul. In this, Christopher Marlowe's *Doctor Faustus* departed from its predecessors in German folklore: the original Faustian pact traded directly with the devil. But Marlowe was speaking to the Renaissance world of knowledge created by the printing press, which had made books more present, more prevalent, and more liable to fall into the wrong hands (that Faust, or Fust, was also the name of Johannes Gutenberg's business partner in his print shop may be a coincidence, but it is a delicious one).

The sense of books' shadowy magic continued to accrue force as the printing press compounded its cultural dominance. Glossing "The Master and His Pupil" in his 1890 compilation of *English Fairy Tales*, folklorist Joseph Jacobs suggests that the magician's spell has "long been used for raising the ———": his omission of the word "devil" reveals that he, like the learned man in the North Country, is invested in the power of the printed word. Jacobs's book, which was also responsible for popularizing such familiar stories as Tom Thumb, Dick Whittington, the Three Little Pigs, and Jack and the Beanstalk, is implied to possess the power of the sorcerer's book of magic: the reader is advised "not [to] read the lines out when alone," since "one never knows what may happen."

In a tale told with pared-down simplicity, the detail of the book's description in "The Master and His Pupil" is striking: we know more about what it looks like than either of the human protagonists, who are scarcely characterized at all. That's because the book is at the center of the story. While its contents are only implied, its outward appearance visualizes its magical powers. Originally, the book features described had a practical purpose, but by the time of the story they had come to connote antique and powerful learning. For example, when books were stored flat rather than upright, as was common practice until the late seventeenth century, their corners needed protection. Metal cornerpieces were thus first practical, and later decorative, aspects of bookbinding. Metal clasps also initially had a practical purpose, preventing pages made from vellum—calfskin—from curling or buckling in damp conditions. Later, when they were no longer needed, because paper leaves were less susceptible to their environment, clasps were nevertheless retained on some volumes to symbolize the important, precious, or secret content between the book's covers. Buy a modern tween a physical diary, for example, and that book may well include a lockable plastic clasp in retro imitation, conferring a heightened sense of privacy on their adolescent confessions.

A clasped book also demanded a certain physical ceremony. Writing in the early fourteenth century, explaining and defending his own ruinously expensive book habit, Richard de Bury admonished careless handling of books: "In the first place as to the opening and closing of books, let there be due moderation, that they be not unclasped in precipitate haste, nor when we have finished our inspection be put away without being duly closed." Opening and closing the clasp was part of a ritual of respect for the book and its contents, a ritual that should be afforded proper care and time. The medieval-ish leather-bound volume with metal clasps described in the story thus has a range of visual connotations, with magic, with scripture and ritual, and with storytelling itself.

In the story, the master is culpable because he left the book unclasped, leaving its esoteric secrets open to the unworthy. And attached to a table, his book evokes the history of chaining valuable books in university and cathedral libraries in the Middle Ages and well beyond (the Bodleian Library in Oxford stopped chaining books in 1769; the last Oxford college unchained theirs in 1799). All these features combine to create a venerable, occult, and valuable book: part Bible, part grimoire, or book of spells. Archetypal and potent, these books look and behave in particular ways. They are large and leather-bound. They are written in Latin, or in other unfamiliar languages or scripts. They are old. And they are actively powerful, especially in the wrong hands.

This darker aspect of books' efficacy has persisted in the numerous reiterations of this story into the modern era. In Disney's 1940 version of the story, retold as the most popular of the animated episodes in *Fantasia*, the sorcerer, complete with long beard and fearsome eyebrows, was allegedly modeled on Walt himself. Wearing a long robe and a pointed hat with astrological symbols, he conjures his spirits from a volume open on his magic desk-altar. Amid the flood caused by his usurpation of these magical powers, Mickey Mouse scrabbles onto this floating book. Surfing the waters aboard the book, he desperately leafs through its pages, looking for the magic antidote. Here, "The Sorcerer's Apprentice" resonates with its own period, and with a contemporary Hollywood transformed aesthetically and culturally by Jewish émigrés from Europe, including the talented abstract animator on *Fantasia*, Oskar Fischinger. The horrifying image of the multiplying broomsticks marching in fascist lockstep, their nightmarish shadows cast menacingly on the wall, echoes the topical iconography of Nazi military power. The apprentice has summoned forth a cinematic sequence from Leni Riefenstahl. The powerfully dangerous sorcerer's book thus resonates with another necromantic volume, *Mein Kampf,* and its dark arts of national resurgence and racial purity (see Chapter 11).

I've begun with the tale of "The Master and His Pupil" for two reasons. The first is a sentimental attachment to this parable of dangerous and transformative bookishness firmly, if unexpectedly, located in Yorkshire, the "north-country." I was born and brought up in Leeds, West Yorkshire, and took my own first, inexperienced forays into the world of books at Bramley library, a pleasure dome unpromisingly concealed within a single-story 1920s brick building in a grimy postindustrial suburb. I can remember the scruffy parquet floor, the low stands of picture books, and the child-sized chairs. My library tactic was a kind of reading triage, quickly assessing which books might be consumed there and then, reserving the precious places on my library card for stories that I could savor during the week. For me, as for many people, it was the public lending library that taught me about books as objects, as well as about fantastic worlds (see Chapter 9).

But the second reason is more significant. The story of "The Master and His Pupil" establishes the central premise of my argument here, because it makes clear that it is the book itself, as much as its contents, that has agency. It's the book that summons the demon, not its clumsy reader. It functions as a material talisman rather than a simple repository for magical information. The case I want to make over the course of this book is that what's superficially evident in the depiction and understanding of books of spells is actually true of all books. All books are magic. All books have agency and power in the real world, the power to summon demons and to dispatch them. They are, as Stephen King puts it in his terrific memoir, *On Writing*, from which I have taken my title, "a uniquely portable magic." And a book's magic always inheres in its form, including that portability, as much as in its content.

A thick paperback with block lettering, or a number of small, neat volumes, or a landscape-format book—these would not work in Joseph Jacobs's story, because their forms conjure other sorts of content than spells. Just as it is vital that the magic book in the fairy tale has a black leather binding with iron furniture, so the apparently incidental forms that our own books take are inseparable from their meanings. And they, too, are talismanic, even if they don't have obviously special finishes. We tend to understand our engagement with books in emotional or cognitive terms, rather than in tactile or sensory ones. We emphasize the encounter with the book's contents rather than the feel of it in our hands, the rustle of its pages, the smell of its binding. But if you think about the books that have been important to you, it may well be that their content is inseparable from the form in which you encountered them.

My much-loved childhood Gerald Durrell, especially

his animal collecting, documented in the fascinating *The Bafut Beagles* and *A Zoo in My Luggage*, for example, will always be in the yellowish wrappers of World Books. This was the mail-order book club from which my unbookish grandparents bought most of their small library in the 1950s. These hardback volumes in their faded dust jackets seem somehow connected to the dry savannas and pith-helmet world of Durrell's colonial expeditions captured within them. I was in awe of my copy of Jan Pieńkowski's wonderful piece of pop-up book architecture, *Haunted House*, forever reminded that its spooky slide transitions, tabs, and flaps were fragile, and always therefore feeling myself too clumsy to ever enjoy its cheerfully ghoulish fairground aesthetic. The edition of Thomas Hardy's *Tess of the d'Urbervilles* we had at school was most remarkable for its transparent cover film that called irresistibly to be peeled back, leaving behind a washed-out still of Nastassja Kinski wearing a straw hat from Roman Polanski's 1979 film: later, weakened by these depredations, I think my copy had to be backed in wallpaper left over from our spare bedroom. My *Tess* is part ghostly reproduction, part blue sprig on a cream background. It is a specific physical edition that thus triggers a quite different reading experience from other versions, such as Hardy's weekly serial, originally published in the illustrated newspaper *The Graphic* in 1891; or the novel released in three volumes that year; or the single volume that followed the year later; or the beautiful collectors' copy bound in purple cloth and illustrated with contemporary woodcuts now available from an upmarket publisher; or the large-format student annotation edition, with extra-wide line spacing and margins for notes and explanatory commentary in preparation for exams.

These editions and copies may all reproduce the same story (although Hardy substantially edited the serial version for the novel), but they are not the same book and thus not the same encounter: we read them differently. Form matters. Form captures a book's historical and cultural moment; form has its own politics and ideology; we read form almost unconsciously as an aggregate of the senses before, and alongside, reading the words on the page.

Portable Magic, then, is a book about books, rather than words. Words can be reissued in numerous forms and are subject to redefinition by those forms; books are stubbornly, irreducibly present. David Scott Kastan calls this distinction the difference between writing as "platonic," or essential, and books as "pragmatic," or contingent. It is this materiality that is our focus here. *Portable Magic* is not a study of platonic writing but a book about pragmatic books. Literary works don't exist in some ideal and immaterial state: they are made of paper and leather and labor and handling. I want us to explore and celebrate this material heft, and the wonderful undersung inseparability of book form and book content. And not just in the hallowed halls of libraries and collectors, where histories of the book have tended to hang out (although there, too): the books here are everyday rather than aristocratic, mass market and marked with a coffee ring rather than unique and kept in a glass case. Still, form works its magic on them all. The saucy cover of Jilly Cooper's blockbuster *Riders*, for instance, with its gold lettering, curvaceous jodhpured bottom, and opulent fan of pages, perfectly establishes its tone and presents its bulk as a pleasurable wodge of leisure time. In the eighth century, the early Christian missionary St. Boniface requested from a monastery a copy of the epistles of St. Peter lettered in gold so that he might present the new religion to wealthy "carnal" men in the Frankish empire in the terms of temporal value that they would understand. The first issues of Dickens's novel *Bleak House*, serialized in nineteen blue-green paper-covered installments in 1852–53, were framed by pages of advertisements. Perhaps the Siphonia pocket raincoat, available from the manufacturers Edmiston's, close by the Adelphi Theatre, was intended as a practical antidote to the "soft black drizzle" and fog that memorably envelops London at the opening of *Bleak House*: one effect of these commercials is to align the novel's appeal with consumer rather than literary culture. What the thick bonkbuster, the luxury scriptures, and the consumerist serial share is the material combination of form and content that I want to call "bookhood."

"Bookhood" is a nineteenth-century coinage on the model of more familiar forms such as "childhood" or "brotherhood," and one due for revival. It suggests the book's physical autonomy and life-ishness: "the state or condition of being a book," as the *Oxford English Dictionary* puts it. I like it because it encourages us to think about books from the perspective of the book itself, and because it helps focus attention on its physical engagement with the senses beyond sight, and with activities beyond reading. Bookhood includes the impact of touch, smell, and hearing on the experience of books. It focuses on paper, on binding, on cover illustrations, on bookselling, libraries, and collections. It explores how size creates meaning and shapes expectations. It registers the particular bodily gestures and vocabulary that we all use with books: long before we learned to swipe or pinch screens, we had to learn to thumb pages. Bookhood is a dog-eared page corner, or spines arranged on a shelf. We acknowledge it when we prefer a stitched binding to one of those glued ones from which the leaves inevitably drift, when we buy a collectors' edition or track down the specific cover of a childhood favorite in a secondhand bookshop, or when we recall, imprinted photographically in our memory, an illustration, or that a particular relevant phrase or reference was on the left-hand page about two thirds of the way down. Bookhood is remembering the smell and feel of a loved story, not just its plot or characters. Instead of making the book somehow transparent, simply a technological means to deliver its words, bookhood renders the book object more opaque, more present, more material. "In normal reading," writes Garrett Stewart, in a book about books made into art objects, "books are to some degree vaporized by attention." Away with this normal reading! *Portable Magic* challenges this immateriality, reminding us instead that our reading is always conditioned by our consciousness of the book itself and its inalienable bookhood.

For bookhood is an intrinsic part of reading, even if often a subconscious one. We all register the size and weight of a book, the texture of the paper and the design of the typeface. We know what it is like to operate: how tight the binding is, and whether it requires two hands to hold it open. We clock the cover and the clues about the content of the book that might be signaled in its design, we know whether its spine is cracked, or its jacket scuffed, or its dark matte finish susceptible to fingerprints (Penguin Classics: I'm looking at you). We may work through it, marking our place with fingers or folded corners, or a bound ribbon, or a train ticket, a postcard, or pressed flowers, between its pages. Or we may use its multidimensional physicality in other ways: yoga block, doorstop, flyswatter, flower press, deportment aid. We are conscious of its smell: the chemical high of ink or treated paper, the vegetal residue of human touch. Researchers have generated a historic book odor wheel, with smell categories including almonds, rotten socks, smoke, vinegar, and musty (top tip: should you want to remove a bad book smell, perhaps of damp or cigarette smoke, leave the volume in a sealed box with some clean cat litter); numerous perfumeries have attempted a book scent, from Demeter Fragrance Library: Paperback to Biblioteca de Babel by Fueguia 1833 ("notes of old book pages turned yellow, book bindings, and the polished wood of book cases").

All these sensory engagements, all these haptic activities, are different depending on the precise contours of the particular book in your hand. It's why buying a new edition of a much-loved book is always somehow alienating, even a betrayal. Jorge Luis Borges, the Argentinian writer and critic whose work is so preoccupied with imaginary books, stories, and impossible libraries, professed himself intellectually uninterested "in the physical aspects of books." Nevertheless, he recalled with warmth what a specific edition of a book that he had studied for a lifetime, *Don Quixote*, had meant to him:

> I still remember the red bindings with gilt titles of the Garnier edition. Eventually, after my father's library was broken up and I read *Don Quixote* in another edition, I had the feeling that it was not the real *Don Quixote*. Later a friend obtained for me a Garnier copy with the same engravings, the same footnotes, and the same errata. For me, all these things were part of the book; in my mind, this was the real *Don Quixote*.

Thus emotions run high where books and book behavior are concerned: posting an image of a thick volume cut in half to make it more portable, the culprit outed himself on social media as a "book-murderer." Ask any group of readers about their habits of writing in the margins of their books or inscribing their name and you will get a range of strongly held views. It's hard to imagine another inanimate object provoking similar outrage. As John Milton put it *Areopagitica*, his 1644 defense of "the liberty of unlicensed printing" prompted by the arrest of the bookseller John Lilburne for importing subversive books, "Books are not absolutely dead things, but do contain a potency of life in them." That life is located in their physical form as much as in their metaphysical content. And as the context for Milton's much-quoted phrase acknowledges, bookhood travels far beyond consumer pleasure: sometimes, as we will see, books become proxies, standing in for human readers and suffering some of their displaced punishments and degradations. Books' materiality places them at the center of larger debates about justice, liberty, and cultural value.

Acknowledging bookhood demands that we resist the tendency to idealize them. Books are wonderful, challenging, transporting—but sometimes also sickening, disturbing, enraging. As in the book of magic with which we began, their meanings, forms, and consequences are not innocent, or sentimental, or always nice. Discussing the books bound in human skin in Chapter 13 transposes bibliophilia, or the love of books, into a distinctly discordant key; thinking about forced conversions in Puritan New England (Chapter 15) fingers the book as a morally compromised agent in the colonial encounter.

Not all books are *The Very Hungry Caterpillar*, although that book's physical playfulness also sounds a note of caution. Eric Carle's first proposal was for a book about Willi the Worm, a bookworm nibbling through pages: this early iteration gives *The Very Hungry Caterpillar* a symbolic quality, in which what is being gobbled eagerly up is not so much the—to me in the 1970s, unspeakably exotic—pickle, watermelon, salami, and cherry pie, but rather the book itself. Carle's allegory of reading makes clear that, as the caterpillar discovers, hungrily consuming books can give us a stomachache.

Often books about books glow with a rosy nostalgia for childhood reading, or map with delight the lifetime companionship of a much-loved novel or the inventive transformations of a canonical text across time and media. That's to say, they are about books as containers for fictional worlds, characters, and ideas, not about books as distinctive manufactured objects conveying their own meanings that shape, and are shaped by, their readers. What's more, books about books tend to be about nice books shaping thoughtful, refined, and creative people rather than about dangerous books with potentially malign effects. The material books in this book you are reading can be tricky, sometimes vicious; they have the power to misinform and manipulate as well as to comfort and educate. They are the symbols and the tools of unequal power relations, inscribing across their horizontal openings vertical social hierarchies—as here between master and pupil, and elsewhere between adult and child, and between colonizer and colonized. As Walter Benjamin, cultural critic, philosopher, and bibliophile, mournfully observed under the shadow of the Third Reich, "there is no document of civilization which is not at the same time a document of barbarism." He wasn't directly talking about books, but he should have been. To understand our long love affair with the book, we need to recognize its dark side. This is a relationship in which each partner has the capacity to abuse the other: books can crack our spines, loosen our leaves, mark us with their dirty fingers, and write in our margins just as much as we can theirs.

So, *Portable Magic* is an alternative, sometimes sideways, history of the book in human hands. It charts and reinterprets key milestones in book history from Gutenberg (Chapter 1) to Kindle (Chapter 16), tracing different patterns of book production and use through different case studies, including a wartime edition of a biography of Queen Victoria designed for a soldier's uniform pocket (Chapter 2); a photograph of Marilyn Monroe reading *Ulysses* (Chapter 4); a rare book recounting a terrible natural disaster sunk with the *Titanic* (Chapter 6). As it is organized neither chronologically nor geographically but by theme, I hope that the chapters can be read in any order, depending on whether you think you are interested in Madame de Pompadour or the Gutenberg Bible, school library censorship or queer collage, diaspora or design. Later in the book (Chapter 7), I discuss the long history of dipping at random into a book to gain insight or advice, known, following the initial deployment of Virgil for this literary and ethical tombola, as *sortes Virgilianae*. In this spirit, you might want to think of reading *Portable Magic* not as a long-term chore but as a kind of *sortes Smithianus.*

You may feel that this book should have been heavily illustrated, but the two-dimensional representation of these irredeemably three-dimensional objects always disappoints. Changing book technology has made pictures—in the manuscript books of hours, or in the modern exhibition catalogue—differently available to book producers at different times, but I hope that here I can draw on the historic capacity of books to describe and make vivid material objects through words, from the clock at the start of *The Life and Opinions of Tristram Shandy, Gentleman* to the richly imagined locations of Genesis, or Gilead, or Gormenghast. An inextricable part of the magic of the book is that it is fertile, generative of other worlds.

My point throughout is that the books that are on your bedside table or propping up your computer monitor, those volumes given to friends or family, inscribed by their givers or scribbled in by children, heavily thumbed and falling apart or pristine and unfingered, inherited, borrowed, devoured, treasured, organized by author, topic, size, color—these books are important. They are vital exemplars of a resilient technology that has barely changed over more than a millennium but that has changed us, our habits, and our culture. Materiality is not just a property of rare or special books, although that's where specialists have tended to cut their teeth. Books are culturally and materially important precisely because they are democratic and everyday, not because they are too valuable to touch. Instead of meeting remarkable manuscripts at one remove, we can all run into amazing books that record rich, varied, sometimes troubled histories, both personal and political.

When I had the great privilege of uncovering a rare Shakespeare first edition in a chilly Scottish library, the thrill as I worked through the minutiae of its watermarks and the details of its printing to check its authenticity was more physical than intellectual. In three large volumes, each propped on a foam rest, the book's linen-rag paper was softened by centuries of fingers turning the pages. An inscription from an eighteenth-century scholar registered it as a bequest from a friend, reminding me of books' unique place as tokens of human affection (Chapter 3). But I'm not sure that that wonderful and valuable once-in-a-lifetime First Folio really meant more to me than many more immediate, mundane, magical book encounters: my battered large-format Asterix comic books, or the anticipatory wedge of unread detective thrillers saved for holidays, or my grandmother's Edwardian school-prize poetry book, its spine repaired by a local bookbinder for her eightieth birthday, or the pleasing compact weight of the cream-and-black Everyman hardbacks with their ribbon bookmarks, or the acrid smell of a new, illustrated exhibition catalogue. While some books do have old-master price tags, really, books are ordinary things that become special in the unpredictable and unique human connections they embody and extend. We all encounter rare and valuable books all the time.

Birdwatchers are alert to the particular, distinctive combination of avian affect, movement, and presence that they call giss: I've tried to transfer that delighted awareness of the specific to my account of books. I hope that *Portable Magic* will make you more appreciative of all the book giss, the bookhood, of your own life and library.

I

Beginnings: East, West, and Gutenberg

A small band of survivors finds sanctuary in the Beaux Arts arcades of the New York Public Library on Fifth Avenue. Outside, a flooded Manhattan is freezing solid in sudden subarctic temperatures. Only the tip of the Statue of Liberty's lamp and her pointed coronet are visible above the ice plains. Far away, politicians argue about their response to the climate catastrophe gripping the northern hemisphere: meanwhile, a grizzled climatologist in parka and snowshoes is trekking through epic cold to keep a promise to his teenage son.

The group ransacks the shelves for fuel to keep warm. Librarians make a vain attempt to protect their collections. A scuffle about the value of Nietzsche—most important nineteenth-century thinker or chauvinist pig in love with his sister?—is averted by the discovery of the tax law section, which all agree can be readily consigned to the fire. The next crisis over resources comes when a librarian (cue buttoned-up duffle coat and heavy glasses screaming "book nerd") refuses to surrender the large leather-bound volume he is clutching on his knees. The Gutenberg Bible. "Do you think God will save you?" is the sarcastic retort. The man's reply makes clear that it is not the scriptural contents he is clinging on to. Rather, he delivers an impromptu eulogy for the importance of this object as an artifact of human ingenuity and progress: "I'm protecting it. This bible is the first book ever printed. It represents the dawn of the age of reason. As far as I'm concerned, the written word is mankind's greatest achievement. If western civilization's finished, I'm going to save at least one little piece of it." In a paradoxical symbolic twist, the NYPL copy of the Gutenberg Bible comes to represent something like the secular enlightenment, or even humanity itself.

The occasion for this heartfelt defense of a book amid a general bibliocide is Roland Emmerich's climate-disaster movie *The Day After Tomorrow* (2004). It seems like a throwaway vignette (and yes, of course they should have burned the chairs and shelves first, given how unsatisfactory books are as fuel) but is in fact a crucial plot pivot. Recognizing the value of this specific book redirects the film from a story of human helplessness in the face of nature to a celebration of human technology and resourcefulness. Hero-dad and Gutenberg (often dubbed the "father of printing") together secure humanity's postapocalyptic future, reassuring us that something important can survive Armageddon. But to understand the role of the Gutenberg Bible in larger narratives of books' and human progress, we need to flesh out the film's hyperbolic cultural and historical claims. Is this the beginning of our long love affair with books? Was this the first book ever printed? Does Gutenberg's Bible represent "mankind's greatest achievement"? And what is its relationship to "western civilization"? As we'll see, the answers to these questions are sometimes disobliging to cherished myths of origin, enmeshing the printed book within a larger, more combative and political narrative. It's good to be reminded from the start that books—their production, their form, and their content—are never neutral.

Johann, or Johannes, Gutenberg has earned his place in history as the inventor of movable type. This enabled text to be set from individual letters and then reproduced multiple times using a printing press. It is to book production what opposable thumbs are to primate evolution. Like all origin stories, this one overlooks a good deal in order to produce a single, heroic starting point, but let's go with it for now. Born in Mainz on the River Rhine around 1400, Gutenberg trained as a goldsmith and was later involved in various enterprises, including wine-making. Both these crafts had an impact on the development of printing, which required both the fine metal work of individual pieces of type known as sorts and the reengineering of a grape-press mechanism to create print impressions. Gutenberg's entrepreneurial attempts to mass-produce relic-viewing mirrors for a popular pilgrimage site also suggest an inclination toward innovative technologies of reproduction. These skills, combined with the capital of a new business partner, the wealthy lawyer-goldsmith Johann Fust, fed his audacious print experiment.

To produce the new commodity of the printed book, everything—from type to appropriately prepared paper to ink—needed to be reengineered. But in some significant ways, the mechanically printed Bible wasn't such a radical break with the handwritten books that came before (and continued after). While the printing press clearly was a game-changer for the speed of book production, preparing the complete Bible for print publication was still a hugely time-consuming enterprise. The Gutenberg Bible ran to 1,282 pages, split across two volumes. Each page had two columns and, with a few exceptions, forty-two lines per column (the book is sometimes known as the 42-line Bible because of this). It probably took six pressmen about two years' work in total to produce the 170 or so copies that were printed. Just like its manuscript forebears, this labor-intensive product was a distinctly elite commodity.

The finished Bibles appeared in 1455. The numbers involved really remind us of the materiality of these books. The majority were printed on paper, but a small proportion were produced on the substrate associated with the work of scribes—vellum, or calfskin—which could be sold at four or five times the price of the paper copies. To make up the Bibles, which measure around 42 by 30 centimeters—a little smaller than modern A3 format—would have required five thousand calf skins from five thousand calves for the vellum copies, and fifty times that number of sheets of rag or linen paper. The paper was produced in Piedmont and sent over the Alps and then by barge to Mainz. It is all a big supply-chain effort.

Gutenberg's Bibles were all printed in the Gothic script associated with missals (priests' service books) and other liturgical volumes, but the neat appearance of the compact type form actually serves to obscure its innovation. The printed pages look like continuous handwritten script. The forty-eight complete or substantially complete extant copies have an appearance that is thus part new world of print, part old world of manuscript. We are used to new technologies adopting the terminology and taxonomic structures of the older ones they apparently supersede. Computing, for instance, has taken up the analogue office iconography of files, folders, directories, desktop, notebook; digital photography includes the redundant but resonant sound of a shutter opening and closing; e-books mimic the layout and page-turning effects of their print antecedents (Chapter 16). This phenomenon of new technologies aping their predecessors is called skeuomorphic design. In similar ways, Gutenberg's printed book doffed its aesthetic and organizational cap to the manuscript predecessors it was attempting to both imitate and unseat. The two text columns and the Gothic typeface aligned the reading experience with that of manuscript—but, beyond this, rubrication (highlighting in red), illuminated capitals, and colorful marginal scrollwork were usually added to the Bibles after they left the print shop. This decorative supplement not only drew on the visual conventions of the manuscript tradition but was in fact supplied by its experienced scribes. Thus the book often credited with being the first in print was actually designed to be completed by hand, inaugurating a long tradition of readers finalizing or perfecting their books (Chapter 14).

In other ways, Gutenberg's return to a large lectern-style Bible also looked backward rather than forward. His retro choice of format recalled popular Bible books of previous centuries, in contrast to the small, portable scriptural books that had recently been popular. Like many technological innovations, then, this printed book was actually a technological and aesthetic step backward (like those stilted early talkies, hampered by the need for the actors to keep close to the microphone). Manuscript books had developed an elaborate visual mise-en-page: the (initially) unadorned and cumbersome Gutenberg was a much less beautiful and decorative book than its predecessors.

Regardless, the new book made an immediate splash. Looking at its printed pages against a strong light, it's possible to see one of three different watermarks—an ox, a bull's head, or a grape cluster. It's clear from these different stocks of papers that Gutenberg made a second order for supplies during the production process, suggesting that he revised his original print forecast upward. This must have been in response to promising presales. One excited cleric, later Pope Pius II, wrote to his superior that he had seen, or heard from others about, some printed quires (bundles of folded sheets) from this new Bible at Frankfurt, and could testify that "the script is extremely neat and legible" such that "your grace would be able to read it without effort, and indeed, without glasses." The book can indeed be read relatively easily from a distance of about a meter, suggesting its practical usefulness in church services in low-light settings. (An alternative history of the book would be via a history of reading glasses, which were first depicted in a 1352 portrait of Hugh of Saint-Cher by the Italian painter Tommaso da Modena.) But the enthusiast reported that it would now be difficult to acquire one of the new Bibles, since it appears that the print run was sold out before publication. Despite this success, Gutenberg's printed books could not balance his account books. Even with the goldsmith's investment, both the Bible and Gutenberg's printing career were over at the same time. The business was bankrupt by the end of 1455, and the printing equipment confiscated by Fust.

So far, then, so familiar. Gutenberg invents printing and everyone flocks to buy the new books. But not so fast. Printing was not simply the work of one entrepreneurial visionary and his banker. There was a broader international context, too. Printing was not, in fact, previously unknown—it just hadn't traveled to Europe, because the demand wasn't there: hitherto, the continent had been broadly content with limited access to literacy and to written texts. The scriptorium method of manuscript production was adequate for this restricted market. We tend to think of printing as leading to the wider circulation of texts, but there's something to be said for flipping cause and effect: the innovation was a response to increased demand. "This book . . . is not written with pen and ink as other books [have been], to the end that every man may have them at once," as William Caxton, Gutenberg's English acolyte, put it in the first book published in London. Early printing was too time intensive to realize this democratic dream, but the direction of travel was clear and irreversible. There was a growing market for the products of the printing press. It was this potential customer base that created the economic and entrepreneurial incentive to develop it.

Gutenberg was a savvy businessman who targeted his market carefully. His decision to produce a complete Latin Bible, based on the Vulgate edition, rather than the more common missals that organized biblical passages around the Church year, reveals that he was aiming at a substantial international readership far beyond the streets of Mainz. He was also plugging a gap in the manuscript market, making use of the new printing technology to produce a substantial text that was relatively rare (most biblical manuscripts were of the Gospels, or the separate Testaments, or Psalms). This doctrinal branding of what was, at heart, a moneymaking project was picked up by John Foxe when he wrote in his expansive sixteenth-century history of the Protestant Reformation that printing was "a divine and miraculous" gift from God, "to convince darkness by light, error by truth, ignorance by learning." Later historians would also align the print revolution with the rise of Protestantism, particularly because the works of the reformist theologian

Martin Luther were among the first international best sellers of the print revolution.

But the immediate religious context was rather different. The ambitious Bible was not Gutenberg's first printing project: his press had already produced a grammar textbook, a poem, a Papal Indulgence (a spiritual voucher allowing time off from Purgatory), and, most interestingly, a topical pamphlet, printed in German in December 1454 as *Eyn manung der cristenheit widder die durken* (*A Warning to Christendom against the Turks*). That this last text includes the first printed New Year greeting ("Eijn gut selig nuwe jar") has tended to obscure the larger geopolitical project to which Gutenberg's press was immediately enlisted: the war against Islam.

In May 1453 the Byzantine Christian capital Constantinople had fallen to the besieging Ottoman army, led by the young Sultan Mehmed II. It became an Islamic city renamed Istanbul, and the Ottoman capital. This event shocked Europe. The fall of Constantinople was feared as a clear and present danger to Christendom, although local rivalries prevented any coordinated response. From the start, Gutenberg's emerging print work was intertwined with discussions about possible military action across the German states, and it capitalized on the fraught relations between Christianity and Islam. The event in Frankfurt from which excited reports of the new printed Bible emerged was on the fringes of a meeting of European nobles and princes of the Church that had been called to discuss ways of rallying public support for a military campaign against the Turks. Just before their Bible emerged from the presses, Gutenberg and his associates were on hand to promote their new product and present some samples. Large-scale Bibles must have looked like a canny sales opportunity at a time when Christendom felt itself under threat: their very size reimposed Christian dominance. In turbulent times, these big books proclaimed that, like the religion they embodied, they were here to stay. We might compare them with the miniature Bibles with small script developed in the different context of the thirteenth century for Dominican and Franciscan friars to carry on their preaching itineraries: the formats tell us something about the state of Christianity as well as the intended use of the volumes.

So it was printed anti-Turkish material, not the Gutenberg Bible, that opened the publishing floodgates—but perhaps we should see the 1455 Bible as an explicit salvo in that religious war. The so-called *Turcica* that followed in its wake was an explosion of print, in genres from woodcuts and ballads to orations and treatises, all designed to meet an insatiable public demand for material about the Ottomans and to debate the question of a new crusade to retake Constantinople. Demand for this Turkish material helped drive print technology rapidly across northern Europe and beyond: within thirty years there were over a hundred printing towns, including London, and by the end of the fifteenth century that number had doubled. The Gutenberg Bible, and the printing industry itself, thus emerged in response to the religious geopolitics of the fifteenth century. It was a more specifically ideological intervention than is often acknowledged, less impartial and more specific and sectarian. That fictional NYPL librarian's claim about "western civilization" takes on a more adversarial quality in this context: East–West conflict shaped his precious Bible and its initial reception in the fifteenth century, and it has continued to shape our print culture in ongoing and indelible ways.

The cultural status of the Gutenberg Bible reproduces a myth of Western superiority. Assertions about Gutenberg's primacy, such as that in Emmerich's fictionalized New York Public Library, have fallen for its original propaganda. We tend systematically to downplay the pre-Gutenberg histories of print and to ignore the prior histories of textual reproduction outside Europe. The resulting incomplete narrative serves to align mechanical printing with the European Renaissance and early humanism in a triumphant story of the dominance of Western Enlightenment values. But although the Bible printed in Mainz in the middle of the fifteenth century is a cultural milestone, it is not the earliest book nor the first to use movable type. Some of the prominent precursors of Gutenberg's Bible should be a bit more famous as print milestones. The British Library has a five-meter scroll of Buddhist scripture, *The Diamond Sutra*, printed in 868 (according to the Western calendar). Found in northwest China at the beginning of

the twentieth century and comprising columns of characters and an illustrative frontispiece, it is the earliest
dated example of block printing. Chinese and Korean
pioneers of print predated Gutenberg by centuries, and
the relatively low cost of bamboo-fiber paper in East
Asia meant that early print was a less elite technology in
these regions. Chinese print technology developed movable type, made of clay and used to make an imprint on
paper without a press. Paper technology was also refined
by Chinese innovation during the Later Han period (by
the second century CE): of course, Buddhist, Jain, and
Hindu book cultures would not adopt parchment, the
skin of young animals, including cows. The paper pioneer Cai Lun (died 121 CE) reported that "silk is dear and
bamboo heavy, so they are not convenient to use," and
had the idea to use tree bark, hemp, rags, and fishnets to
make "silk-like writing material." Paper availability and
widespread literacy drove commercial printing in China
by the Tang Dynasty (seventh–ninth centuries CE), and
the first woodblock edition of the canon of Confucian
classics dates from the tenth century. The oldest datable
book printed using movable type is written in Chinese
by a Korean Buddhist monk. Only the second volume
of the work is extant, now in the Bibliothèque Nationale in Paris. Known by the abbreviated title *Jikji*, it is a
compilation of Buddhist teaching and dates from 1377.
By the beginning of the fifteenth century, printing and
distributing books in the interests of good government
was an explicit policy of King Taejong, who ordered

the casting of sets of metal type to enable widespread print penetration across Korea. So, the idea that print is a European invention simply doesn't stand up: it is a Western myth. Seen from a more global perspective, the question about Gutenberg seems less "How did you do it?" and more "What took you so long?"

The Gutenberg myth is one of the most striking examples of the amnesia intrinsic to traditional narratives of the Renaissance, which have tended to obliterate the role of technical, cultural, and scientific discoveries and scholarship in Islamic and East Asian cultures and to naturalize the spread of Protestantism across northern Europe as the precursor of the Enlightenment. To put it another way, it's a history written by the winners. Observing the overthrow of the Ancien Régime in Revolutionary France, Louis Lavicomterie apostrophized Gutenberg: "Blessed be the inventor of the printing press. It is to him we owe this wondrous revolution." Victor Hugo's comparison of Gutenberg to Jesus—"In the action of Christ bringing forth the loaves, there is Gutenberg bringing forth the books. One sower heralds the other . . . Gutenberg is forever the auxiliary of life"—is a hyperbolic version of the Western-centric framing of the establishment of print.

Gutenberg's central role in stories of cultural progress was retrospectively corroborated by the importance of print technology to European colonization. Religious presses set up in the sixteenth century by the Jesuits in Goa and Macao and by the Spanish in Mexico City and

Lima were the precursors of colonial printing across the global south. It was such a common traveling trope that Thomas More adopted it for his fictional Utopia early in the sixteenth century, supplying his voyagers with book exemplars from Aldus Manutius's Venetian printing house so that the Utopians could teach themselves printing. Later colonists also took with them print technology. The first book published in Australia was a collection of government proclamations and rules prepared by the transported London printer George Howe in 1802; a Maori New Testament in 1837 published by the Cornishman William Colenso on behalf of the Church Missionary Society was the first printed book in New Zealand, followed in short order by *Ropitini Koruhu*, a translation of Defoe's *Robinson Crusoe*; Presbyterian missionaries established printing in Nigeria in the middle of the nineteenth century. Christian evangelists brought printed books as part of a larger assertion of literacy over orality, in an attempt to spread a textual view of the world. As the printed book moved southward it carried its own colonial imprimatur. Printing became a tool of empire, and therefore it was all the more important to its sense of imperial superiority that its own origins should seem securely European.

While the Bibles printed by Gutenberg are fifteenth-century artifacts, the concept of the "Gutenberg Bible," sometimes called the "Mazarine Bible," is a nineteenth-century invention. It was then that the book gained its high cultural and financial value. It is hardly surprising that the veneration of Gutenberg as the father of printing, the willful forgetting of the history of print technology pre-Gutenberg, and the exponential rise in the cultural and economic value of copies of the 42-line Bible all coincided with the age of empire. Just as Europeans asserted the superiority of their technologies as the justification for, and means of, colonial control, so too they erased the technological achievements of the Orient. Mainz erected a statue of Gutenberg in 1837: the bas-relief shows printing across the continents, including Chinese readers of Confucius, Wilberforce and the printing press liberating enslaved African peoples, the artistic achievements of Kant and Schiller, and the signatories to the American Declaration of Independence. More statues followed: Strasbourg and Frankfurt in 1840; Gdansk in 1890; Vienna in 1900. These public assertions of Gutenberg's cultural significance in narratives of human progress—contrary to Gutenberg's own invisibility in his books, which never include his name—set the scene for collectors to bid ever higher prices, making the Gutenberg Bible the most valuable book in the world during most of the nineteenth century.

The New York Public Library does indeed have a copy of this extraordinary book. It acquired it via the famous eighteenth-century French librarian and scholar Abbé John-Joseph Rive. At some relatively early point in its life it lost its first four leaves. We might expect this to have been the story of creation, but the Gutenberg printed St. Jerome's epistles before the book of

Genesis—a reminder that what is included in a Bible continues to fluctuate throughout the history of Christianity. These missing leaves were supplied in facsimile at the beginning of the nineteenth century by the brilliant typographer Firmin Didot, using initial capitals cut from some other volume. This practice, known as sophistication or, more joyously, as vampment, was common as the trade in rare books developed during the nineteenth century. Abbé Rive's Bible spent time in the collection of George Hibbert, an MP, amateur botanist, and book collector whose tastes were bankrolled by Jamaican slavery on his family sugar plantations. When an American collector, James Lenox, bought it for what was described as the "mad price" of £500 in 1847, it became the first copy of a Gutenberg Bible to go across the Atlantic (half of all the extant copies are now in the US). *The Times* described it as "a beautiful work, which, from the extreme care that had been taken of it, appeared to have been but recently issued from the press."

So, the Gutenberg Bible's cultural status draws on and perpetuates a wider narrative of European cultural dominance, even as his press capitalizes on Islamophobia and the anxieties about the survival of Christianity's empire at the end of the Middle Ages. Printing and paper were already available technologies just waiting for their European moment: the combination of Gutenberg's entrepreneurial restlessness, shifting geopolitics, and the wider appetite for reading matter created the occasion. These factors produced a technology that was always and already implicated in social, political, and religious debate.

The Day After Tomorrow ends with mass migration southward: the climate catastrophe means that previously prosperous and dominant northern territories have become too cold to support human life. Scenes of crowds waiting at the US border with Mexico, for instance, overturn the familiar exodus, as it is the Americans who are trying to escape. But amid the devastation, there is hope. Or perhaps not hope exactly, but rather the promise that some things will be preserved in an uncertain future; or maybe even that history repeats itself. As a rescue helicopter picks up the last New York Public Library survivors off the icy plain, we see that the librarian is still carrying the Gutenberg Bible. The film thus reproduces in miniature a larger, and more dangerous, cultural narrative of overvaluation. Emmerich turns this book, and the origin myth it encapsulates, into a kind of fetish. The volume that seemed to represent the first step in human progress toward enlightenment and reason has become, like so many of our books, a deeply irrational material thing.

2

Queen Victoria in the trenches

"Pinned down in a field by mortar and machine gun fire" in northern France in the late summer of 1944, one American infantryman dived into a ditch to sit out the bombardment. He found an unexpected diversion when "a lump in my pocket turned out to be 'Queen Victoria.'" "There was nothing I could do except wait. I started to read and found it a rather good substitute for just 'sweating.' There was a two-way traffic above me, our shells going, theirs coming and bursting, and I kept reading of Victoria's 'dear beautiful Albert' and his soft flowing mustache that she admired so much."

This absorbing book was the biography *Queen Victoria*, published in 1921, by the Bloomsbury aesthete Lytton Strachey. Strachey dedicated it to Virginia Woolf, who, in return, reviewed it as a "triumphant success" that had changed the direction of biography, predicting that "in time to come, Lytton Strachey's Queen Victoria will be Queen Victoria, just as Boswell's Johnson is now Dr. Johnson": the narrative would eclipse its subject. What was so exciting and new about Strachey's approach was his use of the techniques of the novelist in inhabiting and enlivening his subject. One particularly breathless passage ventriloquized Victoria's ardent feelings on seeing her lovely cousin Albert and deciding they must be married:

> the whole structure of her existence crumbled into noth-ingness like a house of cards. He was beautiful—she gasped—she knew no more. Then, in a flash, a thousand mysteries were revealed to her; the past, the present, rushed upon her with a new significance; the delusions of years were abolished, and an extraordinary, an irresist-ible certitude leapt into being in the light of those blue eyes, the smile of that lovely mouth. The succeeding hours passed in a rapture. She was able to observe a few more details—the "exquisite nose," the "delicate mous-tachios and slight but very slight whiskers," the "beautiful figure, broad in the shoulders and a fine waist."

This is the only reference in the book to Albert's facial hair. It and the repeated adjective "beautiful" clearly made a forcible impact on the combatant, whose memory of his reading is preoccupied with those mustaches.

As this example of Strachey channeling a passion-ate young woman shows, both author and topic were deeply incongruous in that dangerous French foxhole. Strachey had made his name with *Eminent Victorians* (1918), his wittily revisionist biography of revered nineteenth-century figures, including Florence Night-ingale and Gordon of Khartoum. As Edmund White was to put it later, Strachey's achievement was "to take down once and for all the pretensions of the Victorian age to moral superiority . . . Something had been punctured for good": his retrospective account of the immediate past was at once a decisive break from its assumptions and habits, and a trumpet blast for modernism. His biography of Queen Victoria was in some ways more reverent and more conventional, a life of the queen understood through her intense relationships with her family and prime ministers. But in combining fictional techniques and psychological speculation with historical research, Strachey revealed his alignment with fellow modernist writers, including Woolf herself, and their shared artistic project of imagining the impulses and discontinuities of the inner life.

This literary technique was not an obvious fit for the battlefield. Nor was Strachey himself. A (mustached and bearded) pacifist and conscientious objector during the First World War, he was a prominent member of the bohemian artistic, intellectual, and sexual coterie that included Virginia and Leonard Woolf, Vanessa and Clive Bell, Duncan Grant, Roger Fry, and J. M. Keynes. You could hardly hope for better companions at, say, an exhibition of post-Impressionist painters, or a lecture at Caxton Hall on the philosophy of intrinsic value, or a house party at Garsington Manor in the Oxfordshire countryside, but they are not necessarily the first choice of fellowship for an injured soldier under heavy fire. The soldier's observation of the "soft flowing mustache" wryly registers the dissonance.

But in one important sense *Queen Victoria* was, quite

literally, made for that combat environment. As one of the Editions for the Armed Services Inc., a series of softback books designed to be carried in a uniform pocket and distributed for free, *Queen Victoria* was part of a sustained attempt to weaponize books during the Second World War. It and more than 1,300 other titles were produced by the American Council on Books in Wartime to recruit publishing to the war effort. President Franklin D. Roosevelt wrote of the "growing power of books as weapons"; they, like ships, "have the toughest armour, the longest cruising range, and . . . the most powerful guns." Under the guidance of the council, he encouraged the book trade to come together to "arm the mind and spirit of the American people with the strongest and most enduring weapons." But the council also had a shrewd eye on the postwar economy. Over the four years during which they were distributed, Armed Services Editions (ASE) would play their part in winning the war. Over a longer span, their impact on the peace was even more substantial. That paperback on the bedside table, the cheap reprint of a classic work, the thick airport blockbuster novel: all are the direct heirs of this pugnacious wartime imprint. In the story of Gutenberg in Chapter 1, we saw how eager readers created the conditions for book innovation; here, the direction of influence is reversed, as new book technologies work to establish their readership.

When *Queen Victoria* was first published, England and America were still recovering from the social, economic, and human catastrophe of the First World War. Victoria's long reign, only two decades past, seemed like another, simpler age. The first edition was a royal-blue clothbound hardback with a plain pale dust jacket and nine black-and-white plates, priced at 15 shillings: a high-end book for a high-end market. The first US edition was printed by Harcourt, Brace the same year, with a cover endorsement calling it "a masterpiece of the new biography," and the dust-jacket title in large, angular, antique-styled lettering against a pale purple background. It won the James Tait Black Memorial Prize, underlining its literary credentials. Twenty years later, when the same text was presented to service personnel, it wore a quite different uniform. Soft-backed with a red cover bearing the roundel "Armed Services Edition" and a banner reassuring readers that "this is the complete book—not a digest," this edition was a little larger than a standard iPhone. Its cover carried a miniature black-and-white image of the Harcourt, Brace cover design—a book within a book—and copied its angular title lettering from the American hardback. (Turn to pages 107–8 for the passage about Albert's hot whiskers.)

The form of the Armed Services Editions was dictated both by their intended use and by the available means of production. There were two size formats produced by different types of rotary press, both designed to be portable and pocket sized and to make use of printing equipment normally used to produce magazines and trade catalogues but currently underemployed owing to shortages of paper supplies and the wartime slowdown in consumer activity. Measuring 5 ½ by 3 ⅞ inches, *Queen Victoria* used a press gauge normally spooling out copies of the *Reader's Digest*, the general-interest mass-market magazine, and copied its familiar two-column layout. The format, that's to say, carried its own connotations, and the books were a long way from Bloomsbury. They were printed one above the other, two to a page, designed to be cut horizontally in half to produce small, wide books stapled on the short side. This method required matching titles by length so that the paired works used the same number of pages. The staples were a distinct and practical innovation: as one officer reporting from a posting in the South Pacific observed, "insects eat the glue, sewed backs moulder, but your stapled books hold up real well." The books often show uneven alignment along the top or bottom margin, sometimes shaving off the page numbers, revealing the mechanics of their making.

Armed Services Editions were produced under license from copyright holders who agreed to a very small royalty in return for substantial circulation, enabling the books to be produced for around 6 cents per copy. Narrow margins and minimal blank space throughout emphasize this economy in an era of paper rationing. The tight spine staple, fibrous pages, and horizontal format allow the books to be held open with a thumb in the gutter. My ASE *Queen Victoria*, bought online from a secondhand-book dealer in Grand Rapids, Michigan, has the lateral mobility of a fan, and thumbs softly. The sound is like a moth chirring; the book nestles in the hand almost like a flick or flip book, as if a series of stick figures of Queen Victoria in its corner could be animated into a jerkily moving analogue to Strachey's prose evocation of her life. Its absorbent, yellowing paper feels like much-washed fabric to the touch, its corners are scuffed from use, and the smell is that slightly musty, woody, hint-of-vanilla scent familiar to me from decades of hanging around cheap secondhand bookshops. It is closer in feel to a comic book than the heavily sized (prepared to give a stiff surface), crisp paper of the original Chatto & Windus edition.

The ASE were the brainchild of the Council on Books in Wartime, a committee of publishers, librarians, and other luminaries of the American book world. The council was formed in the wake of the attacks on Pearl Harbor in 1942 under the chairmanship of W. W. Norton. Its ideological aims were declared in its initial statement of purpose:

> To achieve the widest possible use of books
> contributing to the war effort of the United Peoples:
>
> By the use of books in the building and
> maintenance of the will to win.
>
> By the use of books to expose the true nature of
> the enemy.
>
> By the use of the technical information in books
> on the training, the fighting, the production and the
> home fronts.

By the use of books to sustain morale through relaxation and inspiration.

By the use of books to clarify our war aims and the problems of the peace.

Under the auspices of the council, more than 12 million free copies of 1,324 titles were distributed to service personnel in 1943–47, across the theaters of war. The titles reproduced as Armed Services Editions had to appeal to conspicuously catholic reading tastes. Everything from the *Iliad* to *Superman*, from *The Fireside Book of Dog Stories* to Conrad's *Lord Jim*, and from Voltaire to Hemingway, was included, in a range that consciously prioritized recreational reading over anything more directly didactic. Poetry, westerns, mystery stories, serious nonfiction, humor, and contemporary best sellers contributed to monthly issues of sets of thirty titles, shipped around the world. Longer novels, such as Wilkie Collins's *The Moonstone*, originally published in serial form in 1868, were too long for the economics and practicalities of the edition. These were abridged by freelance editors. Cost prohibited anything but occasional line-drawing illustrations: the ASE of *Queen Victoria* did not include the original photographic plates.

The titles chosen were thus deliberately inclusive. As Colonel Ray L. Trautman of the Army Library Service put it, "the philosophy of this office with regard to book selection consists primarily in giving men what they want to read rather than what we may think is good for them to read." Nevertheless, editorial choices could be bold. Two printings of Lillian Smith's controversial novel *Strange Fruit* (1944), about an interracial romance, which had been banned in Boston and for US postal service delivery, were a topical choice for a still-segregated military. There were, however, some sticking points. George Santayana's book *Persons and Places* was excluded as "dubious as to democracy"; Zane Grey's western *Riders of the Purple Sage* was considered an attack on Mormonism and therefore dropped from consideration for the series; it was suggested that Hemingway was too "salacious," but this was ultimately rejected and his works were kept on the list. Despite these hiccups, the overall commitment of the series to uncensored publication meant that the Council on Books in Wartime played an important role in securing longer-term freedoms to publish. In 1944, the American election was fought by conservatives on an anti-statist platform that aimed to dismantle the public institutions and programs of the New Deal associated with Roosevelt's presidency—among these, the activities of the council. In particular, the proposed Soldier Voting Bill would ban the distribution of government-funded political reading matter to the army. Publicizing this as an "alarming encroachment on freedom," the council lobbied to achieve substantial exemptions, including for the Armed Services Editions, which meant the effective nullification of the legislation.

For some now-classic titles, the reach offered by the Armed Services Editions transformed their standing and readership. Six times the print run by Scribner's between 1925 and 1942, 155,000 copies of Fitzgerald's *The Great Gatsby* were reprinted in this format. Maureen Corrigan notes that in 1940, the year of his death, Fitzgerald's publishing royalties amounted to a meager $13. Armed Services Editions found for the laureate of the gilded age a new and eager readership, contributed to the rediscovery of Fitzgerald in the 1940s and beyond, and established the enduring reputation of a book that has never been out of print since. Lytton Strachey's *Queen Victoria*, like *Gatsby* a product of the early 1920s, had been reprinted a couple of times during the decade, but not since 1928. It had probably reached the end of its print life by wartime, just as the Bloomsbury Group itself was wrecked by the deaths of many prominent associates, including Strachey himself. Selection for ASE republication as edition number 261—in a series including Geoffrey Household's *Rogue Male*, James Thurber's *The Middle-Aged Man on the Flying Trapeze*, and the *Selected Stories* of Katherine Mansfield—gave the work a new lease on life two decades after its original publication.

So pervasive were Armed Services Editions that newspaper reporters placed with active units often commented on their presence. A. J. Liebling, reporting in June 1944 for *The New Yorker* on preparations for D-Day, noted that "the soldiers were spread all over the LCIL [Landing Craft Infantry Large] next door, most of them reading paper-cover, armed-services editions of books." Each soldier was given a book on embarkation on the

D-Day vessels. One of Liebling's interviewees recalled that "these little books are a great thing. They take you away. I remember when my battalion was cut off on top of a hill at El Guettar, I read a whole book in one day. It was called 'Knight Without Armor.' This one I am reading now is called 'Candide.' It is kind of unusual, but I like it." His observation suddenly collides the worlds of Voltaire's satire on optimism and the flesh-and-blood realities of the combat zone: "I think the fellow who wrote it, Voltaire, used the same gag too often, though. The characters are always getting killed and then turning out not to have been killed after all." One soldier wrote, in a comparison much echoed in popular accounts, "to say thanks a million for one of the best deals in the army. Whenever we get them they are welcome as a letter from home. They are as popular as pin-up girls." A copy of Plato's *Republic* now in the Irvin Collection of the University of South Carolina has pencil notes inside the front cover including the names of borrowers, and not only the date but also the precise time of their loan, suggesting both high demand and quick circulation of titles.

The Council on Books in Wartime thus organized mass global distribution of an extraordinary range of books. But their strategic ambitions were also sharply commercial. The book trade in 1940s America had been stultified by problems of distribution and uptake. There was a vicious circle: not enough keen readers, and not enough bookstores to encourage new readers. Norton and his council saw the Armed Services Editions as a unique opportunity to induct a large cohort of service-men and -women into habits of reading and to build the book-buying public for the future. Reassuring publishers who were unwilling to allow their assets to be reprinted in the Armed Services series, Norton suggested that "the very fact that millions of men will have an opportunity to learn what a book is and what it can mean is likely now and in postwar years to exert a tremendous influence on the postwar course of the industry." Indeed, two significant consequences of the Armed Services Editions—one benign, one somewhat less so—can be traced in the course of publishing after 1945.

The first consequence is the development of the paperback as the standard print form for most genres of fiction and nonfiction in the postwar period. Armed Services Editions did not invent the paperbound book, but they popularized the innovations associated with 1930s imprints such as Albatross in Europe (founded in 1932), Allen Lane's Penguins in London (1935), and Pocket Books, established in the US by Robert de Graff (1939). All these radical publishers aimed to produce cheap books and to challenge copyright and distribution monopolies. The Hamburg-based firm Albatross, for instance, pioneered a format familiar to anyone who's read a mid-century Penguin: soft paperback with cover designs of modern type, geometric lines, and a black-and-white avian ornament, with colored covers indicating genre. The inside jacket paragraph blurb, printed in English, French, and German, captures the continental sophistication of the series. Allen Lane, waiting at a railway station with nothing to read and conceiving Penguin books as a similar format of paperback fiction that could be sold by a vending machine or in a retail outlet such as Woolworth's, was Albatross's British equivalent. In the postwar period, the German émigré and typographer Jan Tschichold developed the striking design of colored horizontal bands and Gill Sans Bold lettering, realizing Lane's idea into one of the twentieth century's most iconic consumer items. George Orwell, reviewing a batch of Penguins in 1936, famously noted that they "are splendid value for sixpence, so splendid that if the other publishers had any sense, they would combine against them and suppress them." In the US, it was émigré publishers, including Kurt Enoch, one of the Albatross founders, who brought paperback innovation into American publishing. Robert de Graff worked with the publishers Simon & Schuster to produce 25-cent paperbound books, often movie tie-ins. Pocket Books controlled costs by substantially increasing print runs, using publishers' plates where available, reducing the size of books to 4¼ by 6½ inches, and developing new production techniques, including "perfect binding," a glue system much cheaper than the stitching in hardback books.

In the prewar period these industry disruptors pushing cheap paperbacks were at odds with the publishing worthies who would be co-opted to the Council on Books in Wartime. But during the war the Armed Services Editions proved to doubters that books could be effectively remarketed as a high-volume, low-profit commodity. They turned the paperback into a mass-market and global phenomenon. In 1939 there were fewer than 20,000 paperbacks published in the US. By 1943, that figure had exceeded 40 million. In the UK, Allen Lane began with a print run of 20,000 copies of each of ten titles and was selling millions by the mid-1940s. The book market would never be the same again.

Paperbacks were the baby boomers of the book demographic and, appropriately, it was a baby-care book, Dr. Spock's *Pocket Book of Baby and Child Care*, that was one of the new format's first huge successes. Selling for 25 cents across more than 100,000 retail outlets, including drugstores and railway kiosks, the Pocket books paperback edition sold about a million copies every year in the decade after the war. The huge cultural impact of postwar best sellers like Dr. Spock, or J. D. Salinger's *The Catcher in the Rye* (Chapter 10), or Dale Carnegie's *How to Win Friends and Influence People*, or Rachel Carson's *Silent Spring* (Chapter 5) would never have happened without the innovations of wartime book production.

The second consequence is a darker one. One of the negative claims about the Armed Services Editions during debates on the Soldier Voting Bill in 1944 was the suggestion that they were "communist propaganda." The Cold War cultural compass was already being set. Having been turned so effectively into weapons of war, mass-market books could not easily be demilitarized.

Another council project, Overseas Editions, intended for German prisoners of war, published native-language editions of books by Thomas Mann, Joseph Roth, and Erich Maria Remarque, as well as translations of English-language works, including those by Hemingway and Conrad. At the end of the war, Roosevelt's decision to limit book publication within the former Axis countries, especially Germany, meant that postwar reading matter in Europe was closely controlled by the occupying powers. Overseas editions published in the Bucherreihe Neue Welt series were imported in large quantities to Germany, Austria, and Czechoslovakia as part of denazification and propaganda efforts. Their explicit aim was to export American values and to direct the reeducation of the civilian population about the facts of the war. Both these paperback series were portrait-format books, familiar from the Albatross and Penguin imprints, rather than the landscape-format developed for military use.

American books, from Mark Twain's to *Little House on the Prairie*, poured into Germany. Control of publishing and distribution of books and other printed material in the postwar period was deeply politicized: a recent biography of the disgraced publisher Robert Maxwell suggests that the British Secret Service part-financed his first venture into publishing while he was based in ruined and partitioned Berlin. For the British, Captain Curtis Brown—whose name is familiar from the prominent literary agency founded by his family at the end of the nineteenth century—was the liaison officer for the

Allies' literary program in defeated Germany. One of Denmark's leading publishers and booksellers, Henning Branner, supported by the Office of War Information, had stockpiled US and British books along the Swedish border during 1944. He was able to ship 700 crates of books into Denmark on the day after the liberation of May 5, 1945. Visiting France in 1946, the American publisher Blanche Knopf reported that the country was

> interested in reading, but is hungry for books from England and America, particularly America. There is a terrific cry for books for translation and in the English language. We here cannot conceive how a country like France with no free literature, no free reading for five years, what it means for them to get books again. The most important thing is to make it possible for the French to get our point of view both politically and culturally.

Knopf's unacknowledged slippage here between books that express freedom and books that express "our point of view" encapsulated the Cold War aftermath of wartime propaganda publishing. Both in America and in liberated Europe, anti-Communism drove what books were available. Howard Fast's novel *Spartacus*, about the Roman slave revolt, later made into an Oscar-winning film starring Kirk Douglas, was banned from publication by J. Edgar Hoover, a ban enforced by the FBI. After Little, Brown followed Hoover's prohibition, the manuscript was rejected by seven other publishers because of the pro-Communist sympathies of its author. Fast published it himself in 1950. Books by the anti-Communist Hungarian-born Arthur Koestler were exported into Europe in large numbers under American and British government-funded schemes. And by the 1950s, the CIA was operating an extensive clandestine cultural program across Europe, supporting artists, writers, conferences, theater productions, and concerts, and underwriting the publication of magazines and books under the auspices of the Congress for Cultural Freedom. So, paradoxically, the industrial technologies and networks that enabled the mass circulation of books also restricted their access. Books' democratic promise—the wider dissemination of knowledge; the "free literature" Knopf saw had been missing in occupied France; the commitment to antislavery discussed in Chapter 3—was always a compromise.

3

Christmas, gift books, and abolition

If I said it was a book that invented the modern Christmas, you'd probably already be anticipating a familiar discussion of *A Christmas Carol*, Charles Dickens's 1843 parable of the miserly Ebenezer Scrooge; the visitation of the ghosts of Christmas past, present, and future; and his redemption through holiday generosity. "'God bless us, every one!' said Tiny Tim," etc. But in fact the books that were instrumental in shaping Christmas emerged two decades before Dickens's fable. And like so many other Christmas traditions adopted in Britain during the nineteenth century, from decorated trees to the exchange of cards, the model was German. In 1822 Rudolph Ackermann, an entrepreneurial Anglo-German publishing pioneer who had developed a profitable trade in high-end lithographic prints and illustrated books, created a distinctly new bibliographic product. With *Forget-Me-Not*, the decorative gift book or literary annual had arrived in England. As the preface acknowledged, it drew on the established German literary almanac or pocketbook: "The British Public is here presented with the first attempt to rival the numerous and elegant publications of the Continent, expressly designed to serve as tokens of remembrance, friendship, or affection, at that season of the year which ancient custom has particularly consecrated to the interchange of such memorials." The book was published in November 1822 to catch, and to stimulate, a fledgling holiday-gift market.

Forget-Me-Not was an immediate hit. At this distance, to be honest, it's a little difficult to see why. It's a pocket-sized book decorated with sentimental swags and flowers, with short stories, poems, and wood-cut engravings of podgy Georgian children with saccharine rhyming descriptions. June is illustrated with an image of a toddler making a dash for it through an open gate while his serene young mother looks into the middle distance (the picture does cry out to be a caption competition) and the verse "The Gate's unbarr'd, the jovial cry / Proclaims Young Learning's Liberty / Which does the early mind prepare / To urge again th'improving care." On this evidence, Percy Bysshe Shelley, who drowned earlier in the year, could rest easy in his Rome grave. As Vita Sackville-West noted wryly in 1930, however, the elements designed to appeal to nineteenth-century readers were carefully included: "Switzerland and Caledonia; romantic love and the triumph of virtue; feminine modesty and manly strength; phantoms, ruins, graveyards, and wild valleys; the fruits of sportive fancy and the comfort of an elevated moral tone— nothing was lacking to turn these little offerings into a deserved success." Copycat titles such as *Friendship's Offering: A Literary Album*, *The Literary Souvenir*, and *Keepsake* were quick to appear, as publishers on both sides of the Atlantic developed and commodified seasonal gift-giving habits. The 1820s was the decade in which exchanging Christmas presents went mainstream. Books were in the vanguard of this commercial assault, in cities from London to Boston to Calcutta. In India a colonial *Bengal Annual,* subtitled "a literary keepsake," was published from 1830 for several issues, illustrated with engravings sent from England and with a British editor, and British contributors and readers.

The success of the gift book in the early nineteenth century is the direct antecedent of the modern book-publishing year. This is heavily dominated by late-autumn sales, including so-called Super Thursday, at the beginning of October, when a large number of hardback books intended as Christmas gifts are released. Nowhere is this more evident than in Iceland; the tradition of exchanging book presents on Christmas Eve developed around the time of the country's independence from Denmark in 1944. And the annual as a genre continues too, particularly as a festive gift for children. In 2021, for instance, the *Rupert* annual celebrated the centenary of its eponymous checked-trousered bear, with a new edition of the yearly hardcover compilation of stories and puzzles. Like its gift-book predecessors, the annual makes the year ahead part of its title, fixing it as a topical and up-to-date gift but also issuing a marketing challenge: if the books are not sold that year, it is almost impossible to repurpose them for the following Christmas.

Christmas gift books were a huge publishing phenomenon by the middle decades of the nineteenth century.

Within a few years of Ackermann's first foray into this form, the poet laureate Robert Southey grumbled sniff-ily that "annuals have grievously hurt the sale of all such books as used to be bought for presents." Not since alma-nacs, which circulated in their hundreds of thousands during the sixteenth century, had ephemeral, date-stamped books so captured the popular market. It has been esti-mated that in 1828, the year of Southey's complaint, 100,000 annuals were sold in the UK. Partly responsible for this rapid market takeover was the industry's canny product segmentation. Gift books rapidly spun out into differently priced volumes for separate demographics and interest groups: boys, girls, mothers, temperance advo-cates, Masons. Their miscellany of poetry and prose kept many jobbing writers, especially women, in work, and they also paid sufficiently to snag literary names, many of whom simultaneously expressed deep condescension to the genre and its readers. Sir Walter Scott, Samuel Taylor Coleridge, Charles Lamb, Wordsworth (pleading the expenses of an eye operation), Dickens, Thackeray and—lo and behold—superior Robert Southey himself were all paid for contributions to annuals between the 1820s and 1850s. Never mind Shelley resting easy: had he not drowned, he, too, would doubtless have joined the army of Romantic writers supplying copy to the literary phenomenon of the annual.

These gift books were particularly associated with middle-class women (still seen as the primary reading demographic for major publishing genres, including romance) but, in fact, their reach was surprisingly wide. The Royal Collection has beautifully red- and gilt-bound copies of the 1833 and 1837 volumes of *Forget-Me-Not* given to the young Princess Victoria by her mother. The later edition must have been gifted just months before she became queen. Women dominated the genre, as editors, writers, purchasers, and recipients. Isabelle Lehuu describes the circulation of gift books within "an economy of sentiment, an exchange of beautiful luxury goods for memory and love." Extant copies—the New York Public Library has a great collection—carry the manuscript traces of these now-lost attachments: "Caroline Snelling, from her friend Mrs. Callender"; "Miss E. L. Chapman from her friend S. Shapcock"; "Mrs. E. Marshall with the compliments of her friend A. Hart." These inscriptions, in the curly handwriting of the mid-nineteenth century, capture forgotten interpersonal formalities in their modes of address. The dedication formula, however, reiterates the function of the gift as the affirmation of friendship. Such inscriptions show how gift books managed to repackage mass-produced objects as bespoke tokens within specific and often highly personal relationships. The genre soon pioneered the convention of the blank, illustrated presentation plate on the flyleaf with room for the names of the giver and the receiver. *Forget-Me-Not* opened with a framed plate "To _____," protected by a tissue guard. The American annual *The Token*, published in the 1830s, carried a decorated plate with flowery cartouches and nymphs holding up illuminated capital letters, with pointed blank spaces for the giver to articulate something more intimate: "From _____ as a Token of _____ to _____." One copy records decorously that Waldo Flint gave it to Rebekah Scott Dean as a token of "his regard": Flint was a Republican senator for Massachusetts, and Dean was his sister-in-law. Gift annuals were, as Stephen Nissenbaum suggests in his book on the invention of Christmas, "the *very first* commercial products of any sort that were manufactured specifically, and solely, for the purpose of being given away by the purchaser." Nobody bought an annual for themselves.

Ackermann's inaugural *Forget-Me-Not* was not originally a highly decorated book. It was small, like a bijou clutch purse or prayer book. In its first few years, it was published in turquoise-green paper boards with a matching patterned slipcase, and it carried a few illustrations. Many surviving copies have been bound in leather and, for subsequent editions, Ackermann produced a deluxe full red-morocco-bound version. (Morocco leather, originally goatskin but later calfskin, was favored by bookbinders because it was strong, was workable, and showed off decorative tooling and gilding.) Publishers quickly understood that the genre's luxury sensory qualities were crucial to its success. Within a few years, annuals came in fashionably dyed fabric bindings, including the popular *Keepsake*, bound in gorgeous red silk (this luxury fabric proved appropriately ephemeral, and there is a paradox in these time-sensitive, dated, and fragile objects being deployed to confirm enduring bonds of affection). Before long, gift books developed their own highly decorative and often beautifully bound aesthetic ("like one of Lord Palmerston's cast-off waistcoats," the novelist Thackeray wrote snarkily of the *Book of Beauty*). These diminutive luxurious items were often named and decorated to parallel them with jewels or flowers: *The Garland, The Amaranth, The Violet, The Gem.* Their presentation combined advances in publishing that enabled mass production with the details that suggested artisanal luxury. They were the first mass-market books to have specifically printed wrappers, the forerunner of the modern dust jacket. They thus depended on the very technological developments in steam-powered printing and stereotype printing plates that were making regular books cheaper and more uniform. Although they were published at different price points, they were, overall, distinctly expensive.

The genre's overriding demand for illustrations, surfing technological developments in printing that enabled fine images to be prepared more cheaply, meant that the engravings were commissioned first and led the textual content. Poets and other writers were signed up to write accompanying, largely ekphrastic (the literary device of describing visual material in detail) text. Extensively illustrated with portraits of royalty, celebrity or historical figures, landscapes, and classicized pastoral engravings, gift books were expensive to produce (more than half the publishers' outlay of £10,500 on a single issue of the *Keepsake* was paid to artists and engravers). Several publishers sustained large losses with versions of the genre that did not find success in the marketplace: others developed innovative marketing techniques, including carrying advertisements within the volume, or including verses, especially in children's books, that emphasized brand identity. Southey complained again, to a friend, that "the literary department . . . must be as inferior in its effect upon the sale to the pictorial one, as it is in its cost . . . these Annuals are picture-books for grown children." Thackeray poured scorn on a typical sentimental—and orientalist—engraving in the *Keepsake* in which a "fierce Persian significantly touches his sword; a melancholy girl in front, looks timidly and imploringly at the spectator."

Because gift books were associated with women, their content was assumed to be—and often was—bland and nondescript. What was important to the sentimental economy of the gift book and profitable to the publishing economy was the affection it conveyed, not the content of its pages. These drawing-room or boudoir accessories were primarily decorative, and their content took a while to settle down. The preface to the first issue of *Forget-Me-Not* stated its "aim to unite the agreeable with the useful" and drew "the Reader's attention to the important Tables exhibiting the results of the late Census, compiled from the returns of the Population of Great Britain," alongside "a Genealogy of the European Sovereigns and Living Members of their Families" and a "Historical Chronicle for 1822." But any encyclopedic or almanac content was gradually dropped in favor of literary extracts and sentimental illustrations emphasizing didactic conduct or etiquette for their readers. In *Middlemarch*, her "Study of Provincial Life," George Eliot's narrator sneers at the clumsy attempts of Ned Plymdale ("one of the good matches in Middlemarch, though not one of its leading minds") to woo Rosamond Vincy using an annual. "He had brought the last 'Keepsake,' the gorgeous watered-silk publication which marked modern progress at that time" (the novel, published in 1871–72, is set forty years earlier, in the period leading up to the electoral changes of the 1832 Reform Act). Together, Ned and Rosamond pore over "the ladies and gentlemen with shiny copper-plate cheeks and copper-plate smiles, . . . [he] pointing to comic verses as capital and sentimental stories as interesting." The verdict is devastating: Ned's taste is patronizing and lowbrow, and Rosamond knows it. She "was gracious, and Mr. Ned was satisfied that he had the very best thing in art and literature as a medium for 'paying addresses'—the very thing to please a nice girl." Ned has fallen for the genre's own marketing promise of suitability for respectable middle-class courtship. One annual preface reassured suitors that it could be "given and received without violation of decency." This unobjectionable literary object comes to represent Ned's cheery mediocrity. The narrator's condescension is evident, and the handsome doctor Tertius Lydgate's scorn is bracing, establishing both his superior taste and his sex appeal: "I wonder which would turn out to be the silliest—the engravings or the writing here." Exit poor Ned.

The gift books' association with silliness, perhaps particularly as identified by men such as Southey, Thackeray, and Lydgate, could, however, be effectively subverted. The genre, and its popularity, was before long appropriated as a vehicle for radical ideas. One such appropriation, which hoped to capitalize financially and ideologically on gift books' extensive market penetration, was *Autographs for Freedom*, published in Boston in 1853 on behalf of the Rochester Ladies' Anti-Slavery Society. The Preface expressed the hope that "while it shall prove acceptable as a GIFT BOOK, [it] may help to swell the tide of that sentiment that, by the Divine Blessing, will sweep away from this otherwise happy land, the great sin of SLAVERY." The capitalization serves to connect two perhaps unexpectedly parallel discourses: abolitionism and gift books. Messages of support were compiled from notables from the New York area and beyond, including the formerly enslaved abolitionist leader Frederick Douglass and Harriet Beecher Stowe, apocryphally credited by Abraham Lincoln with starting the American Civil War with her novel *Uncle Tom's Cabin*. The Bishop of Oxford, son of the prominent English abolitionist William Wilberforce, wrote succinctly: "England taught her descendants in America to injure their African brethren. Every Englishman should aid the American to get rid of this cleaving wrong and deep injury to his race and nation."

Autographs for Freedom effectively combined two popular middlebrow genres, the autograph book and the gift

book, using new technology to reproduce facsimile signatures from supporters alongside the literary anthology
typical of the souvenir or gift book. Writing to solicit a
contribution from Ralph Waldo Emerson (he did not
comply), the editor, Julia Griffiths, praised her forthcom-
ing volume: "The beauty of its exterior will commend it
as a suitable Christmas, or New Year's gift." The book
was advertised in plain bound copy (75 cents) or gilt ($1);
its successor, the following year, increased the prices to
"$1.25 in plain muslin; $1.50 gilt edges; $2 full gilt sides
and edges." The most interesting thing about *Autographs
for Freedom* is the way it redirects the sentimental, domestic, and feminized tradition of the gift book. This iteration
of the genre moves it from networks of private affection into a public sphere, to evangelize and fundraise for
the abolitionist cause.

A gift book, therefore, looks as if it operates within
the codes of accepted social conduct for women and
their reading. One with a distinct political and ideological agenda subtly sabotages the conventional expectations
of the form. Abolitionist gift books are therefore quite
similar to the book now held in Oxford that came to the
Bodleian Library with the papers of the South African
activist and trade unionist Ron Press. From the outside,
this volume looks like a copy of the Penguin paperback
edition of Raymond Chandler's *Smart-Aleck Kill*, and,
indeed, the first nine pages proceed in the hard-boiled way
we might expect. But then, nestled inside this short story,
is a hidden bomb-makers' manual titled "Umkhonto We

Sizwe: An Elementary Handbook on Explosives." Issued by the African National Congress to armed operatives, it details practical urban explosive techniques, including how to make petrol bombs, mines, and booby traps. From the cover, no one would know. The incendiary contents of tactical abolitionist gift books such as *Autographs for Freedom* are less literal, but they, too, gained traction from the disjunction between the book and its cover. They mobilized female supporters through pre-existing bonds of affection and friendship, using these to transmit an enhanced consciousness of slavery and the movement for abolition. They weaponized the dull, safe gift book into a more pointed ideological tool. Perhaps if Ned Plymdale could only have offered this, the course of *Middlemarch* would have been rather different.

Christmas gift books developed and democratized a longer history of books exchanged as gifts, particularly in formal or diplomatic contexts. A book gift created in a monastic scriptorium could convey loyalty and gratitude to a king or a prince; in the other direction, the book might signal patronage and favor. In an early-fifteenth-century illustrated manuscript created by the artist known as the Virgil Master, the philosopher Alchandreus, wearing a green robe, kneels before Alexander the Great and presents him with a copy of his tome on astronomy. The courtiers pictured in the throne room are the kind of wealthy patrons who commissioned manuscripts like this one in late-medieval France. Boccaccio sent Petrarch a copy of Dante and received works by Cicero and Varro in return: exchanging books was a key token of Italian humanist friendship. Book gifts are common in the inventories of New Year presents given to Queen Elizabeth I. This formal gifting tradition has, of course, continued into modern times: American college graduations are often marked with a copy of Dr. Seuss's cheerily nonspecific paean to the future, *Oh, the Places You'll Go!*, and a recent poet laureate, Carol Ann Duffy, followed in the footsteps of her poetic predecessors by giving a presentation copy of her work to the sovereign; the Royal Collection shows that a number of modern Shakespeare editions were presented to the queen on a visit to a Scottish cathode-ray-tubes factory in 1997; and a copy of *The Rodgers and Hart Songbook* in a presentation box was given to her by Barack and Michelle Obama in 2009. I like to think, though, that, like my mum, she loyally buys her own children's books: the royal copies of *The Prince's Choice: A Personal Selection from Shakespeare*, *The Old Man of Lochnagar*, and *The Elements of Organic Gardening*, all by HRH Prince Charles, are marked in the catalogue as "acquired by Queen Elizabeth II."

Some of these diplomatic gifts may not have been exactly what their recipients expected (does Her Majesty enjoy musical theater?). What did the Mughal emperor Akbar make of the magnificent polyglot Bible presented to him by a Jesuit delegation to Fatehpur Sikri in 1580? This book, the so-called Plantin Bible, was a tour de force of European printing and scholarship. Published in Antwerp between 1568 and 1573 under the patronage of

Philip II of Spain, the multivolume edition had parallel columns with Hebrew, Greek, Aramaic, Chaldaic, and Syriac, each translated independently into Latin. Published in 1,200 fine paper folio copies and thirteen vellum ones for Philip's own royal use, the book drew on extraordinary multilingual and cutting-edge biblical scholarship, authorized and authenticated by the scholar and theologian Benedictus Arias Montanus, whose signature, in woodcut facsimile, concluded each section. The first five volumes of the paper set were taken up with the text and translations, the last three were the "Apparatus Sacra": grammars, dictionaries, and maps. According to Pierre du Jarric SJ, the chronicler of early Jesuit missionaries, at the time of the gift Akbar was about forty years old, wearing shalwar kameez—"his outer garment reached to his knees, and his breeches to his heels"—and several rows of pearls on his forehead, although in private he enjoyed a Portuguese-style black velvet suit. Intelligent, melancholic, well informed, keen on hunting, and interested in machinery and inventions, he accepted the gift graciously.

> The King received these holy books with great reverence, taking each into his hand one after the other and kissing it, after which he placed it on his head, which, amongst these people, signifies honour and respect. He acted thus in the presence of all his courtiers and captains, the greater part of whom were Mahometans. Afterwards he inquired which of these books contained the Gospels; and when it was pointed out to him, he

looked at it very intently, kissed it a second time, and placed it as before on his head. He then gave orders to his attendants that the books were to be conveyed to his own apartment, and ordered a rich cabinet to be made for their reception.

Akbar had an extensive library of books in Arabic, Latin, Persian, and Sanskrit, and employed a large retinue of scribes, calligraphers, and bookbinders: perhaps this monument of European printing found a place in this multilingual textual culture, but no one knows where this particular copy is now.

Nineteenth-century gift books were, therefore, modifying previous habits of giving away books, which tended to focus attention on authors dedicating and donating particular editions to patrons or other influential readers. They established all books as ways of securing horizontal friendship networks, rather than vertical relationships of patronage and diplomacy. They turned books into the defining gifts of the modern era.

But, as we have seen, buying books for other people can be hit and miss, and an awareness of this risk would grow in the early twentieth century. Based on an anecdotal survey of his friends, the Chatto & Windus publisher Harold Raymond suggested that the Christmas market for book gifts was suppressed by customer anxiety and "the fear of giving an unsuitable book." In 1926 he floated, in the trade magazine for booksellers, a national scheme for "selling books by coupon," better known as book tokens. Raymond identified that gifting worries were greater around books than around other comparable objects, and that "this diffidence is intensified if the recipient is known to be fond of books and to read a lot." The advantages of the coupon, "designed to look more like a Christmas card than a soup ticket," were that it was at the same time a more delicate gift than cash or a postal order and earmarked for a category of item the giver judged appropriate. "Uncle John sends his nephew Fred a coupon. Fred regards the book which he acquires as Uncle John's Christmas gift, and Uncle John is further satisfied in the thought that a postal-order for the same amount would probably have been converted into chocolates or cigarettes." Books, then, are distinct types of gift objects in two ways. Firstly, choosing an appropriate book for Fred is more fraught than choosing a different gift: book presents are freighted with an emotional or interpersonal burden greater than that attached to other gifts. Secondly, a book is something people, including Fred, ought to want but might not choose to buy unless the money was already put aside for it. In 1932 the first tokens were introduced. Early designs and adverts stressed the potential pitfalls of book-giving, obviated by this new, clever biblio-currency: "Your problem solved! No risk then of sending the wrong gift: he can choose any book he likes."

Anthropological theories of the gift help us understand some of these social anxieties around book-giving. In his influential study, *The Gift*, Marcel Mauss identified what he called "inalienability" as a defining characteristic of gift relations: the gift is forever linked to the giver and a means of cementing the relationship between donor and receiver. Gifts bind people, that's to say, rather than simply transfer objects. By contrast, something that can be transferred without ties from one owner to another is pure commodity, alienated from the person who gave it. Natalie Zemon Davis, writing of books as gifts in sixteenth-century France, suggested that while early print technology had begun to turn books into commercial, capitalistic objects, nevertheless, the sixteenth-century gift economy retained some of the aura of the preprint age. In print as well as in manuscript forms, she argues, the book was "a privileged object that resisted permanent appropriation and which it was especially wrong to view only as a source of profit." Some of this special aura still attaches itself to books in ways that could not be said of, say, fashion accessories or cosmetics (other small-format desirable items given as gifts). Although they are commercial objects, books carry emotional and friendship ties that ally them more closely with Mauss's theory of the gift than the commodity.

The practice of inscribing a book with a dedication or message confirms that such a gift witnesses an ongoing relationship rather than a one-off exchange: that is why there is such a mournful, voyeuristic pleasure in finding inscribed books discarded to secondhand bookshops. Having been returned to the realm of the commodity, these books retain their inscribed endearments, but cut loose from the context in which they made sense. Wayne B. Gooderham's online curation of book dedications captures this. What has happened to Paul, given a copy of Marx by Loveday, "with the hope that you will always be fighting, with hand, heart and head, for a world that is politically democratic and socially & economically egalitarian"? Are you, Paul? Did "my dearest wiflet," given a copy of A. S. Byatt's *Babel Tower* "to read when I'm away but dreaming of you," simply toss it into the charity-shop bag and run off with her Pilates instructor? How long after Esther's Valentine's gift of a book of love poems did Andreas keep it before clearing it from his shelves? What's striking about the traces in these secondhand books is their evidence that the gifted book always bears witness to the relationship between giver and recipient. All books are invisibly marked with these histories: inscriptions make these networks visible, like a kind of bibliographic barium meal. Subsequent owners inherit a prehistory of their book and have to recognize that, marked with an emotional dedication, pet name, or private message, it can never fully, or only, belong to them.

The next chapter, however, shows us three book owners who illuminate our long-standing tendency to do just the opposite: to assert claims to our books as part of our unique and strategic self-presentation.

4

Shelfies: Anne, Marilyn, and Madame de Pompadour

One unexpected aspect of the switch to online meet-
ings and interviews during the global pandemic was the
close attention paid to the bibliographical background in
shot behind politicians, pundits, and colleagues. A Twit-
ter account called Bookcase Credibility (bio: "What you
say is not as important as the bookcase behind you")
gathered 100,000 followers for its screen grabs with
witty captions. One caustically interpreted as a cry for
help a book called *What Works* placed upside down in a
bookcase behind a struggling cabinet minister; another
noticed bookshelves organized by color; others gleefully
spotted multiple copies of books written by the speaker,
sometimes even turned cover outward, bookshop-style.
In response to the heightened semiotics of the bookcase background, a secondhand-book business previously
working on film and television sets reported extraordinary domestic sales during lockdown: their pickers
curate for the hesitant bookcase novice a convincing run
of volumes to produce the desired effect on camera.

Our awareness that we all associate particular kinds
of books with particular kinds of people is, however,
centuries old, as the following three portraits of three

bookish women attest. Each woman has chosen a careful composition with a book or books to shape the viewer's perceptions. Each woman's picture sparks with knowing social disruption—of their own public image and, more widely, of stereotypical images of men, rather than women, as intelligent, cultured, and bookish.

The first dates from seventeenth-century England: Lady Anne Clifford's *Great Picture*. Clifford (1590–1676) spent much of her adult life in a legal campaign to secure her hereditary rights to the family's land and estates around Skipton in the north of England. Her tenacity eventually paid off and, when she finally came into her inheritance, she memorialized her struggles in an extraordinary three-panel painting. The *Great Picture* was painted in the style of the fashionable court artist Anthony van Dyck, but on a budget: the artist is unknown but was perhaps the Flemish painter Jan van Belcamp. It was commissioned around 1646, as Charles I surrendered to the Parliamentarian army and John Milton's first collection of poetry was published, but its subject is personal rather than public. The triptych depicts a fifteen-year-old Anne on the left-hand panel at the point when, on her father's death, she should rightfully have come into her inheritance. On the right-hand panel she is in her fifties and finally in sole possession of her estate, accompanied only by a cat and a dog. In the middle stand her parents, George and Margaret Clifford, and her young brothers, whose deaths in childhood left her the heir, according to an entail stating that the Clifford properties

74

must descend in direct line, even, exceptionally, if that was through the female. A somewhat surprising inscription explains that the boys are pictured after Anne's conception but before her birth, so that she is imagined to be invisibly, zygotically—if that's a word—present in the central family portrait. There are thus three ages of Anne: prenatal, teenager, dowager. Numerous painted coats of arms and miniature portraits establish a larger genealogical network, giving a particular prominence to women. The painting, now in Abbot Hall Art Gallery in Kendal, measures around five by three meters, and its human sitters are life-sized. It—and its twin, for there were originally two copies of this picture, *in situ* at the two major seats of the Clifford family—broadcasts the importance of family and inheritance to Lady Anne Clifford's life, a grand visual equivalent to the "Great Books" she dictated to record her family history.

The most significant pictorial element, though, registers another constant in Anne's life. Across the three sections of the triptych there are some fifty books. Like their painted readers, these, too, are life-sized. And these are not just generic background or filler, the seventeenth-century equivalent of by-the-yard books in country pubs. Rather, each is painted with a label with a short, identifying title. Books, and particular books, matter to the picture of herself that Anne wanted to project: she invites this close-up focus on her bookshelves and what they say about her. The books are placed in specific areas of the painting to flesh out her biographical narrative.

Works of geography, history, philosophy, and religion in
the left-hand panel are a youthful reading list including
literary texts alongside works of instructive nonfiction:
Castiglione's *The Book of the Courtier*, Boethius's *Conso-
lation*, St. Augustine's *City of God*, Ovid's *Metamorphoses*,
Montaigne's *Essays*, Cervantes's *Don Quixote*, Chaucer's
Works, and Sidney's *Arcadia*. This composition emphasizes intellectual and spiritual development, majoring in
literary and philosophical works, and draws out Anne's
later cultural networks. In 1620, for example, Anne commissioned a monument to the Elizabethan poet Edmund
Spenser in Westminster Abbey: here on her bookshelf
is a copy of his *Works*, published in 1611. As a young
woman in her late teens, she had been among the courtly
dancers with Queen Anne at Whitehall in Ben Jonson's
lavish entertainments *The Masque of Beauty* (1608) and
The Masque of Queens (1609): Jonson's collected works,
including these texts, are in her painted library. The label
on a book with a red fore-edge locates the volume in
the biography of the sitter: "The Chronicles of England
in Prose by Sa: Daniel Tutour to the Young Lady," or,
more emphatically, "by Sa: Daniel Tutour to This Young
Lady," on a book painted on a shelf alongside a portrait
of a sandy-haired Samuel Daniel, poet, playwright, and
Italianist. There are poems and sermons by John Donne,
who was known to Clifford; she had heard him preach
a sermon at Knole in 1617. The edition of Augustine,
translated by John Healey (1610, 1620) was dedicated
to the Earl of Pembroke Philip Herbert, Anne's second

husband. Surprisingly, Clifford does not, however, seem to have had a copy of the most famous book dedicated to the Herberts: Shakespeare's First Folio of 1623. For a contemporaneous portrait using that volume for self-fashioning we need to look to van Dyck's portrait of the cavalier poet Sir John Suckling.

We know from other sources, including a recently discovered manuscript library list from Appleby Castle, the titles of more than 160 books owned by Anne. This allows us to cross-reference the books in the *Great Picture*, and to appreciate the way her collection was specifically curated for the painting. Practical Christian spiritual development was evidently important. Balanced on top of a copy of Donne's sermons in the top-right-hand corner of the picture is William Austin's *Meditations and Devotions* (1635), a book itself figured on its decorative title page as an act of remembrance by his widow "as a Surviving Monument... of her ever-honoured Husband" and begins with "A Meditation for our Lady-Day." Clifford's household accounts record that she bought eleven folio copies of this in December 1669 for a total of £3 13s 4d. She clearly saw these books as part of her pastoral obligation to her wider community as a large landowner and distributed these and other works of spiritual and religious comfort to members of her household. Clifford also maintained a collection of reference books on legal and land-management issues, useful to a woman who had spent her entire adult life in legal land disputes. Her copy of Sir Henry Wotton's

The Elements of Architecture speaks to her responsibilities as a landowner restoring estate buildings. The overall image given by the painting is of an active rather than a reflective reader, with practical books as proxies for her own tireless pursuit of her legal rights and her lands. Some of her books contain her annotations. In the margin of Anthony Weldon's scandalous insider account *The Court and Character of King James*, published in 1651, she has written "a right description of King James" next to the unbecoming printed detail "his tongue too Large for his mouth." Her diaries record that she enjoyed being read to, and among the works read aloud were the essays of Montaigne and Spenser's *The Faerie Queene*, as well as the Bible and other devotional texts.

The *Great Picture* is, in essence, Clifford's autobiography, capturing her at three points in her life in a multidimensional portrait. These painted bookshelves register Anne's social and cultural milieu as well as her reading and capture her personal itinerary from the retrospective of later middle age. They tell her story in the way she wanted it to be told. These prominently identifiable books chosen for her painting clearly create something we might call a biblio-biography or, more colloquially, a shelfie. While there had been occasional identifiable books in paintings before this, hers is the first in an aspirational autobiographical genre that is recognizable in the twenty-first century: despite predating all the relevant technology, even including the bookcase itself (modern bookcases are often attributed to Samuel

Pepys, who commissioned freestanding glazed book cabinets or presses based on Dutch models from Simpson the joiner in the 1660s), Anne Clifford has found true "bookcase credibility."

So, too, has the second sitter, a century later. Jeanne-Antoinette Poisson, known to history as Madame de Pompadour, was the official mistress of the French king Louis XV from 1745 to 1750. Pompadour had a long professional relationship with the painter François Boucher, and he was the artist, known for his idealizing portraits, to whom she turned for a series known as *femme savante* paintings, designed to rebrand her as a woman valued for her intellect rather than for her sexuality. Boucher's portraits frequently represent Madame de Pompadour with an open book or against a background of bookcases. One of these, now on permanent loan to the Alte Pinakothek in Munich, was commissioned in 1756 to mark the elevation of the thirty-four-year-old Pompadour as a lady-in-waiting to the queen. It is life-sized, showing her semi-reclining on a chaise. She floats above an extensive and elaborate deep-sea-green gown carefully spread out to show its decoration of rose swags, and her pale, unlined décolletage is prominent. She looks to the left, up from a book held in her lap by her right hand: the suggestion that her reading has been momentarily interrupted is conveyed by her thumb, marking the page.

The sense of the painting is of stasis: waiting, Madame de Pompadour looks contemplatively into the middle distance, surrounded by the cluttered luxury of her boudoir. There are more books in a rococo cabinet reflected in the mirror behind her, supervised by a clock and a sulky putto slouching atop. A red leather-bound volume is placed casually under a small writing desk, untidy with an envelope, candle, quill, and other writing paraphernalia; there are loose-leaf papers and two cut roses on the floor at her (surprisingly tiny) slippered feet. A small dog, a King Charles spaniel called Mimi, watches from the bottom-left-hand corner of the picture. The dog's upward gaze creates a diagonal line of sight across the sitter's body. This line bisects the book, and her head reflected in the mirror, and anchors the composition in the top-right-hand of the frame with a heavy gold drape that serves to emphasize the theatricality of Pompadour's self-presentation.

In this portrait, Boucher draws naughtily on the iconographic tradition around the most famous reader of all. In medieval and Renaissance paintings of the Annunciation, the moment when Mary is visited by the Archangel Gabriel and told that she will conceive a son whom she will call Jesus, the Virgin is traditionally depicted reading. She was typically presented seated at the right-hand side of such depictions, as Pompadour is, and other resonant pictorial elements of this genre of painting include a curtain behind her suggesting a domestic setting, a vase of cut flowers, especially lilies, and sometimes a cat or, less frequently, a dog. Most prominent is the repeated trope that the angel's unexpected arrival, with the greeting "Hail, thou that art highly favoured, the Lord is with thee: blessed art thou among women" (Luke 1.28), has interrupted Mary in the act of reading. (The iconographic tradition diverged: Western Christianity developed this imagery of the literate Virgin, while in Byzantine images Mary was pictured spinning, a material metaphor for the generation of matter in the Incarnation.) This activity is not mentioned in the one standard Gospel account of Jesus's divine conception but grew out of the apocryphal gospels that often associated the young Mary with studious sanctity, preferring a withdrawn, proto-monastic life with her books, in preparation for her incarnational destiny. Commentary during the early medieval period developed the theme that Mary was reading either the Psalms or the prophetic passages of the Old Testament, and this tradition was important in legitimizing women's reading of Scripture. Mary's question to the angel, "How shall this be . . . ?," became, for early commentators, including Ambrose and Bede, the model for active, interrogative biblical interpretation. From the twelfth century to the eighteenth, therefore, the template for a woman reading in a painting was this established iconography of the Annunciation.

Aligning herself with this sacred iconography was a daring reconfiguration of her image after the end of her sexual intimacy with the king. Pompadour worked with Boucher on this successful career relaunch. Contemporaries read this iconography as it was intended: one review of the portrait extolled the way "books, drawings and other accessories indicate the taste of Madame la Marquise de Pompadour for the sciences and the arts that she loves and cultivates with success, those to whose study she knows how to consecrate her useful moments." Elise Goodman observes that Boucher combines two genres—the domestic court portrait that emphasized the subject's rank in monumental scale and luxurious accessories and the intellectual portrait of the man or woman of letters in the scholarly privacy of the study or cabinet. But I think I see this portrait at the intersection of two different genres: a scandalous secular annunciation, mashed up with contemporary classicizing portraits of the fleshly goddess of love, Venus. In place of the austere purity of Mary's circumstances at the angel's visitation, Boucher paints an interior marked by wanton intimacy and luxurious consumption. The reading woman here awaits not the spiritual impregnation of the angelic visitation but the temporal pleasures afforded her because of her sexuality: the pearl bracelet Pompadour wears on her right arm, visible just above the open book, was known to carry a cameo of her erstwhile lover the king. Another contemporary portrait of Pompadour, La Tour's 1755 pastel drawing portraying her in the tradition of Enlightenment *philosophes*, made her book titles visible: here, we do not know what volume from her extensive library she has chosen. Let's just say it seems unlikely to be the Psalms.

A *Catalogue des Livres de la Bibliothèque de Feue Madame la Marquise de Pompadour* was published after her death in 1765, listing her books. The sale numbered more than 3,000 volumes, including Perrault's *Fairy Tales*, Prévost's

Manon Lescaut, Defoe's *Robinson Crusoe* and *Moll Flanders*, and Fielding's *Tom Jones* in translation, volumes of French poetry, of philosophy, and of classical literature. There were, as Nancy Mitford observed drily in her biography, "only five books of sermons." Books in Pompadour's library were marked with versions of the three-towered coat of arms bought for her by the king. Mitford suggests that "it is clear that she read her books and did not simply have them as a wallpaper to her rooms." Her favored red and olive morocco bindings are visible in Boucher's portrait, and the two volumes leaning at an angle are suggestive of a collection that is used rather than merely symmetrically decorative. Pompadour was a prominent artistic patron, supporting the visual arts, the Sèvres porcelain factory, the theater, gem carving, and other enterprises. Her interest in books extended to printing and illustration: she had printed, in a press brought into her Versailles apartment, Corneille's tragedy *Rodogune*, and worked on the frontispiece aquatint herself, after Boucher. A copy of this book, bound in red morocco with Pompadour's crest, is in the collection of Ferdinand de Rothschild at the French chateau-inspired mansion of Waddesdon Manor. For a time at the end of the nineteenth century Rothschild also owned the Boucher portrait with the sea-green gown, and displayed it at his house in Piccadilly. Today we can see how that portrait combines sexuality, erudition, and the ironic reworking of pious iconographic traditions to present its reading subject as coolly powerful and assured, owning both her court notoriety and her intelligence.

Just as Pompadour's contemporaries fell back on a binary logic about her—she was either sexual or learned—so, too, we have struggled to reconcile the sexuality and erudition captured in a photograph of Marilyn Monroe taken in 1955 by Eve Arnold (the first woman to join the influential Magnum photo agency). Monroe, backlit by the afternoon sun and wearing a boldly striped vest and shorts, or perhaps a swimming costume, sits barelegged, knees drawn up to her chest, on a children's merry-go-round. She is immersed in the final pages of a book: James Joyce's *Ulysses*. Her full lips are slightly parted. She holds the book in her right hand, by the right-hand cover, steadying it against the crook of her elbow and her left forearm, which is hugging her knees: a pose which, because it does not enable easy page-turning, suggests that she undertakes the work of reading with slow, immersive concentration.

A surprising number of photographic shoots of Monroe depict her reading. Philippe Halsman did a series with Monroe in her apartment making extensive use of a bookcase as a backdrop: the star, draped over the bookcase to show off her curves, was dressed in sheer lingerie. In one she reads an unidentified book positioned suspiciously far from her eyes, mainly in order not to interrupt the view of her magnificent torso, and a Modern Library reprint is facedown on the carpet, next to a vinyl record. In other shoots she reads Walt Whitman's *Leaves of Grass*, or Earl Wilson's humorous travelogue *Look Who's Abroad Now*, or, more archly, her sometime husband Arthur Miller's *Death of a Salesman*. Arnold's photographs from Long Island were Monroe's personal favorites, and she was directly involved in their staging. But that she might actually have been reading Joyce's challenging modernist work, rather than simply holding it as a prop, has been difficult for many commentators to accept. Perhaps this sexist assumption willfully confuses this reading encounter with the one in Jean Negulesco's comedy *How to Marry a Millionaire* (1953), the film role that established her "dumb blonde" persona. Marilyn's ditsy short-sighted character Pola believes that men are not interested in women who wear glasses and therefore doesn't wear hers: she is shown studying an upside-down book on a flight.

Arnold's photo has long been considered a visual paradox—high and low art, Hollywood star and Irish laureate, flibbertigibbet woman and intellectual man—the contrast reflecting contemporary commentary on the Monroe–Miller marriage, summarized in *Variety*'s headline "Egghead marries hourglass." It has prompted extensive debate about whether Monroe was actually reading *Ulysses*. Asked by a Joyce scholar keen to clarify whether Monroe was indeed the book's most glamorous celebrity reader, Arnold recalled that Monroe told her "she kept *Ulysses* in her car and had been reading it for a long time: she said she loved the sound of it and would read it aloud to try to make sense of it—but she found it hard going." It sounds an entirely convincing response to the text's challenges and pleasures. But at the same time *Ulysses* is chosen deliberately. Recognizing it as a theatrical prop also recognizes Monroe's agency in controlling her own image. That same year, the most widely circulated image of Monroe was the shot of her raised skirts over a subway ventilation shaft on Lexington Avenue. A life-sized cutout was widely circulated to movie theaters advertising *The Seven Year Itch* in January 1955. Arnold's *Ulysses* photograph works quite differently. Jeanette Winterson described it as "sexy" because of the sense of autonomy of "the goddess, not needing to please her audience or her man, just living inside the book." Monroe's pose is focused and intimate. The book artist Buzz Spector's comments on the erotic associations of the book seem relevant: "When we read—the conventional distance between eye and page is around fourteen inches—we become the lectern that receives the book: chest, arms, lap, or thighs. This proximity is the territory of embrace, of possession; not to be entered without permission."

That may be true of books in general, but there is also something distinctly racy about the specific edition she chose. Monroe and her copy of *Ulysses* bring together two symbols of sexuality, transgression and American modernity. For readers in the twenty-first century, Joyce's work is known as a modernist masterpiece, a classic in the terms of value, status, and form (see Chapter 5). For readers in the middle of the twentieth, it had not yet shaken off the scandal attached to its early publication history. Serial publication of the novel in 1920 was halted by an obscenity trial, and imported copies of the first edition, published in Paris by Shakespeare and Company, were intercepted and confiscated. In the UK, all we need to know is the name of the Director of Public Prosecutions: Sir Archibald Bodkin. This Victorian name went with Victorian attitudes, and a selective reading of the book's final section was sufficient to convince him that *Ulysses* was obscene and that publication should be banned.

In the early 1930s Random House forced the issue of censorship by openly importing copies to the US. The groundbreaking case of *United States of America v. One Book Entitled Ulysses by James Joyce* was heard in 1933. Judge John M. Woolsey ruled that the book was artistic rather than pornographic and therefore could not be banned under obscenity legislation: a new edition was promptly published, incorporating an account of the struggles toward publication in the prefatory material. Morris L. Ernst, the publishers' lawyer, wrote a preface claiming its publication as "the culmination of a protracted and stubborn struggle against the censors." "Under the *Ulysses* case it should henceforth be impossible for the censors legally to sustain an attack against any book of artistic integrity, no matter how frank and forthright it may be." His phrasing was topical: like Roosevelt's contemporaneous program of federal relief, the book promised "the new deal in the law of letters." The first American edition carries a lengthy synopsis of the legal arguments and a letter from Joyce wishing success to his American publishers, before the text proper begins with an extravagant, page-sized letter S: "Stately, plump Buck Mulligan . . ."

This edition, published in the aftermath of the censorship trial, and reporting on it within its pages, is the edition Monroe is reading. Its pale cloth binding with red-and-black lettering is utterly distinctive. The Modern Library series, which published cheaper texts of *Ulysses* during the 1940s and early 1950s, would also have been available, but Monroe's choice of this particular one carries substantial power. Like her, this specific hardback is a symbol of sexual and intellectual liberation.

And since we can pinpoint some of the meanings of the specific edition, we can go further. The photograph makes it clear that, like the outraged Sir Archibald decades previously, Monroe is reading from the last few pages of the book: the bulk of the pages rest, already turned, against her left forearm. The end of *Ulysses* is "Penelope," Molly Bloom's famous monologue: eight long, unpunctuated paragraphs ending in repeated affirmation: ". . . first I put my arms around him yes and drew him down to me so he could feel my breasts all perfume yes and his heart was going like mad and yes I said yes I will Yes." It's a part of Joyce's text often praised for its recognition of women's autonomous desires and pleasures: appropriate reading matter for Marilyn Monroe as she blitzed Betty Friedan's America with her dynamic platinum-blonde sexuality.

In October 1999 the sale at Christie's, New York, of

the personal property of Marilyn Monroe raised $13 million. Under the hammer were the star's stilettos, denim jeans, a photo of Joe DiMaggio, dresses, scripts—and her books. A large Monroe library included works by Albert Camus, Ralph Ellison, Ian Fleming, George Bernard Shaw, Tennessee Williams, John Steinbeck, Ernest Hemingway, Colette, Dorothy Parker, and Jack Kerouac. Titles including *The New Joy of Cooking*, a book of Hebrew prayers (Monroe converted to Judaism on her marriage to Miller), a Bible, and Watty Piper's children's book *The Little Engine that Could* in a 1930 edition that may have been with her since her childhood round out her self-portrait. Among the book lots was, of course, that 1934 American edition of *Ulysses* as captured by Eve Arnold; it sold for $9,200. Like Anne Clifford and Madame de Pompadour before her, Monroe's self-conscious manipulation of her image showed an astute understanding of books and their social significations. Her *Ulysses* portrait plays on an apparent juxtaposition between sex symbol and literary seriousness to project a bookishly independent woman engaged in and shaped by her own choice of reading.

5

Silent Spring and the making of a classic

"Why read the classics?" asks the playful Italian biblio-phile writer Italo Calvino, and in the course of answering the question proposes fourteen definitions of a classic. My favorites are number six: "a classic is a book which has never exhausted all it has to say to its readers"; and number fourteen: "a classic is a work which persists as background noise even when a present that is totally incompatible with it holds sway." Calvino's definitions all turn on the content of the classic and its impact on its reader, but I'd argue for a supplementary definition for what makes a classic book. A classic is the result of a particular kind of materiality involving format, typeface, length, and binding. These elements shape expectations about the significance of the content. We would find a classic printed in Comic Sans font or on coarse paper incongruous, its form somehow devaluing it. We might instead expect a classic text to be printed on high-quality paper, or to have an elegant typeface, or to be bound with a marker ribbon, to include a tactile cover or other luxury elements that suggest cultural weight. It's not just that these material aspects of the book seem appropri-ate for the seriousness of its content; they actually shape our expectations of—even create—that seriousness. They are what Gérard Genette influentially called "paratexts": those elements of print publication that "enable a text to become a book and to be offered as such to its readers." Genette uses as an example: "Limited to the text alone and without a guiding set of directions, how would we read Joyce's *Ulysses* if it were not entitled *Ulysses*?" We might add, how would we read that text if it were not prepared with a scholarly Introduction, Notes, and Appendices—as in the edition published by Oxford University Press edited by Jeri Johnson and highlighted under its World's Classics imprint?

Since the earliest books prepared by scribes, classics have been framed by commentary or supported by annotation. Biblical glossing layouts were soon adapted for secular texts and classical scholarship. Glossing and on-page commentary were so closely associated with serious and important content that presentation in this form became the entry ticket to the literary canon. The form conferred classic status. Sometimes it takes a spoof to see the shape of the original that is taken for granted: here, Pope's satirical *The Dunciad Variorum* of 1729, which opens by updating Virgil's lines for the Grub Street age—"Books and the Man I sing"—on a page dominated by extensive, parodic footnotes. Pope's page shouts out and simultaneously lampoons "Classic." A classic text in a modern edition—take the familiar classroom staple, the volumes of the Arden Shakespeare—will probably have an introduction by a scholar or other mediator and explanatory notes, either at the foot of the page (more expensive to typeset, so more "classic") or at the back of the book. It may be part of a series with shared print livery explicitly marked as "classic," such as the black-spined paperback Penguin Classics series. When this series agreed to publish Morrissey's *Autobiography* alongside Homer, Austen, and Tolstoy, the mismatch between the novelty of the book and the grave imprimatur of the series was widely noted. A Penguin spokesperson tried valiantly to reconcile the two: "a book could be published as a Penguin Classic because it is a classic in the making. It's something we would like to discuss with Morrissey." The row revealed that the format bestows authority on the contents, as much as vice versa. A classic, that's to say, is about the book as an object as much as it is about the writing within. While Morrissey's autobiography had the black livery, the cover design, and the series title of fellow classics, it was missing the add-ons, or, in Genette's terms, the paratexts: no introduction, no timeline, no annotation, no Further Reading. It looked like a classic but didn't quack like one.

Like women in Simone de Beauvoir's famous formulation, one is not born but rather becomes a classic (unless you are Morrissey). If classic status is registered in material book form, the stages leading up to this are also readable across different editions of the same work. Rachel Carson's devastating account of the human and environmental consequences of chemical pesticides, *Silent Spring*, is a great example of a work that morphs from minor polemic to best seller to masterpiece across half a century of hardback, paperback, mass-market, specialist-bound, and ultimately classic formats. Tracing this work's evolution through different bookhoods reveals how materiality shapes the way we read.

Rachel Carson's clear-sighted analysis of the relationship between big firms, industrial science, and environmental destruction was the first mainstream book to describe the spread of pesticides throughout the food chain. It was first published alongside journalism: as a series of excerpts in *The New Yorker* in June 1962. The magazine pieces, like the book published later the same year, combined poetic techniques, memoir, description, and scientific analysis. The opening makes that clear.

> It was a spring without voices. In the mornings, which had once throbbed with the dawn chorus of robins, catbirds, doves, jays, and wrens, and scores of other bird voices, there was now no sound; only silence lay over the fields and woods and marshes. On the farms, the hens brooded but no chicks hatched.

Carson's platform in the preeminent literary magazine was a mark of her status: she had already written two well-received books on the marine environment.

Letters to *The New Yorker* in the wake of her articles were mostly supportive, but one correspondent suggested that Carson's argument reflected her "Communist sympathies" and remarked, "we can live without birds and animals, but as the current market slump shows, we cannot live without business." In the heated post-McCarthyite period, squaring up to big industry was bound to create a backlash. Some companies threatened to withdraw advertising from the magazine. Fearful of legal challenge, Carson negotiated her American publishing contract carefully to limit her liability.

The Houghton Mifflin hardback edition of 1962 cost $5. It was clothbound in green, with a verdant green dust jacket and large yellow-and-white typography. There is a small, stylized image of a running stream, perhaps a misreading of the title: the first chapter, "A Fable for Tomorrow," makes clear that *Silent Spring* is "an attempt to explain" the absence of birds and "the voices of spring in countless towns in America." The second word refers to the season, not the water course. The tagline "The author of *The Sea around Us* and *The Edge of the Sea* questions our attempt to control the natural world about us" is an inaccurately gentle summary of an urgent and determined book that gained its commercial and ideological power from its combination of science and activism. The design of the book jacket is often the first act of interpretation in the journey of the work to the reading public: the design of the first edition of *Silent Spring* downplays the book's revolutionary message.

The book's interior was similarly muted. *Silent Spring* carried an epigraph from Keats's "La Belle Dame sans Merci," "The sedge is wither'd from the lake / And no

birds sing," as well as line illustrations of botanical spec-
imens and landscape scenes by Lois and Louis Darling.
These suggested a familiar and reassuring Romantic nature book. Long recognized as a pioneer of the ecology
movement, *Silent Spring* also led the way in one of the
later twentieth century's best-selling print genres: popular science. Most of what Carson reported was already
known to scientists and other specialists, even if they
did not always admit it publicly. What was new about
her approach, and the book that promulgated it, was the
presentation of this material for a wider audience. The
scientific underpinning of the account was registered
but not visible on the layout of the page. An "Author's
Note" records, "I have not wished to burden the text
with footnotes"; instead a "List Principal of Sources"
serves as an appendix. The list runs to some sixty pages.
In *Silent Spring* these different elements—epigraph, appendix, illustrations—reveal the book's dynamic and
innovative genre: it is part scientific tract, part nature
writing, part polemic, part popular science—and this
synthesis encapsulates its countercultural content. A
book written by a woman ecologist working outside any
academic or scientific institution, and written as a direct
challenge to the moral bankruptcy of apparently objective, cold laboratory science, its format embodies its
oppositional stance, even as the cover quotation and design seek to modulate Carson's explosive argument.

In the UK, *Silent Spring* was initially presented rather
differently from this American marketing. With a red

cover with the author's name and the title in large letters, it carried endorsements from the evolutionary biologist (and eugenicist) Julian Huxley, and an introduction by Lord Shackleton, who praised "this brilliant and controversial book" and emphasized the relevance of its American examples to the British context. Using more local ecological examples—the decline of the peregrine falcon, the Irish potato famine, the role of the Nature Conservancy in protecting the environment—he advocated "ecological management to promote a natural balance which will also suit the needs of man." Carson's book was thus presented to a British readership framed by (male) authority figures offering both an endorsement of her ideas and some translation from an American to a British environmental context. Within months of its publication, *Silent Spring* was being circulated in book-club editions on both sides of the Atlantic, including the preeminent Book of the Month club. It was also sent to UK subscribers as a Readers Union monthly choice "selected on merit alone from the lists of all leading publishers and issued (at a mere 6s each, plus a small postage charge) in sturdy, well-produced volumes designed to please and endure."

Book-club editions are often overlooked and book-club readers condescended to in cultural histories of reading, which characterize the curated choices as bourgeois and unadventurous. Book clubs are often assumed to distribute books as commodities for the profoundly unbookish; there's a sense that readers merely consume the book rather than commune with it. The ambivalence of the literary novelist Jonathan Franzen about appearing on the modern equivalent of the book-of-the-month club, *The Oprah Winfrey Show*, might be seen as an example of this suspicion. After Franzen withdrew from her show in 2001, the host explained that it was "because he is seemingly uncomfortable and conflicted about being chosen as a book-club selection." Franzen's reluctance seemed to be in part about the branding of the books with the imprimatur of the television show: "I see this as my book, my creation, and I didn't want that logo of corporate ownership on it." Oprah's book choices were marked with an O logo sticker, a badge judged to be worth tens of thousands of sales for a chosen title.

The Antiquarian Booksellers' Association of America defines the book-club edition as "usually an inexpensive reprint utilising poor quality paper and binding and sold by subscription to members of a book club; in general, of little interest to book collectors and of low monetary value." The format, that's to say, has the opposite physical features and connotations of the more desirable and high-end "classic." But book clubs are more powerful than this implies, for they have had a significant impact on sales and reach. Carson's book specifically fitted the Book of the Month's preference for "the populariser of professionally produced knowledge," as Janice Radway puts it in her affectionate analysis of "a club that uses sophisticated marketing techniques to sell not only individual books but the very idea of taste itself."

Nevertheless, the club was anxious about presenting *Silent Spring* to its members. The standard process of choosing via an editorial review from the selection committee had produced a highly positive report. *Silent Spring* was described as "the most revolutionary book since *Uncle Tom's Cabin*." Despite—or perhaps because of—this endorsement, the club president took the rare step of urging readers not to reject October's choice, telling them, in the Cold War rhetoric so effectively deployed by Carson herself, that the book's subject matter was as important and as lethal as "worldwide nuclear warfare." The other Book of the Month club selections for 1962 offer an entirely different context in which to view *Silent Spring* and its publics: the selection judges picked out works by Steinbeck, Faulkner, and Mary Renault in a list that included the year's best-selling novel, Katherine Anne Porter's *Ship of Fools*, alongside Barbara Ward's praised analysis of global economics, *The Rich Nations and the Poor Nations*. Analyses of book-club distribution tend to focus on the disparaged cultural demographic of the "middlebrow" and, even when they attempt to reevaluate the term, do not divert substantially from its condescending implications. But for *Silent Spring*, book-club publication was a triumph. In addressing itself directly to a general readership, the Book of the Month club edition in austere dark green with white lettering was in fact the ultimate symbol of Carson's vital movement, through print, into the mainstream. She had written a book to awaken popular resistance to the dominance of the military-chemical machine: more than any other early edition, it is the book-club version that represents that popular audience in book form.

The controversy around *Silent Spring* was intrinsic to its success. One industrial chemist announced that "if man were to follow the teachings of Miss Carson, we would return to the Dark Ages, and the insects and diseases and vermin would once again inherit the earth." Personal and misogynistic attacks on Carson were commonplace. One jibe suggested that, as a "spinster," her interest in genetics was absurd; another pictured her as a witch on a broomstick flying over Congress as rational, male scientists testified against her book below. *Silent Spring* provoked other publications both for (from her publishers, bolstering its authority with statements from supportive scientists) and against its arguments (from representatives of the chemical industry). Monsanto's 1963 pamphlet "The Desolate Year" rewrote Carson's lyrical opening chapter to depict a world impoverished and starving after the banning of pesticides. The reverberations were widespread and the debates made *Silent Spring* a best seller. The cultural and scientific impact of Carson's work was immediate and expansive, from interviews and Congress committees to Joni Mitchell songs and Peanuts cartoons ("We girls need our heroines," says Lucy after her brother accuses her of "always talking about Rachel Carson"). The ubiquity of Carson and her ideas was registered in later editions, which incorporate information about the reaction to them and sales. A 1964 paperback moved a long way from the genteel summary that "questions our attempt to control the natural world," instead calling *Silent Spring* "the world-famous bestseller about our ravaged environment and the man-made pollution that is imperilling all life on earth." The British Penguin paperback a year later pulled no punches, with a cover design using a photograph of a dead bird and a flash of text highlighting "a persistent and continuous poisoning of the whole human environment." A decade later a Fawcett paperback costing 75 cents had a dramatic black cover with white lettering and a gold rosette advertising "The Explosive Bestseller the whole world is talking about." Indeed, translations into a dozen European languages during the 1960s, and into Chinese, Korean, Thai, and Turkish in the 1970s and '80s, had made *Silent Spring* an international print phenomenon.

Mass-market paperbacks were largely a postwar phenomenon in the US and Britain (see Chapter 2). They were sold outside the normal, limited distribution channels of bookstores, which were mostly confined to big cities. A stand of paperbacks in airport terminals, chain stores, and bus stations captured a much wider demographic. A report on this new format by UNESCO in 1965 registered its disruptive literary and cultural energies and its particular economic model:

The paperback is printed on ordinary, but agreeable, paper, strongly bound in a coloured jacket which is very often illustrated. It is never printed in less than some tens of thousands of copies, and it is seldom sold at more than the equivalent of an hour's wages per volume . . . Its intellectual mobility is enormous: while in 1961 it accounted for 14% of the total output of books in the United States, in 1962 it accounted for 31% and the ratio keeps increasing.

Price, format, and new channels of distribution gave the paperback a natural affinity with youthful, countercultural, or otherwise baby-boomer titles. One anonymous interviewee of Kenneth Davis, who wrote a study of "the paperbacking of America," name-checks an indicative title:

As a youngster, I borrowed the Ballantine edition of Tolkien's *Lord of the Rings* and was promptly transported to Middle-earth. I was enthralled and proceeded to reread the trilogy at regular intervals . . . Such books as the trilogy cannot be properly savored during the day. No, I saved the trilogy for late-night perusal—something to curl up in bed with. This cannot be comfortably accomplished with a hardcover book. The wave of Tolkien's popularity crested during the late-sixties counterculture and was undoubtedly linked with it, since Tolkien's protagonists embraced idealistic causes and saw them through with perseverance and determination. Truly a myth for the times. A hardcover edition would never have attracted such a following, since it would seem too "Establishment," resembling the much-feared textbooks wielded by stodgy professors.

Paperbacking had a similar impact on *Silent Spring*, reinforcing its edgy distance from the establishment and aligning it with the counterculture of the 1960s.

Paperback versions of *Silent Spring* continued to be printed as the ecological crisis depicted in it showed no immediate signs of losing its relevance. The edition published in 1994 with an introduction by the Democratic environmental campaigner Al Gore addresses a different readership and frames the work in new ways. Gore recollects the impact of the work on his political thinking from his early years; it was "one of the books we read at home at my mother's insistence and then discussed around the dinner table." And when the forty-year-anniversary edition was published, it was with a sense of hindsight: "*Silent Spring*: the classic that launched the environmental movement." This edition carried a biographical foreword by Linda Lear (Carson's own life story, including her early death from breast cancer in 1964, had come to the fore in the mythology of her best-selling book) and an afterword by the biologist Edward O. Wilson. In part, Carson's warning was against the passive acceptance of the progress, consumerism, and economic growth that characterized America in the 1960s and beyond: it was an inevitable irony that her book should be co-opted as one of the more lucrative commodities in the publishing industry. But the different editions throughout that decade and afterward embody the spread of Carson's ecological warning, from magazine to best seller, from cautious "question" to angry condemnation.

The fortieth-anniversary edition claimed for *Silent Spring* the status of "classic." The paradox is that it was admitted to this elite category because of its mass success. But if format confers authority, Carson's place in the pantheon of great American writers had been finally secured by the publication of *Silent Spring & Other Writings on the Environment* in the hardback Library of America edition in 2018. This series self-consciously establishes the American canon in handsome, hardback books with the author's name in distinctive cursive script. Their Smyth-sewn bindings ensure that the volumes can be bent back without cracking the spine: an open Library of America book rests flat on the desktop as an authoritative text to refer to rather than curl up with. They are clothbound, with kraft endpapers and an integral ribbon marker: a luxury format in an age of mass production. The publishers boast that the trim format—slightly narrower than expected, with the elegant proportions emphasized by a tricolor horizontal stripe just below the halfway point—is based on Euclid's golden mean of aesthetic beauty. These are volumes that combine visual, tactile, and intellectual pleasures, to produce a library that "will last for generations." That, perhaps, is the ultimate definition of a classic.

The Library of America editions are certainly beautiful, perfectly weighted, smart on the shelf and in the hand. They represent the print apotheosis of the ecological manifesto of *Silent Spring* as it is transmitted from weekly magazine to classic. But perhaps this material acceptance into canonical status takes something of the urgency out of Carson's writing, withdrawing it from the activist realm and instead neutralizing it with the dead hand of the library. Carson began *Silent Spring* acknowledging all those who are fighting to "bring victory for sanity and common sense in our accommodation to the world that surrounds us" and ended with a rallying call to take "The Other Road" from chemical insecticides. Calvino's suggestion that the classic continues "as background noise" seems to condemn *Silent Spring* if not itself to absolute silence then at least to a more muffled presence. A classic is closer to the hushed and guarded life of the book collection, discussed in the following chapter, than to the immediate urgency of the protest line. It is too soon to consign Carson's book to the library: there is still so much work to be done to give spring its voice back.

6

The *Titanic* and book traffic

A portrait of Harry Elkins Widener shows a soft, dreamy-faced young man with a severe center parting, his left forefinger holding his place in a small-format book—perhaps his prized edition of Keats's poems. Born in 1885 to an elite Philadelphia family, Widener grew up in the moneyed leisured class, the same world that gave the economist Thorstein Veblen his insight into what he called, compellingly, "conspicuous consumption." Harry's own conspicuous consumption was bookish. By the age of twenty-four he had a serious book collection of over fifteen hundred volumes. In his application in 1909 to join the Grolier Club, an exclusive New York society for rich bibliophiles, he proudly admitted to collecting "chiefly the books which interest me," especially nineteenth-century writers and illustrators. "At present, the finest art of my library consists of Shakespeare, Extra-Illustrated Books . . . and almost complete sets of the first issues of Swinburne, Pater, Reade, Stevenson, and Robert Browning." All we know about Widener's actual reading, by contrast, is that his go-to book was *Treasure Island*. Helped by an indulgent and wealthy mother, his collecting became more serious with Grolier membership. Philadelphia society bookdealer A. S. W. Rosenbach collaborated with his young protégé and client on a privately printed catalogue of the Widener collection. Pride of place went to a recent acquisition, the Countess of Pembroke's 1613 copy of *Arcadia* inscribed by the author, "Your loving brother, Philip Sidney." The catalogue, as befitted an ambitious bibliophile, was itself a lavish work: a hundred copies on paper and two on vellum in large quarto (printed on four leaves to a sheet) format, with tissue-covered facsimile reproductions. Edmund Gosse congratulated Widener "on the possession of a superb house of books." Their owner made a will leaving them to his mother, with the desire that they should be given as a named collection to Harvard University.

Book-collecting was one of the high-status occupations of wealthy American men in the Gilded Age, when J. Pierpont Morgan, Henry E. Huntington, and Henry C. Folger were all using their libraries to launder the substantial proceeds of corporate finance, railroads, and oil respectively. The sociologist Russell W. Belk defines collecting as "the process of actively, selectively, and passionately acquiring and possessing things removed from ordinary use": the collected book is for show, not for reading. Collecting, Belk observes, is a fundamentally acquisitive and possessive activity, but these impulses are sometimes disguised by the high aesthetic or cultural value of its objects. This should be familiar to us: a person who buys more books than they can possibly read occupies a different place in the anatomy of consumerism than someone who stockpiles designer handbags, or high-performance cars, or branded sneakers. The Western enjoyment of the Japanese term *tsundoku*, meaning the tendency to accumulate unread books, suggests a desire for a category that recognizes book purchases as somehow distinct from the run of material luxury consumption, and underwrites, without stigma, the value of the book beyond reading. Writing in the early fourteenth century, Richard de Bury offered *Philobiblon*, his account of the pleasures of book-collecting, as a means to "clear the love we have had for books from the charge of excess." This charge, and the attempt to counter it, are perennial. The nineteenth-century diagnosis was harsher still than mere excess. "Bibliomania" was typically characterized by an immoderate, even ruinous attachment to books acquired through purchase or theft, with a strong suggestion that these books were to serve an inert and possessive collection, rather than for reading or other direct use. Among other things, this pathology of bibliomania made troublingly little distinction between the collector and the thief: each was programmed to acquire books by whatever means available.

One of the few clinical discussions of bibliomania, published by Norman D. Weiner in the *Psychoanalytic Quarterly*, draws exclusively on literary and historical references. Weiner suggests that there are few clinical case studies since the behavior is "ego-syntonic," that is, it is acceptable to the self because it is compatible or consistent with fundamental beliefs or personality, and therefore not experienced as problematic or presented for therapeutic intervention. A mania for books, just like the justifications for collecting books, sees it as desirable, ethically distinct from other kinds of collecting. Weiner's theory found suggestive analogies between tales of book acquisition and stories of sexual conquest, bringing "to mind the activities of the hypersexual male hysteric who just constantly reassures himself that he has not been castrated." His evidence, perhaps not strictly scientific, was that Casanova's eventual retirement was to gentle employment in the Castle of Dux in Bohemia, as Count Waldstein's librarian. Writing in the great age of book-collecting, P. G. Wodehouse continued this appetitive theme in creating the comic American bibliophile Cooley Paradene of Long Island. Paradene's expensive library "caused bibliophiles on entering it to run around in ecstatic circles, prying and sniffing and uttering short excited whining noises like dogs suddenly plunged into the middle of a hundred entrancing smells." The apparently cerebral activity of book-collecting is clearly more id than superego. Not all book collectors are in fact male: there were significant female American collectors contemporary with Harry Widener, including Abby Ellen Hanscom Pope and Amy Lowell (her collection, like Widener's, is now at Harvard). They are, however, exceptions that tend to prove the rule.

And if collecting expresses something particular

about the collector, it also transforms the essence of the object. The theorist of collecting, Belk, again: "When an object enters a collection it ceases to be a fungible commodity and becomes a singular object that is no longer freely exchangeable for something of similar economic value—its value is in the context of the collection." Collecting thus removes the book from circulation and exchange. It is thus one of many means we have encountered—including gifting, annotation, inscription, and reading itself—of turning mass-produced books into unique relics.

We can see this transformation in progress as Harry Widener goes book-shopping. In late March 1912, he was with his parents in London on a buying spree. It was an extraordinary time to be a wealthy book collector. The shift in economic power from Europe to the US, the decline of landed English families and the break-up of their estates, and the rise of what Bernard Berenson called the "squillionaires" all meant that large sales of rare books commanded intense public interest and high prices. The transfer of valuable books from the libraries of the English aristocracy to the new money palaces of the New World was a source of comment and cultural anxiety in Britain. Widener was in the mood to comfort-buy, having been outbid on everything he wanted at a recent sale by his new, and extremely wealthy, rival Henry Huntington.

At London's foremost antiquarian bookseller, Bernard Quaritch in Grafton Street, he bought many items, including a set of nine quarto half-morocco volumes of Gibbon's *Decline and Fall of the Roman Empire*. In addition, he picked out a 1598 copy of Francis Bacon's *Essaies*, which Quaritch had bought at the sale of Alfred Henry Huth a few months earlier. This first edition of ten of Bacon's essays was a pocket-sized book, some twelve centimeters high, with the full title *Essaies. Religious Meditations*. At the shop of J. Pearson and Co., Widener then bought a rarity from the first century of the printing press, a small, four-leaf octavo (printed on eight leaves to a sheet) news pamphlet printed in black letter type from 1542. With hindsight, it's hard not to see the dramatic irony in this last-minute purchase of a disaster narrative: *Heavy News of a Horrible Earthquake which was in the city of Scarbaria in this present year*. At the time it was believed to be the sole surviving copy. Widener packed it, and his new copy of Bacon, into his traveling bag and joined his family on the maiden voyage of the luxury liner that was to take them home. The name of the ship: RMS *Titanic*.

On the night of April 14, 1912, four days into the crossing and about four hundred miles off Newfoundland, the extent of the damage done to the ship's hull in an iceberg collision became clear. Harry's mother, Eleanor Widener, and her maid were evacuated in lifeboat number 4 at 1:55 a.m. The survival rate of women in first-class accommodation was the highest for all categories of passenger: their lifeboat was picked up by the *Carpathia* and the women were taken to New York.

Neither Harry Widener, aged twenty-seven, nor his father, survived. Their bodies were never recovered.

Although it might jar now, it did not seem tasteless to his friends to point out that one of his book purchases was also lost in the catastrophe. Although most of his London haul was sent across the Atlantic in a tin-lined trunk on RMS *Carpathia* (the ship that navigated the ice floes to respond to the *Titanic* distress call and picked up hundreds of survivors), the book of essays bought from Quaritch was not. "Just before the 'Titanic' sank," his bookdealer friend A. S. W. Rosenbach reported in a posthumous catalogue of Harry's collection of works by Robert Louis Stevenson, "he said to his mother, 'Mother, I have placed the volume in my pocket; little "Bacon" goes with me.'" "This is surely," added Rosenbach, somewhat gratuitously, "the finest anecdote in the whole history of books." The pamphlet about the earthquake was also apparently lost, but not so susceptible to anthropomorphic eulogy.

Widener's tragic story was immediately retold within the terms of his own bibliophilia. The copy of Bacon that sank with him resonated with the story of the poet Shelley. Shelley's drowned body was identified after his boat capsized off Pisa by the copy of Keats's *Lamia* in his pocket, given to him by his friend Leigh Hunt, who had it from Keats. Hunt had marked his favorite passages for Shelley's perusal; the volume, except its binding, was destroyed on Shelley's funeral pyre. Other associations were prominent, too. The *Daily Telegraph* described

Widener as "An American Lycidas," referring to Milton's elegy for a young Cambridge man, Edward King, who drowned aged twenty-five off the Welsh coast in 1637. The Miltonic allusion was echoed by Rosenbach, who ended his eulogy for Widener at his memorial service quoting the poem: "who would not sing for Lycidas?" Widener's library included, of course, a blue-morocco copy of the first edition of this lyric elegy in Milton's 1645 *Poems*, along with first editions of *Paradise Lost*, *Paradise Regained*, and Milton's defense of freedom of the press, *Aeropagitica*.

Ever since the immediate shocked reaction to its loss in the press in 1912, stories of the *Titanic* have tended to emphasize the ironies of its luxury. As a symbol of the opulence of the era, the ship was designed to appeal to the wealthy elites crossing between Europe and America in comfort and style. It attempted to beat its transatlantic rivals for comfort and glamour, with electric elevators to wood-paneled first-class state-rooms, the stylish Café Parisienne on B deck, the mirrored ballrooms, modern gymnasium, and swimming pool: "gilded gear" and "vaingloriousness," as Thomas Hardy put it in his poem on the disaster, "The Convergence of the Twain." But the majority of the passengers on board, as on all such voyages, were not the Wideners, Guggenheims, or Astors. Rather, they traveled in third class, or steerage. Many were traveling to the US in the hope of creating new, prosperous lives for themselves as workers or settlers, sometimes independently, sometimes in family groups, and sometimes to join contacts who had already made this migration. Charlotte Collyer and her husband, Harvey, for instance, traveled with their daughter on the *Titanic* to start a new life on an Idaho fruit farm. Harvey drowned, along with their life savings. Pål Andreasson, aged nineteen, was traveling from Sweden to join his brother, who had emigrated to Chicago some years previously; he, too, was lost in the tragedy. Mrs. Safiyah Ibrahim, who had previously attempted to enter the US from Syria but been refused entry because of a contagious eye infection, was trying to join her husband, Wassuf, who had already settled in Greensburg, Pennsylvania, where he was employed in a metal works. She survived, and the Ibrahims made a successful life for themselves in Pennsylvania, anglicizing their names to Joseph and Sophie Abraham.

The passenger lists recorded at Ellis Island, the entry point for the assessment of immigrants to the United States, give a sense of the scale of new arrivals around the period of the *Titanic*'s doomed voyage. A random search: Josef Bacon of Laczki, Galicia, aged seventeen; Isaac Bacon, twenty-four-year-old Russian, on the *Verdi*, in 1909; in 1910, eighteen-year-old William Bacon from Catfield on the *Baltic*; Jan Bacon, Polish, aged eighteen, from Laczki, Galicia, on the *Main*; the Armenian Louther Bacon, aged eighteen, from Turkey, and his nineteen-year-old brother, Eghia, on the *Niagara* in 1911; Mary Bacon from Nottingham, with her four-year-old son, Albert, on the *Campania*, and Edward Bacon, twenty-two, from Belfast, on the *Celtic* in the same year; Vasilo Bacon, with her children Georges and Nicoleta, from Dauti in Greece, on the *Eugenia* in 1912. To these we could add the doomed Francis Bacon, from London, aged 314, on the *Titanic*, also in 1912, who never reached the New World.

These were women and men who saw in America new possibilities and who uprooted themselves from their families, communities, and networks to strike out for a different life. The parallel with the book conveyed from England to America is suggestive, though, admittedly, the agency is a bit different: Bacon's *Essaies* did not exactly choose to jump down from the shelves of Quaritch's in Bloomsbury and set out for the New World. Nevertheless, the thousands of European books bought by wealthy American magnates in the Gilded Age were economic migrants, too. Like the men and women looking for work, these volumes followed the money, leaving behind them decayed estates, economic austerity, and an Old World that was increasingly becoming the poor relation of the New. Migrant books were shipped to their new lives in New World libraries, museums, and collections on the same vessels as their human counterparts. The westward pull of books was noted with alarm by many aficionados in Britain: a cartoon in a British newspaper in 1922 depicted an Uncle Sam with a copy of Shakespeare's First Folio under one arm and Gainsborough's *The Blue Boy* under the other. Both had been in the news after high-profile sales to America.

Sociologists discussing possessions that relocate with

migrants talk about "diasporic objects"—that's to say, things detached from their place of origin that gain new meanings in their new contexts: they are both familiar and strange. One recent study, for example, discusses the placement of *matryoshka* dolls in the households of the Russian migrant community. Books are particularly appropriate examples in this discussion, since they all fan out from their place of origin, moving to and with their owners. Portability is intrinsic to their technological and cultural success. A recent UNHCR (United Nations High Commissioner for Refugees) photographic project by Brian Sokol includes a portrait of Iman, a Syrian from Aleppo, now in a refugee camp in Turkey with her two children, featuring a large Qur'an she brought with them for protection. The so-called Kennicott Bible, a manuscript prepared in fifteenth-century Galicia by the scribe Moses Ibn Zabarah in the Judaic year 5236, is witness to the exile of Spain's Jews, banished by Ferdinand and Isabella in 1494. Working with an artist who contributed numerous anthropomorphic and zoomorphic illustrations and who signed the book Joseph Ibn Hayyim, Zabarah's bold Sephardi script and delicate shaded shapes created a masterpiece. The family of Isaac di Braga, Zabarah's patron, was exiled first to Portugal and then to North Africa and Gibraltar. Their Bible went with them on this migrant progress and its journey documents their experience of diaspora.

Smaller and less elaborate Bible texts have notably accompanied more recent migrants, too. In 2019 Tom

Kiefer, who worked at a border-force detainment center on the US/Mexico border in Arizona, took a moving series of photographs of migrants' possessions confiscated and thrown away by officials. What is so powerful about these images, exhibited under the ironic title "El Sueño Americano" ("The American Dream"), is the individual lives hinted at by these cheap, common but personal items and the utter callousness of treating these possessions as trash. Among the portraits of toothbrushes and children's toys is a picture of six small-format blue books laid out in rows on a paisley handkerchief. They are copies of the *Nuevo testamento*. These Spanish-language New Testaments published with Psalms and Proverbs are distributed by Gideons International, an evangelical Christian publisher based in Nashville, Tennessee, best known for its placement of free Bibles in hotel rooms. At first, Kiefer's symmetrical photographic arrangement suggests that they are simply multiple copies of a mass-produced and mass-distributed book: the Gideon website claims that it has given out over 2 billion copies in multiple languages over the past century. But a closer look shows that these books give a heartbreaking glimpse of their social and emotional lives. They are proxies for their forgotten owners. One blue Bible is carefully marked with a flutter of fluorescent Post-it notes; another apparently contains photographs or other mementoes and is kept closed with elastic bands; one has a cover bleached from sunlight; another has been curved around the contours of a body, having been carried in a pocket. Even the most mass-market book takes on an individual shape and character through use; even these migrants' identical Spanish-language Bibles are each, preciously, one of a kind. In this particularity they are quite different kinds of objects from the repeated combs, toothpaste, and soap of Kiefer's other images.

Just as for human migrants, the prospect of books returning home is highly emotional. In 1982 a Mexican journalist took from the Bibliothèque Nationale in Paris an ancient eighteen-page Aztec codex, handing it to Mexico City's Museum of Anthropology as an act of guerrilla restitution. A more diplomatic solution was achieved by the newly independent republic of Iceland, which began negotiations with its former ruler, Denmark, about the repatriation of manuscripts taken to the University of Copenhagen in the seventeenth century. Iceland argued that there was a strong moral obligation to return the manuscripts after the ending of the union with Denmark in 1944. The counterarguments proposed by the Danish political and cultural authorities are familiar from other debates about the restitution of cultural property: opponents argued that the manuscripts were relevant to a larger Scandinavian heritage rather than the nation-state of Iceland, and further that Iceland had no appropriate heritage infrastructure to house, conserve, and study the treasures.

In 1971 a live television broadcast showed a large crowd lining the harbor in Reykjavík greeting the arrival of a Danish naval frigate and the Danish Minister of

Education returning two Icelandic texts, *Flateyjarbok* and *Konungsbok eddukvaeda*. (By contrast, the flag at the Copenhagen Royal Library was flown at half-mast.) *Flateyjarbok* is a lavishly illustrated, large-format medieval compilation of sagas of Norse kings in two volumes. It is written on vellum in a black glossy ink made by boiling bear-berry plants and has particularly beautiful illuminated capitals. The *Poetic Edda* is an "unprepossessing" small-format brown-bound book containing some ninety pages of verse written as prose to save space on its browning vellum pages (the description is by Carolyne Larrington, its most recent translator). Sent as a gift to King Frederick of Denmark (hence *Konungsbok*) in 1662, it is the sole early witness to the poetic depiction of pre-Christian Scandinavia and has been vital to our understanding of Norse mythology and heroic legend. The *Poetic Edda* has influenced culture from Wagner's *Ring* cycle to *Lord of the Rings* and *Game of Thrones*. Well over a thousand other literary and administrative Icelandic manuscripts held by Denmark were returned over the subsequent twenty-five years, making this small, bookish, independent nation at the forefront of debates about the restitution of cultural artifacts from former colonial rulers. In 2021, the fiftieth anniversary of the beginning of the manuscripts' return, Iceland began construction work on a new "Icelandic House" at the university in Reykjavík for their conservation. This is, writes Jeanette Greenfield, "the outstanding example of a major state-to-state return of cultural property":

a potential model for claims for restitution of objects from colonial museums recently dubbed "brutish" by the activist curator Dan Hicks.

The Icelandic manuscripts were unique books. But, unlike Harry Widener and the other 1,495 victims of the *Titanic*, his 1542 earthquake pamphlet lost at sea was not irreplaceable. If you look in the catalogue of the Widener collection now at Harvard University, it's there. A copy emerged at auction that had been in the collection of the ardent Victorian collector Thomas Phillipps. Phillipps had left a will stating that his huge library must remain in perpetuity in his house, that no bookseller or other stranger should rearrange it, and that no Roman Catholic, nor his daughter and son-in-law (James Halliwell-Phillipps, a fellow collector a little too free with his scissors to be an entirely reassuring presence in a library), be admitted to see the books. The will was contested and declared too restrictive. Phillipps's collection was sold in numerous sales right up until the 1990s. The earthquake volume was sold by William H. Robinson, booksellers in Pall Mall, in 1950. The buyer was, again, a man called Widener: George Jr., who donated this replacement of the book lost with his brother Harry to join the collection at Harvard. Buying a replacement for the Widener collection acknowledges the young collector's books as an expression of the man himself: his tastes, his ambitions, his presence—an early-twentieth-century "shelfie." But it is also a poignant reminder that, bluntly, books, unlike people, are usually replaceable.

By collecting, Belk suggests, "the collector brings order to a controllable portion of the world. Collected objects form a small world where the collector rules." It may be a fantasy of control and order that underpins many instances of book collection. But the kingdom of book-collecting tries to erect borders where books resist them. Books' intrinsic portability means they are always on the move, always migratory, always displaced. They are the ultimate diasporic objects.

7

Religions of the book

At the turn of the twenty-first century a campaign for fans of the *Star Wars* film franchise to identify as "Jedi" when asked about their religion in the UK census resulted in almost 400,000 protestations of faith. Some years later the Charity Commission ruled that Jedi was not a religion as it did not promote moral or ethical improvement and therefore the Temple of the Jedi Order did not qualify for charitable status. But in one important sense the evolving *Star Wars* universe revealed that the morphology of Jediism did follow the shape of many more established religions. Later episodes of the film franchise retrofitted Jedi as—like Judaism, Islam, and Christianity—a religion of the book. In *The Last Jedi (Episode VIII)*, a disillusioned and grizzled Luke Skywalker has retreated to Ahch-To, a distant planet that was the birthplace of the Jedi order. Like an interplanetary Prospero from Shakespeare's *The Tempest*, he has his library for company: eight bound volumes of the Jedi's ancient scriptures stored on a shelf in a hollow tree trunk. Like all iconic libraries since Alexandria, the collection is destroyed by fire. Yoda, with his characteristic syntax, is unperturbed by the conflagration and dismissive of the value of the books: "page-turners they were not." He suggests rather that the future of the Jedi will be secured by humans passing on their wisdom not by written but by oral transmission. But in the last moments of the film the scriptures, along with a handful of the rebel fighters, are found to have survived and been stowed carefully in the Millennium Falcon. We have, Princess Leia encourages the depleted resistance, "all we need" to rebuild, and that includes the ancient books.

Star Wars fans will see the contrast with the series' representation of the Jedi Archives, a repository of advanced digital knowledge based on the Long Room in Trinity College Dublin. Books of scripture are not, it seems, these immaterial packages of information. Rather, these sacred items were lovingly created for the film set by artisans "who designed and printed painstakingly detailed vellum-like sheets then bound them in the cast of a hand-carved cover." Official Lucasfilm archivist Madlyn Burkert describes "a host of individual pages, designed and lettered as if they truly held the knowledge of those first Jedi practitioners. There's incredible attention to detail on each page, layers of gold leaf mixed with blue pigments and an unidentified script, perhaps inspired by some of the earliest scrolls and scribbles from our own human history." The invented Jedi scriptures establish themselves with the visual shorthand of established protocols for sacred or magic texts: ancient leather bindings, vellum, gold leaf, blue pigments, ancient scripts. The iconography of scripture has remained remarkably stable. These film props are books that would have been as recognizable as religious texts to the Christian convert Emperor Constantine in the fourth century or the modern scribe who created a handwritten Bible for Saint John's Abbey in Minnesota in the twenty-first as they are to Rey and Luke Skywalker. But if books help to establish religions, the reverse is also true. Religions established the book, shaping its form and encouraging its global dissemination.

There are many theories about why the book triumphed over the clay tablets and papyrus scrolls that predated it. One is convenience. The book was the original and most significant reading hack roughly three millennia after the earliest forms of writing developed in Mesopotamia. If you've ever tried to do your own wallpapering, you already have some sense of the difficulties of the scroll. Scrolls, or rolls, were the information-delivery system for classical antiquity. They comprised long sheets of papyrus or parchment divided along their length into pages, which were read by moving the text between two rollers, like frames on analogue photographic film. In China, silk and paper scrolls opened from right to left; elsewhere, the unfurling went from left to right. Manipulating a scroll took two hands. It was hard to find a specific reference or place and almost impossible to refer to two parts of the scroll simultaneously (although sutra-folded binding of Chinese texts by the early Tang Dynasty produced a concertinaed scroll that was easier to consult). The roll had to be rewound at the end of reading to be ready for the next reader. Only one side could be inscribed with information, so it was wasteful, and longer texts needed multiple scrolls. Nevertheless, scroll technology was used to record all kinds of material, from early texts of the *Iliad* or plays by Sophocles and Aeschylus to scriptures, histories, and administrative documents. Tabs helped divide a long text into sections and labels allowed the title to be read without unwinding the scroll. Best of all, it was perceived to be durable. As the sixth-century scholar and statesman Cassiodorus wrote, papyrus "keeps a faithful witness of human deeds; it speaks of the past and is the enemy of oblivion."

But the new technology of the book—gathered sheets folded and fastened at the back or spine, often protected by covers—made a different kind of reading experience possible. Readers could immerse themselves and interact in new ways with the text: skimming, flipping back and forth, or flicking through pages to find a particular bit. Neuroscientists have investigated the ways we use smartphones to explore the human brain's plasticity and the interconnectedness of the fingertips and cortical processing in the brain: their professional ancestors in the early centuries of the Christian era might have used books for similar experiments. Books inaugurated a gestural vocabulary of handling that is now so familiar to us as to seem entirely natural: turning the pages from the corner or far edge; using a finger or other convenient marker to refer to several different points, flexing the spine or cover to make it stay open with minimum effort. Elaborating on his famous dictum that "the medium is the message," Marshall McLuhan identified that "the 'message' of any medium or technology is the change of scale or pace or pattern that it introduces into human affairs." The medium of the book was transformative in human affairs at every scale, from the physical habits of reading to the understanding of the world.

One history of the adoption of the book claims that Julius Caesar invented its early form, known as the codex, as a convenient medium for his dispatches to the Senate. An epigram by the Roman poet Martial dating from around 100 BCE encourages readers to try out this handy newfangled codex in terms that characterize the physical appeal of the book for its readers to this day: "You who want my little books to keep you company wherever you may be and desire their companionship on a long journey, buy these, that parchment compresses in small pages. Give book boxes to the great, one hand grasps *me*." He ends with a cheeky advert for the vendor of these desirable biblio-artifacts: "But in case you don't know where I am on sale, . . . look for Secundus, freedman of lettered Lucensis, behind Peace's entrance and Pallas' Forum." Martial's emphasis on mobility puts portability at the start of the book revolution. He advertises a Roman precedent for those later railway bookshops and handy paperback formats that confirmed books as the ideal travel companion. When publisher Allen Lane, in transit from a meeting with Agatha Christie, wished for something to read on a journey, he was channeling Martial (see Chapter 2).

Still, for many historians the most plausible narrative about the coming of the book is ideological—or doctrinal. Pioneering historical scholarship on adoption of the codices in the early CE period demonstrated that Christian Scriptures and non-biblical religious literature drove the preference for the codex over the roll. By contrast, the reading market for literary texts seemed content with scrolls. Without religion, no book. Christianity and the codex seem to have marched in step through the first centuries of the Christian Era. The case of one particular early Bible, known now as the *Codex Sinaiticus*, illustrates their reciprocity—and also has a story to tell, via Orthodox monks and Joseph Stalin, about books and cultural value in more recent times.

In 331 CE Emperor Constantine wrote to Eusebius, the scholar and bishop of Caesarea, an important center for early Christianity in modern-day Israel. He ordered fifty Bibles from the scriptorium at the theological library in Caesarea for his new churches in Constantinople. It is just possible that one of these mail-order parchment Bibles is still extant in the elaborate handwritten Bible known as the *Codex Sinaiticus*. This book, dating from the fourth century CE, takes its name from the Greek Orthodox Monastery of St. Catherine on Mount Sinai in Egypt, founded around 330 CE and later named after the Christian martyr St. Catherine. The current monastery buildings date from the sixth century. Here, the *Codex* was "discovered" in the nineteenth century (like many narratives of discovery before and since, this seems to have involved a European traveler coming across something of which a local community was well aware and then appropriating it). Some leaves remain at the monastery, but the bulk of the now-incomplete book is held in the British Library, with portions in Leipzig and St. Petersburg.

The *Codex* is a large, almost square volume on parchment, handwritten by three, or possibly four, scribes, in continuous majuscule (uppercase) script without spaces between the words. Each page is about 38 by 34 cm (it's a bit bigger than an old LP) and has four columns of text, so each double-page opening has eight columns, visually equivalent to a scroll with its horizontal frames of text—a sign that this book represents a transitional document between reading technologies. The book is a vital text for biblical scholars as the earliest witness to the Greek text of the Bible and as a source of early textual corrections. It also demonstrates an alternative canon of biblical books, before the Christian Bible had established its authorized form, including the little-known visionary texts known collectively as the Shepherd of Hermas, books from the Old Testament now considered apocryphal (such as the Wisdom of Sirach) and the Epistle of Barnabas, claimed to be by the apostle. The *Codex* witnesses the struggles within Christianity to create canonical Scripture: under the surface of the authoritative Bible text, in any format, are centuries of dispute and argument about its content.

The discovery of the *Codex Sinaiticus* and the book's subsequent itinerary have been controversial. Constantin von Tischendorf, a German scholar working under the patronage of the Russian tsar, removed it from St. Catherine's in the middle of the nineteenth century. Whether this was by stealth or agreement is now unknowable, though the former seems more likely. Documents in the possession of the monastery suggest they loaned the codex in order that it might be copied; von Tischendorf claimed to have saved it from the monks' kindling basket and seems to have considered it his grateful gift to his patron as the defender of Orthodox Christianity. He undertook a detailed study of the work in Russia, presenting both the manuscript and his own lavish facsimile edition to the Imperial Library.

In a further twist, the work was sold by Stalin in 1933 to raise hard-currency funding for his second Five-Year Plan. The London booksellers Maggs were the brokers. Ernest Maggs, who had been to Leningrad to secure the deal, maintained that they had beaten the Russians down from double the price: at the same time he also bought from the Russian government a Gutenberg Bible, on behalf of the Swiss collector Martin Bodmer; it still resides in his foundation in Cologny. The *Codex Sinaiticus* was bought for £100,000, paid by the British government (and aided by public subscriptions managed by a campaign by the British Museum). The Bible manuscript was carried up the steps of the British Museum on December 27, 1933, to the sound of cheering and a brass band. *The Times* reported that a long queue developed to view the manuscript in its glass case and described a crowd "drawn from all sorts and conditions of men and women, and of many nations and languages." Claims that it had been unlawfully alienated from St. Catherine's continue to rumble; perhaps the museum's initial fundraising appeal comparing it to "such famous possessions as the Elgin Marbles" did not help. To this day, the monastery's website maintains with melancholic restraint that von Tischendorf took it unlawfully and that the community "laments the loss of this manuscript."

The *Codex Sinaiticus* offers a significant insight into the needs driving the development of book technology early in the life of the codex. A single book of the Bible would have taken up an entire scroll of manageable length; the codex enabled a collection of biblical books to be bound together as a continuous text. Papyrus, the material used for scrolls, was adopted for early Christian codices in Egypt (each page was cut from a roll, so early papyrus codices were upcycled scrolls), and the practical limits of this technology can be seen in the division of longer Old Testament books into, for example, 1 and 2 Samuel, or 1 and 2 Chronicles. The word "Bible" comes from the plural Greek *biblio*, "books," attesting to its composite nature. Since biblical study does not primarily rely on sequential reading (unlike, say, the reading of a serialized novel), the codex would also allow for the comparison of particular passages for scholarly or liturgical purposes. In time, parchment became more common for these larger volumes. By the time of the *Codex Sinaiticus* and Emperor Constantine's bulk purchase of manuscript Bibles, Greek biblical codices were being copied onto parchment rather than papyrus, a substrate that was lighter, stronger, more flexible, and less inclined to grow brittle with time (although some of the advantages of parchment over papyrus have been overstated, perhaps as part of the downplaying of the story of the codex before it reached Western Europe).

Christianity and the book continued their interconnection through the first centuries CE, deploying new developments in technology to transmit the Scriptures and to establish Christianity as a religion of the book. Early Gospel books were elaborately decorative, often written in gold or silver on parchment dyed purple to signify God as king of creation. Byzantine mosaics dating from the sixth century show Christ Pantocrator at the east end of the church, blessing his people while holding a decorated book of the New Testament. Sometimes this is open, facing outward, to show a carefully depicted script. The St. Cuthbert Gospel, found in the coffin of the early Christian saint and bishop of Lindisfarne, dates from the early eighth century. Its red goatskin binding preserves a Latin manuscript of St. John's Gospel that can claim to be the earliest intact European book. In the eighth-century parchment book of rules for the order of St. Benedict, now in the Bodleian Library, are preserved not only the illuminated capitals and beautiful script of its unknown monastic scribe but the finger marks, in the middle of each page, indicating where it was held and its pages turned. The book, now a library treasure, was a manual for communal and godly living: these dirty smudges seem almost to symbolize the fallen world into which its unblemished rules were issued. Appropriately, among those rules were daily reading, including reading a book in Lent and carrying a small book to consult when traveling. Books, that's to say, were both instructional and devotional for these Christian communities, recording temporal rules alongside divine inspiration.

The necessity for, and development of, bookbinding techniques to hold the extended volumes together triggered doctrinal debates. Instead of the miscellaneous ordering of individual scrolls, the codex fixed for the first time the order of the books of the Bible and thus subjected it to confessional argument. This can be seen in the ongoing differences in what is included and in what order between Protestant and Catholic Bibles. As we saw in Chapter 1, Gutenberg began his Bible not with Genesis but with the letter of St. Jerome to Paulinus: this edition of the Vulgate, compiled by St. Jerome, comprised seventy-three books of Scripture and still forms the official scriptural canon of the Catholic Church. The Authorized Version of the Bible published in Protestant England in 1611 included eighty books. Contested books such as Esdras (included in the Bibles of Orthodox Christianity), or Enoch (canonical in the Ethiopian church), or the Book of Revelation (Luther attempted to have it removed from a reformed canon) are all textual versions of doctrinal differences and schisms.

What's included, or excluded, depends on theology: for example, Catholic canons tend to include Maccabees, which refers to Purgatory; Protestant canons exclude it.

Christianity is not the only religion of the book, of course. Other religions, too, have books at their authoritative center, including the "Mother of Books," *Umm al-kitab*, which is preserved in the presence of God and on which Muslims believe the revelation of the Qur'an is based. But the centrality of print is distinctive to Christian history. In Islam, the "Mother of Books" was written by angelic scribes on pure sheets with a celestial reed pen, and dictated by the Angel Gabriel to Muhammad, bit by bit, in rhymed prose. Muslims thus joined Jews and Christians as people of the book, simultaneously demoting these prior religions, arguing that Muhammad was the last recipient of the Word in its final and conclusive state. After the Prophet's death, these divine revelations were compiled into the Qur'an. A major aspect of Islamic teaching is learning by rote rather than reading, and this preference for oral transmission has historically suppressed Islamic book production, particularly in print. Nevertheless, sumptuously worked calligraphic Qur'ans embody the reverence for the holy book. Early Qur'ans from the eighth to the tenth century used parchment, and Arabic entrepreneurs developed paper, borrowing techniques from China that used mulberry bark and adapting them for fine linen rag paper, around the year 800, long before these technologies reached the Western scriptorium. Until the nineteenth century,

Qur'ans were typically transmitted in manuscript, often with fine calligraphy: earlier printed copies tend to come from European rather than Arabic traditions. It was not until 1870 that the Ottoman emperor allowed Muslim publishers to print the entire Qur'an, and these nineteenth-century books were often produced not through movable type but by lithography, which allowed scribally produced text to be transferred to limestone from which print impressions were taken.

While the scroll was to the Jewish Talmud what the codex was to the Christian Bible, the development of rabbinic scholarship and annotation meant that the codex became more important, too, for Judaic religious texts. Perhaps the first book printed on the continent of Africa is a 1516 rabbinical commentary in Hebrew, published in Fez, Morocco, by émigré printers from Portugal. Traditional orthodox Torah scrolls are still made on parchment on wooden rollers. Although many New Testament translations have Jesus consulting the book of Isaiah in the synagogue in Nazareth, according to Luke's Gospel, this text would have been in scroll format. The medieval bibliophile Richard de Bury, assuming that the text was in codex form, divined from it general instructions for the appropriate handling of books. Christ was recruited against Bury's own hobbyhorse, book carelessness: "The Saviour also has warned us by His example against all unbecoming carelessness in the handling of books, as we read in St. Luke. For when He had read the scriptural prophecy of Himself in the book that was delivered to

Him, he did not give it again to the minister until He had closed it with His own most sacred hands." In Bury's reading, Christ was the first scary librarian.

According to the Pew Foundation, more than half the world's population is identified with one of the three religions of the book: disrespecting their books is profane. The history of religious intolerance is punctuated by symbolic acts of destruction of rival scriptures, from the burning of the Torah by the Roman Emperor Hadrian, the annihilation of the Cathar textual tradition as heretical by the thirteenth-century Catholic Church, and the Florida pastor Terry Jones's provocative "burn-a-Koran day" in twenty-first-century America. That our earliest books are religious has been decisive in shaping attitudes to the book itself. All our books are Bibles in the etymological sense (that shared root of *biblio* and "Bible") and they carry with them that significance. Even nonreligious books are marked by an instinctive respect for the book object and an implicit prohibition on destroying it. Many people feel very strongly indeed about writing in books, or tearing pages, or otherwise damaging them, seeing these as forms of desecration of a sacralized object. However ordinary, books still retain an aura, a vitality, that is always in excess of their actual contents. The destruction of books is an emotive subject for many reasons, not least, as we will see in the following chapter, because it seems to attack sacred—even animate—matter, something that has its own life and deserves respect.

8

May 10, 1933: burning books

Godwin's Law provides the facetious but useful observation that the longer an online debate lasts, the more
exponentially likely a comparison to Hitler or the Nazis
becomes. There should be an annex to the law that sus-
pends its operation whenever the topic being discussed
is book burning. The Nazi bonfires of May 10, 1933,
have established themselves in popular culture as the
establishing instance, and the high (or low) point of
bibliocide. This is despite, or perhaps because of, the fact
that book burning for ideological reasons is almost as
old as the book form itself. As the British Jewish essayist
Isaac D'Israeli, father of the Prime Minister Benjamin
Disraeli, put it at the end of the eighteenth century with
gleeful circularity: "The Romans burnt the books of the
Jews, of the Christians, and the Philosophers; the Jews
burnt the books of the Christians and the Pagans; and
the Christians burnt the books of the Pagans and the
Jews."

Book burning can serve a number of purposes, from
waste management or destruction by the books' authors,
to publicity or rituals affirming specific identity or community values. It can be publicly organized as a spectacle

to shame the authors and their acolytes or a private activity to purge individual guilt. Samuel Pepys spent the early part of Sunday, February 9, 1668—marked in his diary as "Lord's day"—"at my chamber all the morning and the office doing business, and also reading a little of 'L'escholle des filles,' which is a mighty lewd book, but yet not amiss for a sober man once to read over to inform himself in the villainy of the world." The pornographic French pamphlet *L'Escole des filles* had been the target of sustained attempts at censorship, gaining it considerable notoriety, and sales, in the process. The few extant early copies show many of the telltale evasive markers of illicit literature, which include false imprints, bogus places of publication, fictitious names of printers, pirated or copycat editions, and a muddled publishing genealogy. *L'Escole des filles* was a byword for libertinism in Restoration comedy and had an ongoing, checkered life in different print formats through the eighteenth century and beyond, including now as a popular Amazon e-book.

Pepys had bought his copy at Martin's booksellers on The Strand the day before, describing it an "idle, rogueish book" and explaining, "I have bought [it] in plain binding, avoiding the buying of it better bound, because I resolve, as soon as I have read it, to burn it, that it may not stand in the list of books, nor among them, to disgrace them if it should be found." Pepys clearly bought an imported French-language edition, because he says he was originally planning to have his wife translate it, but realized on consultation of the volume that it was much too bawdy to be suitable for a woman. Two decades later, the London publishers of a translation, *The School of Venus, or The Ladies Delight*, were prosecuted for "printing divers obscene and lascivious books, one called The School of Venus" and "for selling several obscene and lascivious books." Joseph Streeter and Benjamin Crayle were fined 40 shillings and 20 shillings respectively. Perhaps Pepys acquired the 1668 edition that stated, incorrectly, that it was "imprinté à Fribourg" by the nonexistent and suggestively named publisher "Roger Bon Temps." This furtive little book is easily concealed and suggests onanistic privacy. (Only one copy is now known to exist: the combination of its small size and fragility and its contested content has driven this early edition to near-extinction.) Pepys's purchase was attentive to the book form: this desirable but transgressive text was explicitly purchased as a disposable object, in plain binding, rather than as a contribution to his growing library. The end of his diary entry repeats that he read the book "for information sake," then burned it and went, in his characteristic sign-off, "to supper and to bed." Pepys enacted his own moral censorship on a book that had evaded the authorities' attempts to burn it publicly in Paris in 1655. But not until after he had eagerly consumed its overheated erotic contents. It's the book equivalent of Augustine's famous prayer "Lord, make me chaste, but not yet."

Private book burning such as this by Pepys, however, seems relatively unusual: more often book burning is a theatrical activity designed to communicate to an audience as much as, or more than, to destroy specific titles. In classical antiquity, book burning served as a kind of ritualized purification of works whose content was deemed dangerous or seditious. In the third century BCE, the Chinese emperor Qin Shi Huang ordered the burning of books of history to consolidate his imperial power and remove material from which unfavorable comparisons might be made. Hebrew books were burned across the Italian states in 1553 as part of the Inquisition. A Norfolk subscription library in 1836 burned George Borrow's translation of a Faust book, since the disloyal son of the county gratuitously transposed Faustus and the Devil to a town whose citizens had "such ugly figures and flat features, that the devil owned he had never seen them equalled, except by the inhabitants of an English town called Norwich, when dressed in their Sunday's best." Thomas Hardy reported that the Bishop of Wakefield burned a copy of *Jude the Obscure*, a book often dubbed "the Obscene" (the bishop actually said that he had thrown it into the fireplace in disgust), "probably in his despair at not being able to burn me." Protesters at the Soviet invasion of Hungary in 1956 burned copies of Russian classics and works by Stalin and Lenin. Different individuals and groups turned to public conflagration to publicize their disapproval of a writer or their affiliations.

One notable bonfire smoldered throughout the European Reformation. Early Modern Protestantism and the

printing press had gone hand in hand across the continent. Martin Luther's challenge to Catholic orthodoxy,
pinned as his Theses to the door of the church in Wittenberg in October 1517, quickly flashed around Europe.
The Basel printer John Froben exported Luther's works
to England, and Erasmus, writing to his friend Thomas
More and sending him a copy, reported on Luther's
increasing popularity among the English elite. John
Dorne, an Oxford bookseller carrying a wide-ranging
stock of academic, literary, and leisure reading, sold a
dozen copies of eight different titles by Luther in 1520.
By then, though, the tide was turning against Luther
across both England and Europe. A Cambridge University order the same year records payment of two shillings
"to Dr. Nycolas, deputy Vice chancellor, for drink and
other expenses about the burning of the books of Martin Luther": it's not absolutely clear what this refers to,
but it does suggest that book burning might be accompanied by a party. By early spring 1521, Cardinal Wolsey
had forbidden the import of Luther books, and the
Pope amplified this command, suggesting that a bonfire
would be a more decisive solution to "extirpate . . . the
Lutheran heresy." The Diet of Worms (a formal assem-
bly of the Holy Roman Empire) in April 1521 confirmed
this edict: "All the books of Martin, wheresoever found,
should be burnt." The following month, the hierarchies
of Church and state attended the burning of Luther
volumes in St. Paul's Churchyard in London as a show
of diplomatic and religious solidarity. An elaborate and

stately procession of clergy, ambassadors, and other dignitaries arrived at St. Paul's. A platform covered with a golden canopy had been erected where Wolsey, with the Papal Nuncio, the Archbishop of Canterbury, the ambassador of the Holy Roman Empire, and the Bishop of Durham seated below him, listened to a two-hour sermon denouncing Luther by John Fisher, during which "there were many burned in the said churchyard of the said Luther's books."

Like many instances of book burning before and since, this bonfire of Luther's works in May 1521 was symbolic rather than effectual. After all, a staggering number of Luther's books and pamphlets were published during his lifetime: Christopher de Hamel gives a figure of more than 3,700 separate editions, or two a week throughout his adult life. When the Wittenberg printer Hans Lufft retired in 1572, he claimed he had printed almost 100,000 Bibles in Luther's translation; counterfeit colophons claiming Wittenberg as the place of publication were also common, sometimes to give a false Lutheran imprimatur to boost authority and sales, sometimes to deflect suspicion in territories that had banned the publication of Luther's works. This flow of printed volumes could never be entirely incinerated: book burning was a fleabite rather than a body blow. In some ways, the 1521 burning wasn't even about Luther's books but about the delicate and shifting alliances between Europe's monarchs and the papacy during the early sixteenth century. These burning books were not a substantive issue but rather props in a pageant intended to implicate, unite, and intimidate a range of spectators. This was less about censorship than about political theater. And the ironies of this particular event are resonant. Within weeks of the book burning, King Henry VIII adopted the title of Defender of the Faith, a first step in his establishment of himself as head of the Church in England and thus of the break with Rome. The prolix preacher at the burning, Bishop Fisher, would eventually be executed for refusing to acknowledge Henry as head of the Church. Lutheranism never was contained, or containable, in the books.

Book burning is powerfully symbolic and practically almost entirely ineffectual. Since the development of print, the dominant characteristic of the printed book has been its reproducibility. It is what sociologists call a "protocol object," something standardized and mechanically produced, as opposed to a "biographical object," something individual, bespoke, or one-off. (We might think here of the replaceability of Widener's books, but not of Widener himself, discussed in Chapter 6.) The colonial explorer Henry M. Stanley—of "Dr. Livingstone, I presume" fame—told an anecdote about his field notebook, "with a vast number of valuable notes; plans of falls, creeks, sketches of localities, ethnological and philological details sufficient to fill two octavo volumes—everything was of general interest to the public." The Mowa people took exception to his note-taking and required that the book "fetish" must be

burnt to avoid ill luck. Rummaging among his belong-
ings, Stanley "came across a volume of Shakespeare
(Chandos edition), much worn and well-thumbed." Sub-
stituting a printed book existing in thousands of copies
for his unique notebook, he "consigned the innocent
Shakespeare to the flames," to a sigh of relief from the
"poor deluded natives." Stanley manipulated the symbolic power of book burning to his own ends, while
playing on the replaceability of print. We might well
notice that, while the notion of the book as a powerful
fetish is attributed to "the childish caprice of savages,"
Stanley's own heavily used copy of Shakespeare has
something of the same talismanic or religious properties for the Englishman in equatorial Africa.

In the era of print, burning books can never extirpate
their heresies. The book bonfire merely stages communal
or partisan disapproval of them. And, further, book
burning—as Stanley's sacrifice of one disposable book
in place of the unique manuscript demonstrates—is a
spectacle that can easily be repurposed, escaping the
control of the authorities imposing it. One Tudor reader
of Luther who rewrote the book-burning narrative is
memorialized by John Foxe in his book of Protestant
martyrology, *Acts and Monuments*. Foxe recounts the
actions of the merchant Thomas Sommers, who, as
punishment for his ownership of Lutheran works, was
to be shamed by public penance and forced to toss his
transgressive theological books into a bonfire. But Sommers took control of the event, riding to Cheapside on

a finely trimmed horse donated by a supporter instead of the ignominious "colliers' nag" intended by Wolsey. Instead of condemning the forbidden books to the flames, he flaunted them by turning them into clothing: "Taking the books and opening them, he bound them together by the strings and cast them about his neck (the leaves being all open) like a collar." Sommers threw Luther's translation of the New Testament over, rather than into, the fire, three times, at which point "a stander by took it up, and saved it from burning." The book was actually saved rather than destroyed by this repurposing of spectacular censorship: Foxe's story is about the ultimate victory of Protestantism, as symbolized by its books.

This trope of ideological theater has persisted. At least two waves of burning have targeted J. K. Rowling's Harry Potter novels in the twenty-first century. Both conservative and progressive communities have focused on the material book as the symbol of disapproval. The first included pyres supervised by Catholic priests in Poland and by evangelical Christians in New Mexico, attacking the books' depiction of magic and the occult; the second was a social media phenomenon sharing images of charred pages in protest of views expressed by the author that have been labeled transphobic. One tweet in response smartly activated Godwin's Law: "1930s Nazis called. They want their book burning policy back."

Recourse to those 1930s Nazis is unavoidable, so let's

investigate. On the evening of May 10, 1933, choreo-graphed pageants of book burning took place in thirty-four university towns across Germany, organized by Nazi student groups as the climax of their campaign of "Action against the Un-German spirit." From Ham-burg to Munich, and from Bonn to Berlin, where Joseph Goebbels addressed a large crowd, works by promi-nent Jewish writers were targeted. So, too, was the more expansive ethical category of "anything that works sub-versively on family life, married life or love, or the ethics of our youth, or our future, or strikes at the roots of German thought, the German home, and the driving forces in our people." Confiscated and donated books, plus volumes removed or deaccessioned from library collections, were gathered for burning: in the event, too many books were contributed to be consumed in the time available, and many were sold on in bulk to paper mills for recycling.

The roll call of authors whose books were burned is both shocking and familiar: Einstein, Freud, Gide, Marx, Zola, Wells, Brecht, Kafka, Mann, Hemingway, and London; copies of the Hebrew scriptures were also burned. Erich Kästner, an author now better known for his children's fiction, including *Emil and the Detectives*, was present in the Berlin crowd to see his depiction of Wei-mar hedonism, *Fabian*, among the books burned. (An uncensored translation of this book, reverting to Käst-ner's initial title *Going to the Dogs*, was printed only in 2013.) Fire oaths committing spectators to the ongoing work of purifying German Aryan culture were signed by the jumping firelight. Under the heading "Bibliocaust," *Time* magazine described the scene in Berlin, where a "black mass of criss-crossed logs insulated from the pavement by sand" had been prepared, "a thumping band blared out old military marches" to accompany a uniformed procession late in the night of students wearing "blue tunics, white breeches, plush tam-o-shanters and spurred patent-leather jack boots. Behind them came other students and a line of motor trucks piled high with books." The students formed a chain, with "the books passed from hand to hand while a leather-lunged student roared out the names of the authors." Like the 1521 burning, it was a piece of theater. Staged at night to amplify the visual impact of the flames, it was part student initiation, part fascist spectacle, part witches' sabbath or black Mass.

The US Holocaust Memorial Museum estimates that around 90,000 volumes were consumed by flames in the coordinated burnings. Micha Ullman's 1995 sculpture memorial to the burnings in Berlin's Bebelplatz sets a glass panel into the square with a view of an underground room of empty bookshelves, with space for the 20,000 volumes estimated to have been burnt in Berlin. These numbers, like the theater of burning, were largely symbolic. The greater and more effectual purge came in the ensuing weeks and months, during which millions of books were withdrawn from German libraries and bookshops.

In 1933 the international response to the events of May 10 was relatively low-key. Only Jewish communities sounded the alarm. In the US, the Union of Jewish Orthodox Congregations announced special services in protest. The following day, 100,000 protesters mobilized by Jewish organizations marched in New York and there were demonstrations in Chicago, St. Louis, and other American cities against what *Newsweek* called "a holocaust of books." Although many commentators were, rightly, deeply alarmed by what they saw, this night of symbolic bibliocidal pageantry had not yet taken on the retrospective horror of the Holocaust: the word was used in *Newsweek* with its literal meaning of "a sacrifice wholly consumed by fire." American responses tended to emphasize the youth and immaturity of the protagonists and to dismiss the escapade as "senseless," "ineffective," and "infantile": the poet Archibald MacLeish described "the misled and ignorant boys" of the Nazi Party. One columnist threatened an avuncular "box on the ear" to those involved: "Somebody ought to tell Adolph's adolescents that it isn't funny anymore." Howard Mumford Jones, addressing the American Library Association in October 1933, was typical in treating book burning as trivial and immature rather than ominous: "The barbarities of Hitlerism have been equalled only by its stupidities, among which I count the childish burning of books."

It was the coalition of prominent American publishers who formed the Council on Books in Wartime

(Chapter 2) who would really seize on the 1933 book burnings as the iconic image of Nazism. The council prepared a range of publicity material that fixed cultural censorship as the primary symptom of the totalitarianism against which the Allies were fighting. Bookshops were sent display packs for the anniversaries of 1943 and 1944, clergy were urged to denounce book burning from the pulpit, and Eleanor Roosevelt used her popular syndicated newspaper column "My Day" on May 11, 1943, to cite "freedom of speech and thought" as crucial to democracy and to note that book burning had had the opposite effect: banned authors' "contributions to the thinking of the world are probably far greater than they would have been without Hitler's effort at suppression." Roosevelt's column coincided with a commemoration of the burnings that took place on the steps of the New York Public Library, its flag flying at half-mast. *The Library Journal*, the official journal for the profession, took as its wartime motto "In America we do not burn books, we build libraries." Frank Capra's propaganda film for American service personnel, *Prelude to War*, cited the freedom to read books as one of a handful of symbolic key freedoms for which the war was being fought, and included newsreel footage of the Berlin book burnings and a spinning collage of forbidden titles. Among the changes made in Frank Borzage's 1940 MGM film *The Mortal Storm* to Phyllis Bottome's 1937 novel of the same name was to include an extensive sequence of book burning—something that didn't seem relevant to the story of Nazi ascendance in 1937 was indispensable by 1940.

Under the auspices of the council's publicity program, the Pulitzer Prize winner Stephen Vincent Benét wrote a play for national radio in 1942, *They Burned the Books*. In an ironic echo of Shylock's famous speech about the shared humanity of Christian and Jew from Shakespeare's *The Merchant of Venice*, Benét's narrator proposed:

> A book's a book. It's paper, ink and print.
> If you stab it, it won't bleed.
> If you beat it, it won't bruise.
> If you burn it, it won't scream.
> Burn a few books—burn hundreds—burn a million—
> What difference does that make?

Benét brought in a sequence of literary voices from Schiller to Milton to Whitman to explain that very difference. Interestingly, while he includes Heinrich Heine, whose works had been included in the 1933 book burning, he does not attribute to the Jewish Romantic poet and literary critic the phrase that has forever linked him to the book bonfires. Tucked away in Heine's early and unsuccessful play *Almansor* (written in 1821–22), an orientalist love story set in Moorish Granada in the reign of Ferdinand and Isabella, the eponymous hero reports the burning of "the Holy Koran on a flaming pyre." His servant Hassan's reply, "A prelude only, that. Where men burn books, / They will burn people also in the end," has resonated far beyond the Bonn theater world of the early eighteenth century. Written under the weight of Prussian antisemitism that would prompt Heine's own unwilling conversion to Protestantism, *Almansor* gave this epigram to a mid-twentieth century slow to acknowledge the terrible truth about Nazi death camps. Linking the book burnings with the extermination chambers of the concentration camps, the holocaust with the Holocaust, Heine's prediction established the stakes of bibliocide as a prelude to genocide.

Heine's quotation forms part of contemporary Berlin's memorial to the events of May 10, 1933, and it has established a now-conventional historical elision of bibliocide and genocide. Correlation, though, is not causation. An efficient bureaucracy, the railway network, hyperinflation, centuries of antisemitism—these and many other precedent causes or contexts for the Holocaust could each have provided a hypothetical first clause in a rewritten version of Heine. As it is, the centrality of Heine's quotation creates a perverse, unethical equation that anthropomorphizes the book. The stakes could not be higher. As Ray Bradbury put it in a later commentary to *Fahrenheit 451*, "when Hitler burned a book I felt it as keenly, please forgive me, as his killing a human, for in the long sum of history they are one in the same flesh." I'm not sure we should forgive this false equivalence, nor fall for this rhetorical trick.

Book burning did happen in May 1933 across German towns, but it was in America almost a decade later that the spectacle gathered its true ideological weight, as part of a US narrative of its own values that has spread around the world to inform contemporary attitudes. For many, book burning has become the most highly charged and visible form of attacks on culture: the phrase is often used as a synonym not simply for the destruction of the material book but for any censorship of its text. In fact, as we have seen, burning books is a deeply inefficient way of eradicating them and a failure as a means of censorship. To even begin to try to cancel the products of the modern printing press, you'd need a different tactic—something like large-scale industrial pulping.

Destruction by pulping is, as it happens, a common fate of the modern book. In the US in the early twenty-first century, returns of unsold books run at between 30 and 40 percent; the large majority are pulped. The contemporary book industry has a short attention span and its products need to move quickly or they will be withdrawn; publishing economics spreads its bets across a large number of titles and makes the majority of its profits from a small proportion of best sellers. And books, unlike most consumer items, are taken by retailers on a sale-or-return basis, meaning that unsold books, or at least their covers (proving they have not been sold: you may have noticed the clause inside many books restricting circulation "in any form of binding or cover other than that in which it is published"), are returned to the publishers for refunds. The largest destroyers of books are, therefore, publishers themselves. In the UK,

Penguin Random House owns a large "centralized returns processing site" in Manningtree, Essex (the US publishing industry is less candid about its recycling). It's a great euphemism: processing, in this context, means shredding, crushing, and baling around 25,000 books a day for paper recycling. Some of this paper is reused for new books, just as, in the early decades of the printing press, printed or manuscript leaves were reused to stiffen the bindings of later volumes. But there are other uses, too. Some 2.5 million pulped copies of Mills and Boon romantic novels were used to create an absorbent, noise-reducing layer for surfacing the M6 toll motorway in the English Midlands. A spokesman for Tarmac reassured "Mills and Boon readers that we're not just picking on their favourite books—other books are down there too."

Pulping books for road substrate is not, of course, the same as the ideologically charged spectacle of book burning. But it is worth remembering amid our careful curation of books on our own shelves and in libraries that it is the fate of most books to be destroyed, one way or another (Chapter 9 discusses book destruction in the context of library curation). Book burning is a highly emotive trope and is visually and symbolically compelling for those who burn and those who deplore it. But, in itself, burning a book is irrelevant. Where people burn books, they are usually inadequate attention-seekers rather than genocidal tyrants. In the end, books are not people, and it is morally repugnant to bracket their destruction together in the same breath.

9

Library books, camp, and malicious damage

As Banksy is to a wall in Clerkenwell, so Joe Orton and Kenneth Halliwell were to the mid-twentieth-century library books of Islington: fringe, or graffiti artists, whose work has been transformed from vandalism to art. In the years after their move to Noel Road, Islington, in 1959, the couple began an extended art project, or, if you prefer, a campaign of malicious damage, with the disappointingly limited selection of books in their local library branch. This involved excising illustrations for the decoration of their flat and repurposing some of them, adding scurrilous false blurbs and re-illustrated jackets. The doctored books were then returned to the library for ongoing circulation. Today, we can see how they propose a kind of queer, surreal collage that anticipates Terry Gilliam's stop-motion montage animations for *Monty Python* at the end of the 1960s; they also preempted the vogue for unique or handmade artists' books that became prominent around the same time. We might call it a prank performance or guerrilla art, particularly in retrospect, given that Joe Orton went on to have a notable career as a subversive and audaciously funny playwright. But, at the time, Orton and Halliwell's work on the Islington Library collection was not considered art: the pair were caught and put on trial. What Orton and Halliwell did, and how their book transformations were received, reveals much about the spoken and unspoken book rules of the lending library, and about our attitudes to the appropriate treatment of books.

A 1960 romance by Phyllis Hambledon, *Queen's Favourite*, published by Ward Lock is a good example of both the underlying form of the books Orton and Halliwell chose for retrofitting and the kitsch way in which they transformed them. Hambledon's original dust jacket pictured a winsome young wasp-waisted woman in a ruff and long gown standing in front of the gatehouse of a Tudorish castle. In its place, Orton and Halliwell have produced a collage of two bare-chested young men wrestling against a Mughal wall. The flowing script of the title in the original suggested that the pictured woman had a privileged position at court; cut out and entirely repurposed by its repasted proximity to the homoerotic scene it becomes a piece of queer innuendo. The back of the dust jacket goes full absurdist, with a semi-naked man bowing at the feet of an empress while a large goose looks on.

The couple's collages play with scale and incongruity to shock the unsuspecting library visitor. In a study of John Betjeman they replaced a photograph of the respected and respectable English poet in a straw boater and three-piece suit with one of a pot-bellied man in underpants, his body covered in tattoos. Some interventions were more explicitly daring: the pair doctored the cover of an adventure novel by Bentz Plagemann about the navy in wartime, replacing a naval cap and a stethoscope with a prominent male torso and groin. Others were plainly surreal: a large goose (again!) sits companionably at the knee of a solemn, bearded Edwardian on the cover of a book on yoga; Orton and Halliwell adorned a play by John Osborne with a large budgerigar; and inserted a monkey's head at the heart of a flower in a guide to roses. Orton suggested that it was this last treatment that was truly unforgivable and caused "the greatest outrage, the one for which I think I was sent to prison." The *Daily Mirror* report of the trial came under the headline "The Gorilla in the Roses."

A red Heinemann hardback of *The Collected Plays of Emlyn Williams* had alternative typewritten titles posted over the originals on its cover. These ranged from the Carry On-saucy (this contemporaneous, seaside-postcard-comedy film franchise set in, and fondly against, British institutions is another analogue to Orton and Halliwell's handiwork) "Knickers Must Fall" (in place of Williams's *Night Must Fall*) to the more brusquely explicit "Fucked by Monty" (*The Light of Heart*). Sometimes the joke ran in the opposite direction from what might have been anticipated. Williams's *He Was Born Gay* was changed to "He Was Born Grey." In other examples, too, part of the joke seems to have been precisely in not making an obvious intervention: some self-control must have gone into their work on a biography of a theater couple called *The Lunts* that left the title unchanged while replacing the portrait of the subjects with a tray of tacky ornaments. The yellow dust jackets of Dorothy L. Sayers's detective novels were thoroughly and debauchedly rewritten, promising the author "at her most queer, and needless to say, at her most crude!" Orton later pointed out that these blank yellow flaps in Gollancz books were ideal for producing "mildly obscene" "false blurbs," since they could be removed from the book, typewritten on, and reinserted.

Not all the reworked covers dealt in camp juxtapositions and kitsch artifice: a series of Shakespeares revitalized the dull jackets of the Arden textbooks with classical sculpture and baroque painting illustrating *Antony and Cleopatra*, while an inspired collage for *Othello* juxtaposed a cutout of Giorgione's *Sleeping Venus* with an image of the Moorish St. Maurice by Matthias Grünewald. No one could deny that these are a clear improvement on the plain originals (and on subsequent Arden cover art). The deft cut-and-paste montages of the Shakespeare covers are an example of the cleverness and the care, almost reverence, that characterized the couple's work. Their interactions with the books show considerable precision and deliberation. Appropriate images are sourced and clipped, positioned and pasted; dust jackets are painstakingly removed, typed upon, and put back on; lettering is repositioned. These graffitied library books clearly took up a lot of their time and creative energy.

This project anticipated the centrality of books to

radical art movements in the later twentieth century. Only a few years later John Latham, hailed as a pioneer of conceptual art, borrowed a book called *Art and Culture* from St. Martin's School of Art Library, where he was teaching. He divided it between a group of friends, and they each chewed a number of pages then spat them into a phial containing yeast and acid. He took the fermented result, *Still and Chew*, back to the library; they rejected it. He was sacked from the college, but *Still and Chew* is now owned by the Museum of Modern Art in New York. Among his book sculptures, which he called *skoob*, was a controversial piece called *God is Great (No. 2)*, consisting of copies of the Bible, Talmud, and Qur'an sawed in half and attached to a sheet of glass. It was intended for an exhibition at Tate Britain in 2005 but was withdrawn, causing considerable debate, because of fears of religiously motivated retaliation at the disrespect shown to holy books.

In a later interview Orton suggested that he had been infuriated that Islington Library did not have Gibbon's *Decline and Fall of the Roman Empire*: "I was enraged that there were so many rubbishy novels and rubbishy books." He linked his own creative biblioclasm with Gibbon's famous counterintuitive take on the fate of the ancient Library of Alexandria: "They used the contents of the library to provide fuel for the baths and Gibbon thought that probably the books were doing more good being so used than they were when being read." Most of the repurposed library books might be said to do more good in their Orton–Halliwell form than when being read. Most are titles that are now long forgotten. The point of the intervention was to disrupt the stultifying norms of middlebrow judgment. Susan Sontag's "Notes on Camp," written around the same time as their library interventions and first printed in the *Partisan Review* in 1964, could almost be a commentary on their debauched découpage. Her elevation of the artifice and extravagance of camp, an aesthetic in which "homosexuals ... constitute the vanguard," observes: "One is drawn to Camp when one realizes that 'sincerity' is not enough. Sincerity can be simple philistinism, intellectual narrowness"—or the Islington Library *c.* 1960. "I don't think," Orton remarked in an interview in 1967, "there's such a thing as good taste and bad taste."

At the men's trial, their probation officer described them as "frustrated actors and frustrated authors": the adapted texts are indeed a flamboyant theater, with books as players and the couple as directors and, later, audience. Orton recalled, "I used to stand in the corners after I'd smuggled the doctored books back into the library and then watch people read them. It was very funny, very interesting." That this was a joke was widely recognized, even if it was not found entirely funny. The *Daily Mirror* emphasized the ludic elements of the prank: "Strange things began to happen to books borrowed from a public library." Mr. Harold Sturge, the presiding magistrate at the men's trial, most certainly did not see what was amusing. Telling them, "You showed sheer malice towards fellow users of this library, who have been deprived of the pleasure of these books," he sentenced Joe Orton and Kenneth Halliwell to six months in prison.

Two things seem striking at this historical distance. The first is the length of the sentence. The *Daily Express* reported, on the same page as the Orton–Halliwell book trial, the same term for a drunken driver who killed his passenger. "Because we're queers" was Orton's caustic assessment of the severity of the custodial punishment, and institutional homophobia in the period before the legalization of consensual sex between men in 1967 must have been a significant factor in the couple's treatment. But there is also more than a whiff of a curious cultural overinvestment in the book as a sacred object that makes acts described in court as "malicious damage" somehow morally equivalent, within the criminal justice system of England in May 1962, with causing death by dangerous driving. "What I am anxious to see," said Sturge, "is that the decision of this Court should make it abundantly clear that those who think they may be clever enough to write criticisms in other people's books—public library books—or to deface or ruin them in this way are made to understand very clearly that it is disastrous." Sturge's pompous summary of the crimes compresses various offenses, including over-cleverness, readers acting as writers, expropriation of property, and destruction of books. Only some of these are against the law. His ultimate equation—defacing library books and disaster—is asserted rather than argued.

Book vandalism and theft often capture a particular form of outrage among those who partly enjoy the spectacle and the nerdy intrigue and at the same time are partly horrified by them. The tone of *American Animals*, Bart Layton's crime docudrama about the attempted theft of rare books from a Kentucky university library, captures this wobble. Bored college students plan an unlikely heist to steal a first edition of Darwin and John James Audubon's huge, valuable *Birds of America*, an early-nineteenth-century collection of bird illustrations. *Birds of America* pushes the "portable" of *Portable Magic* to its extreme, as the would-be robbers discovered. A slapstick scene in which the book—a so-called double elephant folio measuring a meter long—is too large to fit in the lift and has to be manhandled down a fire escape brings out the queasy comedy often attached to book theft (although Layton's film does tone down the callousness of the would-be thieves in dealing violently with the librarian on duty). That sense of circus was fatal in the case of another book crook, Raymond Scott. He walked, wearing flip-flops, as the librarians later recalled in bemusement, into the Folger, the world's foremost Shakespeare library, in Washington, DC, with a copy of the first edition of Shakespeare's plays. The First Folio is one of the world's most-coveted books: I've been fascinated by it, and by the stories it contains and generates, for years. Of course, Scott was promptly arrested: First Folios don't just appear out of nowhere. Perhaps out of naïveté, he had taken it to the most expert place on the planet for an opinion, and their opinion was it must have been stolen. It did indeed belong to Durham Cathedral Library, from where it had been stolen while on display a decade earlier. Scott arrived at Newcastle Crown Court in a stretch limo, smoking a cigar and eating Pot Noodles, and quoting from *Richard III*, "a horse, a horse, my kingdom for a horse." Although there was no suspicion of violence in the case, he was sentenced to eight years in prison. As for Orton and Halliwell, the sentence seemed grossly disproportionate. In the same month as Scott's conviction, two teenagers were sentenced to five years for inflicting fatal injuries on a grandfather on his way home from the mosque, and a man whose company knowingly sold lethally unfit body armor to British troops in the Iraq War received a two-year suspended prison sentence. Something is happening when harm to books comes up for judgment.

In Scott's case, something about the intrinsic cultural value of the specific book, combined with its elevated price tag (First Folios sell at auction for millions of dollars), had inflated the seriousness of this nonviolent crime. Or maybe it is more that injuries done to the book during its absence from Durham, including the removal of preliminary leaves to conceal its provenance, are punished as if they were equal to, or more heinous than, equivalent acts of violence on a person. Back to, perhaps, Ray Bradbury's morally dubious equivalence between books and bodies discussed in Chapter 8. The consequence of the sentence was horrible. Scott took his own life in prison some eighteen months later, over-whelmed by the prospect of his jail term. The publicity for this desperately sad case was, throughout, much more concerned with the fate of the iconic book than with the unstable man, and the book's preservation was implicitly prioritized over that of Scott himself.

In Orton and Halliwell's case, the books they reappro-priated were not really intrinsically valuable, culturally or financially, in their original state. The pair were not preparing collages from rare books or slicing out valu-able illustrations or leaves from manuscripts. They were cutting and pasting onto some indifferent mass-market publications that could easily be replaced. Nevertheless, these library books were ascribed a value in excess of their actual status. The books' value lay—then as now—in their very bookhood. Unexpectedly, *Queen's Favourite* and *The Lunts* turn out to be the mid-twentieth-century equivalent of the talismanic books circulating in the medieval period (Chapter 12), or the misappropriated grimoire of the magus in *The Sorcerer's Apprentice* (Intro-duction). Regardless of their bland content, they are significant, effective, even magical, and therefore deserve veneration and respect by virtue of their form.

If the length of the sentence, and the implied impor-tance of the book objects in both cases, is one standout from this case, the second is the ambivalent role of the library. It was Islington Library who called in the police about the attacks on their books, after "elderly ladies started returning books at arm's length by their fingertips, saying 'this is revolting—it should never be in a public library.'" One of their employees, in an Agatha Christie twist (Orton and Halliwell had brightened up a drab edition of her *The Secret of Chimneys* with a collage of St. Mark's Square in Venice and a giant pair of simpering cats dressed as bride and groom), had traced the malefactors through a sting that drew an angry typed letter from Halliwell denying a trumped-up parking offense. Examining the damaged type in this letter and matching it to the offending false blurbs led to Orton and Halliwell's flat. At first, then, the library were energetic defenders of their property, and ingenious, if unethical, in finding the perpetrators. But it was also Islington Library that retained this doctored material, rather than discarding it as mere vandalism. Despite prosecuting a case that suggested the books had been damaged, the library now preserved them as works of art. The Orton–Halliwell collages are now on permanent display there, as the library's most significant treasures. The library's mission to preserve its books, that's to say, prompted both its prosecution of the vandals and its retention of their work.

The role of the public or lending library in policing the life of the book and endorsing its appropriate usage is a vital one: for many of us, libraries were foundational in learning habits not only of reading but of book handling and preservation. For centuries, the library was the private property of the nobleman or scholar. University and other institutional libraries catered to a narrow elite, frequently even among their own populations (for centuries, Oxford's Bodleian Library did not admit undergraduate readers who had not received their MA degree). The rules for appropriate book treatment in these elite libraries demonstrate their importance in regulating behaviors. Among the initial list of library matters requiring codification as he developed his plans for the Oxford library that would bear his name, Thomas Bodley pondered "the punishment of suche as shall embezel any booke, cutte out any tract or leafs, or raze any line or worde, or in any other sort corrupt or abuse any autour." This list of book depredations ballooned into the declaration demanded of each reader before admittance to the collection:

> that you conforme your self to studie with modestie and silence, and use . . . the bookes . . . with a carefull respect to their longest conservation; and that neither your self in person, nor any other whosoever, by your procurement or privitie, shall either openly or underhand, by way of embezeling, changing, razing, defacing, tearing, cutting, noting, interlining, or by voluntarie corrupting, blotting, slurring, or any other other manner of mangling, or misusing, any one or more of the saied bookes.

(The modern version of this oath, disappointingly, commits the reader only not to "mark, deface or injure in any way" any of the library's holdings; the loss of embezzling, corrupting, and mangling is grievous.) To be admitted to a library was, from the early modern period onward, to agree to a specific range of constraints over how books should be used. Libraries gave access to specific books, but in a wider sense they structured for readers what a book was and how it should properly be used.

In the eighteenth century, subscription libraries were established for the English middle classes on a shareholder basis: the oldest surviving example in the UK is Leeds Subscription Library, which opened in 1768 and still operates above a bank and a stationery shop on the city's busy Commercial Street. Other membership organizations also ran libraries, including philosophical and literary societies and mechanics' institutes. Subscription libraries predated public lending libraries, and will perhaps postdate them, too: the Chinese e-book subscription service backed by the Tencent media company had 192 million users in 2020; Amazon's Kindle Unlimited subscription is its attempt at a similarly large, recurrent income, set against the background of public library closures (20 percent shut their doors in the UK in the decade from 2010).

The Public Libraries Act of 1850, which established in Britain the principle of free libraries open to all and funded by public taxation, was a consequence of profound social change. Increased prosperity, higher levels of education, and more leisure time for working people created by legally protected working conditions, including limits on laboring hours, prepared the ground for reading for self-improvement and relaxation. The

Forster Act of 1880 turbocharged this emphasis on literacy and reading. Leeds clergymen agitated the city council in 1861 to provide "a free library, where men of all grades might resort, and from which books of an instructive and elevating character could be circulated without charge, [which] would greatly improve the social, morale and intellectual condition of the people of this populous and important borough." Public library provision expanded across these growing industrial towns first, making the library as much a part of the industrial landscape as workers' terraced housing and poor air quality. By 1886 there were 125 public libraries, almost a third of them in Lancashire, Staffordshire, or the West Riding of Yorkshire. The next wave of library provision reached county towns such as Truro, Winchester, Oxford, and Aberystwyth from the 1880s. The Scottish-born philanthropist Andrew Carnegie funded more than 2,800 public libraries across the English-speaking world. Almost four hundred library buildings in Britain are associated with his name, including Islington, the scene of Orton and Halliwell's artistic crimes. Carnegie's gift of £40,000 in 1904 established the borough's central library against the resistance of local ratepayers.

Those Yorkshire clerics advocating a library as a moral resource have cast a long shadow over the public library and its operations. A meeting of public librarians in Brighton in 1908 attempted to codify the aims of a public lending collection and reiterated strongly didactic principles:

1) That the function of a Public Lending Library is to provide good literature, and the same test must be applied to works of fiction as to books in other departments—they must have literary or educational value; 2) that every library should be amply supplied with fiction that has attained the position of classical literature; and 3) that the purchase of mere ephemeral fiction of no literary or moral value, even if without offence, is not within their proper province.

Public libraries, then, established and controlled appropriate reading matter: they were vectors for both book transmission and book restriction. And they were crucial, for the millions of readers who used them, in making the book a shared, communal property rather than an individual one.

Public lending libraries thus developed in growing urban cities that were shaped by Victorian commerce and industry, drawing on public funds and philanthropy, in particular the transformative gifts of the great apostle of capitalism, Andrew Carnegie. And yet the paradox is that libraries are countercultural, rejecting precisely those commodity relations that were their enabling condition. No other consumer item is routinely borrowed (and for free) rather than bought outright. Despite being commodities, produced by the market, books have also resisted those frameworks of value for more than 150 years. Uniquely among comparable consumer objects, books circulate, for free, borrowed from the lending library and returned for checking out by the next reader.

Borrowed books trace material connections between members of a community, gathering symbolic weight and cumulative identity through their anonymous circulation. One influential collection of essays in the field of object biography has the title "The Social Life of Things": the books in a lending library might be thought to be the extroverts of this model of material sociability, always gadding about. Of course, there are potential downsides to this gregariousness. Nineteenth-century journalist and library reformer Frederick Greenwood campaigned for the wide adoption of his "book disinfecting apparatus"—a metal fumigator in which "compound sulphurous acid is burned in a small lamp, and a very little suffices to disinfect the books." Anxieties that books were transmitters of disease came at the same time as the smallpox, tuberculosis, and scarlet fever epidemics of the later nineteenth century. Library books and their appropriate disposal became part of statutory reporting under the Infectious Diseases (Notification) Act of 1889. Public Health Acts Amendments in 1907 explicitly restricted book circulation from households or individuals who had been exposed to infectious disease and legislated that any book suspected of bearing germs should be disinfected or destroyed. The prominence of books in these anxious narratives of disease is noteworthy, and not confined to the pre-antibiotic period. Public Health England issued reassurance early in the

Covid-19 pandemic that the risk of viral transmission from a paper or card cover was minimal after twenty-four hours' quarantine and that seventy-two hours was sufficient to decontaminate plastic-backed books.

Fears about infection through the circulation of library books reimagine familiar anxieties about the power of books in the wrong hands. As Leah Price puts it, "the traditional fear that 'unhealthy' texts could 'poison' their readers was literalized by the worry that book objects could spread disease, older concerns about the communion of a reader with a text gave way to newer ones about readers' contact with one another." That unsuspecting readers at Islington Library might be put into proximity with the queer imagination that produced the doctored books was the unspoken charge at the trial of Orton and Halliwell. Lending libraries had established protocols for book-handling and for book circulation that were decisively subverted by Orton and Halliwell's scissors-and-paste guerrilla action. The social etiquette of libraries as networks of readers, the role of the library as moral arbiter (discussed in the following chapter), the sense that the library book is, uniquely among consumer commodities, not the private possession of a reader but the shared property of the library community, and the cultural investment in the sanctity of bookhood—these weighty matters of book ethics all tumbled onto Joe Orton and Kenneth Halliwell in that London courtroom.

10

Censored books: "237 goddams, 58 bastards, 31 Chrissakes, and 1 fart"

Ai Weiwei's exhibition at London's Royal Academy in 2015 was full of characteristic works charting China's rapid economic development and its accompanying restriction of individual liberties, devastation of the environment, and destruction of its built heritage. *Fragments* used architectural salvage from destroyed historical temples; a pair of handcuffs carved in jade and a monumental marble surveillance camera were also displayed, riffing on the traditional materials of Chinese art. One exhibit consisted of two apparently identical copies of Phaidon's popular *The Art Book*, a wide-ranging alphabetical account of art across the centuries and the globe. This chunky paperback with a zany selection of fonts on its cover exudes approachability and unpretentiousness, promising "a fresh and original approach to art" that breaks with "traditional classifications."

Both copies of *The Art Book* are open at a yellow shaded rectangle by the abstract German painter Josef Albers on the recto (right-hand page), but the facing versos carry different images. One has a short biography of Ai Weiwei and a photograph of his installation *Template*, made of temple salvage. This is the edition sold in the UK. In the other, published in English for the Chinese market, a minor Umbrian Renaissance sculptor, Agostino di Duccio, replaces Ai Weiwei. (Di Duccio's other claim to fame is also as a substitute for someone more famous: having lost the commission to provide a statue of David for the Duomo in Florence, he left a partly carved block of Carerra marble to his successor, Michelangelo.) Presumably di Duccio was included in the Chinese *Art Book* not for any particular artistic claim but because Agostino was least disruptive alphabetically. Only the comparison with the Western edition of the book makes clear the censorship in the Chinese edition.

Although at first sight the setting out of these two books for comparison may seem like background information on the place of the dissident artist in his native China, its glass exhibition case holds its own artwork. As *objets trouvés* from a global bookshelf, these two interconnected books together produce a narrative that displays the different pressures under which they are produced. The excision scar is neat, the patch barely visible, but the apparently global commodity of the English language book here conceals a distinct local variant.

We tend to think that censorship obliterates or erases texts so that they are completely lost from view, and perhaps that is the fantasy of censors themselves. Ray Bradbury's *Fahrenheit 451* imagines an off-kilter dystopian world in which books are summarily destroyed by fire crews employed to cause, not extinguish, flames. The alienated fireman Guy Montag is reassured that this is a recipe for civil peace and serenity across communities. Bradbury's examples invoke real-world instances of controversial or censored books: "If Colored people don't like *Little Black Sambo*. Burn it. White people don't feel good about *Uncle Tom's Cabin*. Burn it. Someone's written a book on tobacco and cancer of the lungs? The cigarette people are weeping? Burn the book." His superintendent, Beatty, instructs him in the art of igniting the pages of a book "delicately, like the petals of a flower," their charred remains like "swarms of black moths that had died in a single storm." Bradbury later discovered that his own parable of censorship had itself been censored for use in American schools. During the 1970s and '80s, Ballantine, his publishers, gradually scrubbed away seventy-five instances of "damn" and "hell" to make the novel more acceptable for the lucrative education market. Censorship here is designed to maximize circulation of the text, not minimize it.

That books could be canceled as if they had never existed is barely possible in the era of print (see Chapter 8). More often, censorship is exerted on the extant book, which survives as a witness to the attempt to censor it. This produces a particular kind of object that, like the Chinese edition of *The Art Book*, captures between its pages something of the wider conflicts in which it is embroiled. Rather than canceling it, censorship can preserve, or transform, or reimagine, the printed book that is its target. Censored books are not absences or gaps but often deeply and insistently present. Take a copy of

Shakespeare's collected plays. (Not literally: we have seen what happened to Raymond Scott in Chapter 9.) This time, not the prized First Folio, but the second edition, originally published for John Smethwick and sold at his Fleet Street shop in London in 1632, which found its way to the Jesuit seminary of St. Alban's College, known as the English College, in Valladolid. From the late sixteenth century onward St. Alban's trained missionary Jesuits, sleeper cells for the long task of reconverting England to Catholicism. The college counts many martyrs among its alumni. Perhaps surprisingly, Jesuit seminaries made extensive pedagogical use of appropriate drama to teach the crucial evangelical tool kit of rhetoric, memory, and persuasion, either adapting existing texts or producing new plays for the trainees. Shakespeare—or at least some Shakespeare—was included in this missionary curriculum, as the Valladolid copy of the 1632 edition makes clear.

This copy shows how, under his Hispanified name of Guillermo Sanchez, the Englishman William Sankey, later the rector of the college, undertook to prepare the book for devout seminarians. Sankey had form in the role of sectarian censor: he had already scored out a poem on the defeat of the (Catholic) Spanish Armada and removed the pages recounting the Gunpowder Plot (the attempt by Catholics to blow up King James in Parliament) from a book of recent English history acquired by the library. That this book existed at St. Alban's at all—most recent English history, in the seventeenth century, was distinctly unpalatable to Catholics—illuminates the paradox of book censorship and its instinct, often, to make the book better rather than obliterating it. On the Shakespeare volume, Sankey exerted his most sustained—and perversely delicate—piece of censorship, again with the clear aim of preserving as much of the book as possible. Censorship becomes, paradoxically, an attempt to enable rather than entirely suppress the book. It is a creative process that makes a new book, better fitted to and more expressive of its own context.

Sankey's methods, and the resulting pages, are familiar to anyone who has seen redacted documents in the political realm. He uses a heavy ink to blot out words, lines, or whole scenes, producing page openings that alternate blocked-out rectangles with the two-column print of the surviving text. That the text has been censored is absolutely visible on the page: there is no attempt to suture up the edges of a deletion to preserve the sense or shape of a scene, and no alternatives for the objectionable material are offered. In this way, the book displays its own adaptation to its context: drawing forth the material relevant to the seventeenth-century seminarian and eliding the rest. Such adaptation is an implicit feature of all reading: we all ignore or repress or simply glide over the bits we find dull, repetitive, or even offensive. But what Sankey's censorship does here is mark these elisions on the physical book. Contrast this with another famous case of censoring Shakespeare. Thomas Bowdler, with his sister Henrietta, produced the *Family Shakespeare* for the respectable early-nineteenth-century drawing room with a title page advertising that "nothing is added to the original text; but those words and expressions are omitted which cannot with propriety be read aloud in a family." The power of this original instance of bowdlerization is that the book itself gives no indication of the extent or location of suppressed material.

By contrast, any reader of the Valladolid Shakespeare cannot fail to clock the work of the censor, since the heavy ink of what's been blocked out is the most visible aspect of the book's pages. Did readers accept that the redacted material was unsuitable and irrecoverable, or was there a Jesuit equivalent of what social media calls the Streisand effect (named after the actor who attempted, counterproductively, to restrict online circulation of images of her Malibu beach home)? This is the inadvertent consequence of censorship: it draws attention to the censored material and makes access to the uncensored version all the more desirable.

Visibly redacted material in similar publishing genres is sometimes deliberately inserted to heighten the perceived drama of the revelations in the book. Asked at the obscenity trial of D. H. Lawrence's *Lady Chatterley's Lover* in 1960 about the possibility of sidestepping the question of offense by publishing a redacted version, one expert recognized the unintended consequences: "As for asterisks in place of incidents in the sexual scenes, Sir William thought that 'would make the thing just a dirty book,' while dashes instead of the four-letter words would also create unwholesome associations."

Copies of the uncensored version of Lieutenant Colonel Anthony Shaffer's account of American operations in Afghanistan, *Operation Dark Heart*, sold for thousands of dollars in 2010 once the US government had paid the publishers to withdraw the first edition and to replace it with a heavily and visibly redacted one. Some of the blocking out in the second edition is strikingly specific: Shaffer's description of how he took one of his undercover aliases from a John Wayne movie, for example, creates from two paragraphs of his chatty prose the virtually incomprehensibly staccato "I glanced down at my baggage tags, where I'd scrawled . . . The blue ink was partially smeared . . . I picked up the name . . . from a . . . movie . . . who moulds his company into a combat-ready machine." The effect is to draw attention to what is missing and to make the redacted material the dominant reading experience. The censored text becomes a military memoir ghost-written by Samuel Beckett or Harold Pinter: a curious mash-up of tough talk and weighty silences.

Much of William Sankey's effort on his copy of Shakespeare is, understandably, given the context, directed at religious disputes. In particular, he takes his expurgating pen to anti-Catholic statements in *King John* (Pandulph, the papal legate, gets some stick in this history play) and to pro-Protestant statements in *Henry VIII*. On page nine of the first play in the volume, *The Tempest*, the shipwrecked jester Trinculo encounters the native islander Caliban for the first time and plans to make money out of him by showing this exotic prize at fairs for "holiday fools." The text's original spelling reveals the etymology of the word—"holy-day." Sankey blacks out this word so it is unreadable: presumably it was disrespectful to the Christian calendar. Elsewhere he is attentive to sexual innuendo, but not exhaustively so. Only a few lines later, in the same column of text of *The Tempest*, he makes no intervention in a cheerfully bawdy song about the good-time girl Kate, her "tongue with a tang," whom "a tailor might scratch . . . where'er she did itch." Indeed, Sankey finds nothing to trouble his seminarian sensibilities in the rest of the play, nor in the immediately following comedies, until, some hundred pages later, he reaches the witty Margaret in *Much Ado About Nothing* remarking on the eve of her marriage that Hero's heart will be "heavier soon, by the weight of a man." You can almost hear his sigh of disapproval (but also, perhaps, of self-validating relief—at last! Something to cross out!) as he picks up his quill, loaded with dark ink.

Sankey's censoring work on the Shakespeare folio is interesting precisely because it aims at preserving the plays for the seminarians, minus their offensive parts. It is an enabling strategy at least as much as it is a restrictive one. Almost half the plays in the volume are unmarked. This is both an act of censorship and an act of remediation, resulting in a unique copy of the plays. It anticipates, in highly original ways, the work of making Shakespeare more decorous, or more relevant, or more suitable for children that has prompted theatrical adaptations and new editions, including Bowdler's, right down to the twenty-first century. Only one play is beyond remedy at St. Alban's (just as it was, coincidentally, for Bowdler, who did not include it in his collection): the "vicars and tarts" party that is the problem play *Measure for Measure*. In this sleazy drama, the ruler pretends to be a friar, and a nun is propositioned within a morally compromised urban environment of corruption and commodification. Although later critics have argued for the play as a religious allegory in which the friar-duke comes, Christlike, to restore a fallen people, this does not wash with William Sankey. At this point in his reading of the Second Folio's nine hundred pages, he swapped his censoring quill for a razor and simply excised the offending pages, cutting as close as he could to the center binding to eradicate traces of the play. Only the remaining narrow stubs in the book's bound margin reveal that anything is missing. This Catholic Shakespeare, replete with Jesuit signatures, excisions, doodles, and some evaluative commentary and still in its dark-brown seventeenth-century calf binding, is now in the Folger Shakespeare Library in Washington, DC. It takes its place (as copy number 7) amid the fifty-seven other copies of this edition collected by the foliophile and oil millionaire Henry Clay Folger, each one with its distinctly individual life story inscribed on its pages.

A more wholesale attempt at censorship under the auspices of the Catholic Church was the *Index Librorum Prohibitorum*—the Index of Forbidden Books, compiled and published by the Vatican across four centuries. It began amid the religious turmoil of the mid-sixteenth century that attempted to suppress the works of Martin Luther and was finally abandoned in 1966, three years after, as Philip Larkin rather mournfully timetabled progressive attitudes in his poem "Annus Mirabilis," "Sexual intercourse began . . . Between the end of the 'Chatterley' ban / And the Beatles' first LP." Drawing on biblical precedent, the *Index* took as its epigraph the verse from Acts 19: "And many of them who had followed curious arts, brought together their books, and burnt them before all."

Busy with the Catholic Church's response to the Reformation, the Council of Trent, convened in 1545, was particularly concerned with books. It established the Latin Vulgate as the definitive edition of the Bible (see Chapter 7 on the debates over the canonical books of the Bible) and formed a Congregation of the Inquisition to identify dangerous books and compile an official list of forbidden works. After many revisions this was issued in print in 1564 by Pope Pius IV. The first edition of the *Index* was printed in Rome by a publisher with a considerable pedigree. Paulus Manutius was the son of the most famous sixteenth-century humanist printer, Aldus Manutius, whose pioneering books in meticulous Latin and Greek were revolutionary in form and content. For some scholars, these Aldine books are the true forerunners of the modern paperback; they are also credited with securing the survival of many classical texts in accurate print editions. Paulus inherited the anchor motif of his father's Venetian Aldine Press. Given its associations with the widespread dissemination of literature and its commitment to circulating classical texts, it is unexpected to see the trademark logo on a book dedicated to censorship.

The *Index* initially focused on theological controversies and on volumes that, frankly, have lost their power to shock for all but the most dogmatic of readers. Luther, of course, was included (see Chapter 8), as was the Protestant reformer John Calvin and the biblical translator William Tyndale. However, the Vatican's list-compilers became increasingly interested in obscene or explicit literature that could corrupt a reader's morals, and that Catholics could read only with permission. Condemned books judged heretical, lascivious, or obscene, as well as those on sorcery or magic, had to be approved by Church officials prior to printing. Anyone reading or possessing books listed in the *Index* was threatened with excommunication. The *Index* was always running to catch up, continually trying to update in the face of a tide of immoral or irreligious titles as new fronts opened up in its moral crusade. In 1596 the Talmud and other Jewish works were added. New editions of the *Index* were issued in 1664 (now as a cross-referenced alphabetical list), 1758, and 1900, by which time Voltaire, Locke, Diderot, Rousseau, Kant, and Leibniz had joined, the list now attempting to police Enlightenment thought. An addendum of specific passages in books that should be excised to make the remainder canonically acceptable was published as the *Index Expurgatorius*. But, like all acts of censorship, it had that Streisand effect. It was suggested by Thomas James in 1627 that the *Index Expurgatorius* was an invaluable reference work of books worthy of collecting by the Bodleian Library, on a librarian's sectarian version of the old adage that my enemy's enemy is my friend. The fiercely anti-Catholic (that's saying something in the seventeenth century) bishop Thomas Barlow agreed that the censors had provided an invaluable service: since "we are directed to the book, chapters and line where anything is spoken against any superstition or error of Rome, . . . he who has the *Indexes* cannot want testimonies against Rome." The recently opened archive of the *Index* deliberations shows numerous notable authors, including Harriet Beecher Stowe, Charles Darwin, and Adolf Hitler, among hundreds scrutinized but not ultimately placed on the prohibited list. Among the last authors to be included were Jean-Paul Sartre and Simone de Beauvoir, but by the 1960s the Church effectively admitted defeat on the task of policing print publication. Always unevenly applied, and probably never successful, the *Index* was finally a casualty of Vatican II reforms: a notification from Cardinal Ottaviani in June 1966 explained that it was putting its trust in "the mature conscience of the faithful, and especially the authors, the Catholic publishers and those concerned with the education of the youth" to prevent the circulation of harmful books, and that while the *Index* was still morally binding it no longer carried the force of ecclesiastical censure.

The liberalization of the 1960s had an impact on book censorship beyond the Vatican. Books, including Allen Ginsberg's *Howl*, Vladimir Nabokov's *Lolita*, and William S. Burroughs's *Naked Lunch*, which had fallen foul of censorship in the 1950s, were published. The most iconic case was the *Lady Chatterley* trial, in which Penguin Books were charged in the UK under the Obscene Publications Act. D. H. Lawrence's novel challenged taboos about class, sex, and explicit language by depicting the relationship between married aristocrat Constance, Lady Chatterley, and gamekeeper Oliver Mellors. Since its publication in the late 1920s, the book had been banned in Ireland, Poland, Australia, Canada, and India, as well as by US Customs in 1929. A trial in Japan in 1951–52 found the translation guilty of obscenity and fined the publisher and translator, Sei Ito. However, Penguin was emboldened by a recent US judgment in 1959 that the book's "literary merit" outweighed any offense from the "candor and realism" of its language. Federal Judge Frederick Bryan judged that the book did not appeal to prurience or express "dirt for dirt's sake" and so the ban contravened the First Amendment on freedom of speech. An American edition with a preface was published in 1960. A new obscenity law in the UK allowed publishers to make the case for literary merit to avoid censorship, and Penguin decided to road-test the new Act by presenting copies of the banned *Lady Chatterley's Lover* to a London police station to precipitate prosecution.

The trial and its assumptions about sex, gender, class, and reading were widely understood as a cultural watershed. Mervyn Griffith-Jones's famously patrician peroration for the prosecution sounded like an elegy for a bygone age: "Would you approve of your young sons, young daughters—because girls can read as well as boys—reading this book? Is it a book you would have lying around in your own house? Is it a book you would even wish your wife or your servants to read?" This was greeted with laughter from the jury. Griffith-Jones's bald enumeration of the book's obscenity is comic in its banality: "The word 'fuck' or 'fucking' occurs no less than thirty times . . . 'cunt' fourteen times; 'balls' thirteen times; 'shit' and 'arse' six times apiece; 'cock' four times; 'piss' three times, and so on." Penguin's unexpurgated paperback edition, with the publisher's distinctive vertical orange bands, black lettering, and the price, 3/6, marked on the cover, was a prominent exhibit in the theater of the trial. That it was "published by Penguin for the ordinary reader" and at a low cost was part of the prosecution's case. This was a trial of a paperback, and of paperbacking itself. The summary of the defense called out this elitism and the "attitude that it is all right to publish a special edition at five or ten guineas, so that people who are less well-off cannot read what other people do." During the trial, witnesses were asked to turn to particular pages of the Penguin edition and explain specific episodes or phrases. The jury were not allowed to take it home to read but had to read it in the jury room. Even the judge carried his copy to and from court discreetly stowed in a damask bag stitched by his wife to avoid causing offense on the Tube.

After Penguin was cleared of obscenity and the book ban rescinded, the print run of 20,000 copies sold out in days. A second edition, identical except for an introduction by Richard Hoggart, was published in 1961. Hoggart had given detailed evidence about the book and analysis of key passages under cross-examination at the trial, describing it as "virtuous and, if anything, puritanical." He contrasted its literary merits with the pornographic books of which "you can buy two dozen in the Charing Cross Road in the morning. They are paperback books at two and sixpence. In every one of those there are almost as though by recipe two or three sexual encounters . . . they are there presumably because they sell the book." By contrast, Lawrence's sex scenes were aesthetically and morally integrated into a literary whole. The dedication to the second edition memorialized its recent publication travails:

For having published this book, Penguin Books was prosecuted under the Obscene Publications Act 1959, at the Old Bailey in London from 20 October to 2 November 1960. This edition is therefore dedicated to the twelve jurors, three women and nine men, who returned a verdict of "not guilty" and thus made D. H. Lawrence's last novel available for the first time to the public in the United Kingdom.

As the case of *Lady Chatterley's Lover* shows, efforts to ban books are good for sales. Surely at least some of the Oklahomans who in 1961 encountered the group Mothers United for Decency, who used a trailer full of objectionable books dubbed a "smutmobile" to draw attention to their moral crusade, must have used this as a handy curation of the titles for future acquisition, just like those Protestant librarians piggybacking on the Catholic *Index*. The academic Indologist Wendy Doniger observed that the lawsuit against her book *The Hindus: An Alternative History* (US publication 2009, Indian publication 2010) and its publishers, Penguin India, had the effect of making it an unexpected best seller. The allegation that the book contained "defamatory, derogatory, insulting, and objectionable passages referring to freedom fighters of Indian National movement and also to Hindu Gods and Goddesses" was initially challenged by the publishers, but eventually Penguin agreed to cease publication. Their commitment to pulp the remaining copies was, however, never actioned, because readers alerted to its existence by the controversy flocked to buy them up. If the aim was to restrict circulation of Doniger's book through an appeal to the Indian Penal Code, it backfired. Doniger and her book went from quiet academic niche to front-page news, with sales to match.

Accounts of book censorship—including this one so far—are often comfortably, complacently distanced, by either history or geography. Censorship is the work of Chinese bureaucrats, or the early modern papacy, or Indian religious zealots, or the English legal system before the dawn of the permissive society, with its quaintly patronizing claim to protect the innocent. Freedom of publishing has become an iconic Western value and, with it, the reassuring fiction that censorship is done by them, not us. However, it is striking to acknowledge that the late twentieth century's hotspot for literary censorship is not, as might perhaps be expected, in Iran, China, or Georgia, but in the American schoolroom, one of the most contested of modern bookscapes.

Debates about the books thought unsuitable for juvenile readers have coincided with the development of a new genre directed at them and their concerns: Young Adult (YA) fiction is appropriately named because it often deals with issues of sexuality, relationships, and identity. S. E. Hinton's 1967 novel *The Outsiders* is often credited with inaugurating the genre and, alongside it, an ongoing and fractious reception by education boards. By the 1980s, another coming-of-age novel, J. D. Salinger's *The Catcher in the Rye*, had the dual distinction of being both one of the books most likely to be taught in public schools and the most frequently censored book in American schools and libraries. Censorship had dogged the novel since its publication, when the National Organization for Decent Literature, organized by Catholic bishops, attempted to have it banned. A perennial complaint was about the language ("237 goddams, 58 bastards, 31 Chrissakes, and 1 fart," as one complaint enumerated with more outraged mathematical bathos). Its notoriety was amplified by its apparent role in the murder of John Lennon. Lennon's killer, Mark David Chapman, bought a copy shortly before he shot the singer, presumably the late 1970s paperback by Little, Brown, with the title emphasizing the words "Catcher" and "Rye" against a brown-orange Expressionist depiction of a galloping horse. Chapman wrote inside it, "This is my statement," signing it Holden Caulfield: he also read out a passage from the novel at his trial. A copy was also found in the hotel room of the man who attempted to assassinate Ronald Reagan the following year. (Mel Gibson's character in the 1997 film *Conspiracy Theory* was preoccupied with the book as a CIA assassination trigger, a paranoid conspiracy that has substantial internet presence.) *The Catcher in the Rye* has been banned in schools from South Carolina to California on grounds of profanity, immorality, sexual references and because it is "centered around negative activity." Not unrelatedly, it has sold over 10 million copies in fifty years.

The American Library Association's (ALA) Banned Books Week has, since 1982, highlighted books that have been challenged in the school system, with a range of promotional posters, stickers, and badges encouraging freedom of reading: librarians have become the frontline troops in the battle for publishing freedom. The statistics suggest, however, that the war on book censorship has moved away from federal or state jurisdiction to local, community, and parental pressure. The

most commonly challenged titles in this heated environment deal with LGBTQ+ identities. *Briar Rose*, a
YA novel by Jane Yolen, takes the fairy tale of Sleeping Beauty and twists it carefully with Holocaust themes
and a gentle, gay Prince Charming. It was burned in
1993, with two other books touching on homosexual-
ity, by the Reverend John Birmingham on the steps of
the Kansas City Board of Education. Top of the ALA's
charts for 2016, 2017, 2018, 2019, and 2020 was Alex
Gino's *George*. The central character, Melissa, is known
to everyone as George: her battle to be accepted as a girl
is articulated against her audition for the part of Charlotte in the school play *Charlotte's Web*. Requests for this
book to be withdrawn on religious grounds and for con-
flicting with "traditional family structure" meant that in
several contexts the book was restricted or hidden to
avoid controversy. One complaint stated that libraries
should not "put books in a child's hand that require discussion." At least one school district required explicit
parental permission to allow pupils access to *George*; the
American Family Association encouraged a letter-writing
campaign to the publishers to have the book withdrawn;
in contrast, a crowd-sourcing campaign organized by its
author to provide copies to school districts in Kansas in
which it had been banned reached its target within an
hour. The book's clean white cover with rainbow lettering gives little sense of this ongoing controversy.

So, book censorship is certainly not over. The examples from the American schoolroom tend to emphasize

conservative parents or education boards objecting to books with radical or progressive themes. The more liberal tend to be in favor of both freedom to publish and the right of, say, George to become Melissa. However, for them, the real challenge comes when, supporting freedom to publish, liberals have to allow reactionary, offensive, racist, or phobic literature into the world: these book censors are likely to object to books that transgress modern views on diversity, inclusion, and authenticity. The case of *American Dirt*, a novel about a Mexican migrant (and former bookseller) trying to get to America with her son, created controversy in part because its author, Jeanine Cummins, was not, or not primarily, Latina (the coverage was a little unclear on this point): the book tour and associated events were canceled because of the adverse publicity. Woody Allen's memoir was signed up and then dropped after intense opposition from the publisher Hachette's employees because of the ongoing allegations of sexual abuse against the veteran film director. Shock-jock commentator Julie Burchill had her publishing contract ripped up after she posted racist tweets. Censorship here preempts the book object rather than being enacted upon the book itself, as publishing freedoms are becoming more complicated and contested. The following chapter discusses one case that encapsulates the dilemma: the publishing history of Hitler's *Mein Kampf*.

11

Mein Kampf: freedom to publish?

When America entered the Second World War the cultural work of establishing what was being fought for leaned heavily on resistance to Nazi book censorship (Chapter 8). "This is America," proclaimed one US propaganda poster, "where you can read any paper, any magazine, any book you please. Where freedom of the press is a guarantee of your liberty." It was an important ideological principle, but it obscured some of the more complicated overlaps in forms of book censorship across the divide. Theodore Dreiser's *An American Tragedy*, among those burned by the Nazis, had also been banned in Boston a few years earlier. Ernest Hemingway's *The Sun Also Rises* was likewise censored in both America and Nazi Germany. Steinbeck's *The Grapes of Wrath* was burned in a publicity stunt in the 1930s in California by an organization of farmers opposed to labor law reform and banned from public libraries in Illinois, Kansas, and New York State. Not all Americans had got that freedom-to-publish memo.

There were other forms of book restriction, too. Archibald MacLeish, speaking on the anniversary of the book burning, in May 1942, wondered whether Americans took books as seriously as the Nazis. His suggestion that books had been cheapened by marketing, pricing, and the bypassing of booksellers for other commercial outlets seemed to be a eulogy for more elite reading practices and narrower book circulation. For others, the idea that books were only so much paper pulp was the problem. Alerting fellow library professionals to the scale of book loss in bombed Europe and the disruption to paper supplies in wartime England, Verna Bayles of Princeton University Library noted almost in passing that a current newsreel (April 1941) depicted "a postal or customs official in San Francisco burning tons of 'subversive' material." Bayles was unconcerned about censorship, or perhaps felt it was ineffectual, but was perturbed by the waste of a precious resource, recognizing that "paper is a munition of war." In Britain, a pamphlet published by the National Book Council encouraged citizens to send unwanted books for repulping, noting nevertheless that "those who love books find it hard to think of them merely as inked paper protected by stiff covers."

Banning books was not, therefore, unthinkable in America, although of course it was on a vastly different scale from the attacks on book ownership, selling, and libraries that were common in Nazi Germany. American condemnation of Nazi book burning, particularly in retrospect, was rhetorically simple. What was more difficult was agreeing what was owed to those books in which Nazi ideology was most promulgated. An American poster produced by the War Production Board in

1942–43 urged, "Do it right, but fast, make this year Hitler's last," and carried an image of a match setting alight a copy of *Mein Kampf*, deploying the very iconography of violent censorship that had been constructed as anathema to American values. It was a foretaste of the regulatory difficulties ahead. How to deal with this handbook of Nazism and blueprint for unspeakable genocide was the test case for the ideals of publishing freedom during the Second World War and beyond. The history of this title since the war is a fascinating example of the ways the material book embodies larger ideological and cultural pressures.

Nazism had developed as a cult of the book. As in other totalitarian regimes of the twentieth century, under Stalin or Mao for instance, an influential print manifesto was at the symbolic center of the new polis. Hitler wrote his autobiographical and antisemitic account while in prison in Munich in the early 1920s, dedicating it to the Nazi Party casualties of the failed coup in November 1923. The book was published in two volumes in 1925 and 1926, with the subtitle "A Reckoning." These hardback volumes with red dust jackets, art deco lettering, and a swastika on the spine are an indigestible read and had slow sales. It was not until Hitler's rise to power that *Mein Kampf* became a single-volume best seller. Three formats became widely available in Germany during the 1930s, each targeting a different market.

Most iconic and immediately recognizable was the Eher Verlag edition, with a dust jacket featuring a large portrait of Hitler scowling out, a red spine, and a red banner displaying the title. This mass-market version is the bibliographic equivalent of the large annual Nuremberg rallies, complete with the red-and-black livery and swastika iconography indicative of the Nazi Party's increasing confidence. A second edition, quarter-bound in leather with gold Gothic titling and the image of an acorn and oak leaves on pale boards and offered in a slipcase, was like a prayer book. It included a form in which local officials could mark the names of wedding couples and the date of their marriage, while conveying the best wishes of the Reich for their happy union. Thousands of copies were distributed to couples at the state's expense. A third popular edition, the "knapsack" version, was designed for soldiers serving at the front—it came in a smaller format and was printed on thinner paper.

Copies of these different mass-market editions embodied the spread of Nazism across different sectors of society, but high-end editions were also released, including a blue-morocco hardback published to mark Hitler's fiftieth birthday in 1939—again with the title marked in black letter. Most elaborate of all was a huge, medieval-style edition lettered in gold and decorated with clasps (remember the magic book and the demon it summoned in the Introduction). Printed in a limited edition of around fifty copies for top party officials, it was allegedly displayed as if it were a Nazi Bible, open on a lectern in the entrance hall of the home of Hermann Göring, commander of the Luftwaffe.

The original black letter Gothic lettering used across several editions of *Mein Kampf* was a font called Fraktur, the typographic counterpart of the mythic medievalism deployed by the Nazis to illustrate their racial and nationalist ambitions for the Reich. In Germany the twentieth-century rivalry between Fraktur and the roman typeface Antiqua could be broadly understood as a debate between the two seams of politics: black letter was associated with the right, traditionalism, and nationalism; roman with the left, modernity, and cosmopolitanism. However, in 1941 the Nazi Party issued an interdiction on Fraktur, declaring that, far from being an authentically German letterform, it was in fact Jewish: "Just as they later took possession of newspapers, so the Jews living in Germany owned the printing offices at the introduction of printing and this there came about the strong influx into Germany of Schwabacher-Jewish letters." Roman was thus designated the standard letter of the Reich; black letter was reclassified as degenerate. Subsequent editions of the Eher Verlag *Mein Kampf* were produced with a standard Latin typeface on the cover.

In all, 12 million copies of *Mein Kampf* are estimated to have circulated in Germany, a copy for every other household. Most were paid for by the state.

As the manifesto for the appalling Nazi doctrines of racial superiority and antisemitism that would lead to the gas chambers, *Mein Kampf*'s mass distribution is a sign of national complicity. The ubiquity of the book in German culture during Hitler's rule marked the spread of this ideology across society. It is, in this way, a text, a collection of words, conveying a set of ideas—in the terms used in the Introduction, it is writing as platonic. But it is also clear that the book itself became the symbol of that ideology rather than merely its carrier, a pragmatic and even talismanic object as much as a collection of words. It is striking, for instance, that no authorized abridged account or collection of quotations from the work was published in Germany, which might have been expected were the transmission of the key messages of this lengthy book the priority. Most people, after all, will not study eight hundred pages of any book. *Mein Kampf* was, rather, a ritual object, a portable bibliographic manifestation of Hitlerism, the symbolic center of the Reich. Hitler's signature is reproduced in facsimile at the end of the dedication and many extant copies are signed by him in person: one English translation now in the Wiener Holocaust Library was presented to the Führer for signing by British tourists to the Alps in 1939, just before war broke out. A tipped-in photograph captures the blurry occasion, with pencil arrows naming "M Bormann?," "Hitler," and "Karen." Something about this jaunty captioning recalls Hannah Arendt's unforgettable phrase about the banality of evil, here in chillingly mundane hardback form.

The question of what to do with this book in the countries opposed to Nazism and to its totalitarian values first emerged in the 1930s and is still a live one. An abridged American edition of *Mein Kampf* translated by E. T. S. Dugdale was published in the USA as *My Battle* in 1933, the same year as the book burnings. It prompted widespread public criticism of its publisher, Houghton Mifflin, in part for giving voice to Hitler's ideology in any form but then, more specifically, for releasing an edited text. The American edition whitewashed the ideology by omitting some of its most extreme manifestations. Dugdale cut Hitler's text from 780 pages to just under three hundred. F. D. Roosevelt wrote on the flyleaf of his copy, "This translation is so expurgated as to give a wholly false view of what Hitler is or says." Publishing the book in a form that minimized Hitler's genocidal plans while German rearmament and war preparations continued was widely condemned. A petition condemning Houghton Mifflin for "spreading the propaganda of a common gangster" agitated for the publisher to lose its public contract for textbooks in New York schools. This was rejected by the Board of Education on grounds of free speech: "The issue before us is not Hitler or Hitlerism, but the freedom of the press." From the outset, *Mein Kampf* was exhibit A in debates about press freedom.

But as well as these ethical and political questions, clearly there were commercial considerations, too. Publishers were not necessarily unhappy with the controversy. A memo in the Houghton Mifflin company archives at Harvard records a letter from the chief executive to Chancellor Hitler: "Our announcement of this publication has aroused great interest, and in some quarters opposition. We have, nevertheless, persisted in our plans, and we believe that the actual publication of the book will result in wide discussion and, we hope, in satisfactory sale." In fact, sales were disappointing, and a second, popular edition was published in 1937 at a lower price to try to stimulate the market. This second edition cut the photograph of Hitler saluting from the cover and framed the text in a more explicitly oppositional way. It featured a jacket endorsement by Dorothy Thompson, an American journalist and Berlin correspondent who had written a book warning of the dangers of Hitlerism, *I Saw Hitler*. Her description of Hitler as "the very prototype of the little man" was among the reasons for her expulsion from Germany in 1934. Thompson, therefore, gave her authority as a European expert and known opponent of Hitler to the second American edition of *Mein Kampf*. Her endorsement made critical distance its key selling point: "As a liberal and democrat I deprecate every idea in this book," but "the reading of this book is a duty for all who would understand the fantastic era in which we live, and particularly is it the duty of all who cherish freedom, democracy and the liberal spirit." A cynic might suggest that having failed to make a sales success of the first edition from those readers who might be tempted by its fascist premise, Houghton Mifflin now sought to recover its losses by repackaging *Mein Kampf* as an indispensable read for those who opposed it. George Orwell called out the translation as "edited from a pro-Hitler angle . . . to tone down the book's ferocity and present Hitler in as kindly a light as possible."

Before the outbreak of war, *Mein Kampf* was published in an unauthorized French translation; Hitler's German publishers sued for breach of copyright. They were successful and the book was nominally withdrawn, although it was later reprinted in an authorized and reduced edition in 1938. By 1939 the book had been translated into fourteen more languages. Another English translation, by James Murphy, was published in 1939. It claimed to be an "unexpurgated edition" and was published without the approval of the German publishers. The translator's preface went to considerable lengths to explain the post-Versailles frustrations of the German people as a context for the writing of the book, describing it as produced under conditions of "emotional stress" and bearing "the imprint of its own time." Murphy repeated Hitler's assertions that "Germany has no territorial claims against France" and that his book "does not implicate him as Chancellor of the Reich." The preface, written in the quiet country village of Abbots Langley in February 1939, did not age well. Within months, Murphy's edition was itself to be directly corralled to the Nazi war machine. It was used as the basis of the so-called Sea Lion edition prepared by the Nazis for distribution in England after the successful invasion of the same name. The proposed rollout of *Mein Kampf* as part of the occupation makes clear the central role of the book in Nazi administration. The previously disgraced and expurgated translation was also published in the UK in a serial format during the war. The eighteen parts cost 6d each, with a yellow-and-red softback cover that described *Mein*

Kampf "as the blue-print of German imperialism—the most widely discussed book of the modern world," with "200 full-page plates." It carried a small, unflattering photograph of Hitler, two swastikas on the front, and, most surprisingly, claimed that "royalties on all sales will go to The British Red Cross Society." The Red Cross had not been consulted about this and were uncertain that they wanted to be complicit in the publication, but in the end accepted £500 in royalties.

The question of how to allocate royalties from the work has continued to dog those publishers who reprint editions of *Mein Kampf* and those charities, often related to Jewish culture or welfare, in the US and the UK to whom the money has been offered. Early American publishers fought over the distribution of royalties and whether they went to Hitler or to charity. One estimate suggests that Houghton Mifflin has made hundreds of thousands of dollars of profit from their editions, but, under public pressure, it has given this to charities. Controversy about how directly these funds benefited Holocaust education has continued. In 2001 the German Welfare Council in London returned royalty payments saying it no longer worked directly with victims of the Holocaust. The Wiener Holocaust Library was offered the royalties but refused the gift and, in 2016, Jewish leaders in Boston called Houghton Mifflin out for shifting its focus away from charities dealing directly with antisemitism. Who should profit from the continued sales of this book is an ongoing difficulty.

After the death of Hitler the copyright in *Mein Kampf* passed from his estate to the Bavarian State Ministry of Finance. There was no official ban on *Mein Kampf* in postwar Germany (unlike the ban on the swastika and the Heil Hitler salute). However, the copyright holders chose not to reprint it and thus the book was out of print until the expiry of copyright in 2016. Two editions were immediately planned for publication in 2017. The first, by the Institute for Contemporary History in Munich, aimed to preempt Nazi sympathizers by producing *Mein Kampf: Eine Kritische Edition* (a critical edition). The project was subsidized by the Bavarian government to the tune of half a million euros (both to bankroll the academic work and to avoid the question of profit and those troubling royalties), despite some nervousness about the implications of being seen to underwrite the book's ideology. The Institute for Contemporary History publication acknowledged that careful framing, explanation, and exegesis were needed if this work were to return responsibly to the print marketplace after many decades. It deploys specific aspects of book formatting and history to reshape and reframe its content.

First, the extended title modifies the book's original and iconic two words: even the wide spines of the two volumes are marked with the important qualifying subtitle. And though "critical" in this context generally signifies a careful, objective edition, the word also carries some of its more common use of judgment, censoriousness, fault-finding. The format continues the modification. The two large volumes, bound in plain cloth, amount to almost two thousand pages in total, including more than three thousand footnotes. The page design literally frames Hitler's original text on three sides: the left and right margins of each opening and the foot of the page are given over to explanatory and corrective commentary. This critical apparatus explores sources, corrects factual errors, reins in exaggerations, and dissects the style of the writing (although criticizing *Mein Kampf* for the quality of its prose seems rather like complaining about a landmine that it is not aesthetically pleasing—that is, wildly, offensively, beside the point).

This academic page layout draws on long traditions of biblical glossing, first developed by Anselm of Laon in the early twelfth century. Two distinct blocks of text, visually differentiated by size, script, and position on the page, and later by typeface or color, work together in parallel. The reader accesses the primary text and the framing narrative of later scholarship and commentary simultaneously, toggling between texts of different status and being implicitly instructed how to do this by their arrangement on the page. In the era of print this model for presenting and mediating important texts shaped the mise-en-page of Reformation Bibles. The Geneva Bible, for instance, first published in 1560, has two columns of Bible text with the outer margins reserved for commentary in smaller type. The margins stage the religious disputes of the sixteenth century. The Geneva Bible gloss makes clear the Protestant interpretation of the Whore of Babylon in the Book of Revelation in a marginal note at the description of her dressed in purple and scarlet: "Surely it was not without cause that the Romish clergie were so much delighted with this colour." It identifies Babylon with Rome in the teasing note:

> Very children knowe, what that seven hilled citie is, which is so much spoken of, and whereof Virgil thus reporteth. And compassed seven towres within one wall: that citie it is, which when John wrote these things, had rule over the Kings of the earth: It was, and is not, and yet it remaineth to this day, but it is declining to destruction.

The Douai Rheims Bible of 1582, adopting a similar layout, uses the glossing to promote a Catholic biblical analysis and argues instead that Babylon is "Either the city of the devil in general; or, if this place be to be understood of any particular city, pagan Rome, which then and for three hundred years persecuted the church; and was the principal seat both of empire and idolatry." The framing of the text for specific purposes and readerships amid the wars of religion is one prominent purpose of the commentary.

The cultural weight of these predecessors was a problem for the critical edition of *Mein Kampf.* While the framing commentary placed the work and its pernicious ideology in an insulated context and prevented its being read without this additional information and fact-checking, it also risked conferring an elevated or academic status on a book that did not deserve it. A quick library catalogue search for "a critical edition" brings up erudite volumes of biblical commentary and manuscript studies. Presenting Hitler's work in a form associated with canonical thinkers implicitly praised it as worthy of extended engagement—even as it interrupted a straightforward or unreflective encounter with its content. Perhaps the scholarly apparatus dignified Hitler's murderous racism by embedding it in authoritative historical and intellectual traditions. Perhaps its high price put it beyond the readership of those who might most benefit from its careful ideological dismantling (although the price was intended to limit the book's popularity). How to deal with Hitler's book continued to raise ethical and commercial dilemmas.

There was further controversy about a German edition printed after the lapsing of copyright. Right-wing Leipzig publisher Der Schelm released a cheap single-volume hardback edition in 2016. This was marketed as an "unchanged reprint," did not offer any framing commentary, and reproduced the Hitler portrait and red flash of the popular 1930s editions, although with roman rather than black letter script, on a glossy laminated cover. Der Schelm's website trumpets the rights of individual freedom while distancing the company from "any defamatory, inflammatory, insulting and human dignity–attacking passages, in particular any defamatory criticism of Judaism." It's a tough balance to retain. Amazon banned *Mein Kampf* from sale on its platform, along with other right-wing and antisemitic titles, in March 2020, then retracted its ban, inadvertently but inevitably raising the profile of the book and selling thousands of copies. Modern India is one of the most prominent territories for the distribution of *Mein Kampf*; extreme right-wing Hindu nationalism finds its echo in the fantasy of strong, patriotic leadership. Cheap, unlicensed editions sold on the street and commercial versions in many languages are widespread: one report suggests it is particularly popular as a textbook on strong leadership among students of management and business.

The wartime clarity that pitched freedom of the press as the most visible expression of American ideology, as opposed to the book burning intolerances of Nazi Germany, was always tactical, and always fictional. The ongoing place of *Mein Kampf* in the world's bookshops continues to focus issues of disagreement, hatred, and dissent on the physical book itself and how it should be handled. In researching this book, I have read lots of banned volumes. But calling up *Mein Kampf* from the library stacks, or taking it down from the shelves, I was troubled by the chill shadow I felt it cast. I wanted to write to the librarians to reassure them that my interest was not sympathetic; I wondered whether there were colleagues who might not want to handle the book on its journey from storage to my desk. I felt, like the sorcerer's apprentice faced with the grimoire, that this was a book that might escape my grasp and dance malignly off into the world. Like the books discussed in the following chapter, *Mein Kampf* has a power in excess of, or separate from, its content. I told myself it was only a book, but, as *Portable Magic* proceeds, I'm less sure that a book is ever only a book.

12

Talismanic books

Amid paintings by Bellini, sculpture by Canova, and chandeliers of antique Murano glass, the Correr Museum of Venice holds one curious artifact, once in the possession of the seventeenth-century Doge, admiral and cat-lover Francesco Morosini. It looks like an unremarkable thick leather-bound Latin prayer book, printed with rubricated (red-ink) phrases. But this appearance is deceptive. The second half of the book is a box shaped to fit a small pistol; when the volume is closed, the silk bookmark can act as a trigger and fire the gun.

Morosini's gun-book is the opposite of the common trope of the volume that stops a bullet. This familiar notion, dating from at least the American Civil War, speaks to a longer tradition of books' healing and talismanic protection. The American book dealer A. S. W. Rosenbach recalled that he had been offered so many bullet-hole-scarred Bibles that he suffered from nightmares that armies were charging at him, "each soldier wearing a protecting copy of the Holy Scriptures over his heart." But as Rosenbach's humor points out, that number of miraculous books is probably unlikely. Nor are they only Bibles. In the Library of Congress rests a copy of Kipling's *Kim* that saved a French legionnaire near Verdun in the First World War "by a mere 20 pages." The yellow-paper-covered French edition, with a stitched soft binding and red lettering, hardly seems sufficient to have stopped a bullet, which has pierced the top left-hand margin, just above the imprint "Collection D'Auteurs Étrangers." The contemporary Greek artist Christina Mitrentse has developed a series called "Wounded Books" drawing on the visual conventions of these venerated volumes. Her work initially responded to a car-bombing in Baghdad's cultural and bookselling center and comprises paperbacks "shot with Winchester 4.8 Caliber, under licensed conditions": the wounded books show neat, precise entry holes and ripped and tattered exit wounds.

Also drawing on the myth of the protective book were the steel-covered pocket Bibles widely advertised during the First World War as gifts for servicemen. These hedged their protective bets by combining the superstitious or religious belief in the Bible as a metaphorical shield with the practical addition of a bulletproof cover. Miniature Qur'ans were presented to Indian Muslim troops in the First World War and one example turned up in an unexpected place. Lawrence of Arabia writes that the Bedouin Chief Auda attributed his survival of a volley of bullets that had killed his horse and sliced through his clothing to "an amulet Koran [bought] for one hundred and twenty pounds" that had protected him for thirteen years. "The book," wrote Lawrence, "was a Glasgow reproduction, costing eighteen pence." The publishers, David Bryce and Sons of Glasgow, were experts in miniature book publication, with a large (small) range including Shakespeare, Tennyson, Scottish songs in a tartan cover, a dictionary, and children's titles. *The Allies' Miniature Bible*, also published with an attached magnifying glass, was bound in military khaki. Recalling the development of his specialized printing business, Bryce "descended to the miniature, mite, and midget size, producing a little dictionary, the smallest in the world, in a locket accompanied by a magnifying glass." Bryce's Qur'an was also sold for wearing in a locket and came with the magnifier. It echoed Mughal and earlier examples of tiny Qur'ans and Arabic amulets, was printed in Arabic, and measured about an inch square. With an eye to Islamic markets in Africa, Asia, and the Ottoman empire, and particularly to Hajj pilgrimage, Bryce had a certificate of authenticity included in each copy, claiming that the text was derived from an authoritative manuscript recorded by the calligrapher Hafiz Osman and approved by the Islamic authorities. Those who mocked his miniaturizing enterprise were soon proved wrong, as an early order for 3,000 copies grew into sales of over 100,000.

Bibles have long been adopted for a range of nonreading purposes, from healing to record-keeping, exorcism, and oath-taking. The eighth-century monk and historian Bede reports the use of a book to cure snake bites. St. Augustine wrote that the Gospel of St. John was laid on the heads of those suffering from fever. In the Middle Ages and beyond, this particular biblical book was still judged to have particular protective powers, and tiny manuscript versions, intended to be worn or carried on the person for maximum efficacy, survive as witness to this belief. Around 1600, residents of Nottingham were being encouraged to buy copies of the Gospel as a preservative against witchcraft, at the considerable sum of ten shillings. In Puritan New England, where we might expect superstitions about religious objects to be off-limits, Bibles were used for registering births, curing the sick, making decisions, predicting the future, and warding off devils. The historian David Cressy even reports on a Bible attached to a pole used as a battle standard in a local conflict. Recording that John Osgood of Andover, Massachusetts, left eighteen shillings in his will to the meeting house of Newbury "to buy a cushion for the minister to lay his book upon," Cressy notes that "even in austere New England, in a religious culture set firm against superstition, the physical bound volume possessed some of the attributes of a religious icon or talisman."

In these anecdotes, the Bible as a material object does work equivalent to that ascribed to Scripture as text. Scripture's claims of salvation become attached to the book itself. Some powers attributed to the material book move further from canonical theology. A ritual performed with a Bible and a key was supposed to be a guide to detect a thief:

A Bible having a key fastened in the middle, and being held between the two forefingers of two persons, will turn round after some words said; as, if one wishes to find out a thief, a certain verse taken out of a Psalm is to be repeated, and those who are suspected nominated, and if they are guilty, the Book and key will turn, else not.

A variant of this divination allowed young women to identify the name of their future lover. A nineteenth-century Kentucky belief held that cracking the baby's first louse on the Bible would enhance its reading abilities (the baby's, not the louse's); the use of a hymnal or songbook would produce a good singer.

These uses of the Bible do not require it to be opened or its pages turned: they are about the book as a material block possessing special powers. By contrast, the parallel tradition of bibliomancy—the term for the practice of consulting a book opened at random for prophetic wisdom—imbued material books with the magic power of divination. The practice was popular in early modern Europe, and first drew on classical, or pagan, texts, before later adapting to use Bibles and other works. This tradition was rather more esoteric, as an early anecdote by the gossipy biographer John Aubrey suggests. In 1648, while Charles I was imprisoned, awaiting the trial that would result in his execution, his son Charles, Prince of Wales, asked the poet Abraham Cowley to come and entertain him. "His Highnesse asked him whether he would play at Cards, to diverte his sad thoughts," Aubrey tells us. "Mr. Cowley replied, he did not care to play at Cards; but if his Highnesse pleasd, they would use Sortes Virgilianae (Mr. Cowley alwaies had a Virgil in his pocket); the Prince accepted the proposal, and prick't his pinne in the fourth booke of the Aeneids at this place [IV 615–20]."

Aubrey precedes this story with an explanation of the process, suggesting that it's not altogether common knowledge:

> These divinations are performed after this manner, viz.: the Party that has an earnest desire to be resolved in such an Event takes a pinne, and thrusts it between the leaves of [Virgil, Horace, or the Bible], and choose which of the pages she or he will take, and then open the booke and begin to read at the beginning of that period. The booke at the prickinge is held in another's hand.

This elaborate bit of collaborative book-handling produced a grim prophecy for the young prince. The passage pricked out began, "Let him be vext with a bold people's war, / Exil'd . . . die before his day, the sand his grave." Aubrey observed with an air of morbid prophetic triumph that after his execution Charles's body was "privately putt into the Sand about White-hall." Other versions of the story place it in Royalist Oxford in 1642, when the king went one day to see the Publick Library, where he was show'd among other Books, a Virgil nobly printed and exquisitely bound. The Lord Falkland, to divert the King, would have his Majesty make a trial of his fortune by the Sortes Virgilianae, which everybody knows was an usual kind of augury some ages past. Whereupon the King opening the book, the period which happen'd to come up was that part of Dido's imprecation against Aeneas.

No one has been able to identify which noble and exquisite copy of Virgil this could have been, but the implication is clear: Virgil knew it all.

Sortes Virgilianae, or Virgilian lots, was a form of bibliomancy. Readers went to the book with a particular question, "an earnest desire to be resolved," or, more speculatively, to "make a trial of his fortune." Virgil was deemed an appropriate place to seek information about the future because he was often credited with predicting the coming of Christ and the sack of Rome. Magical powers hung around his mythical biography: in medieval legend he was said to have been the tutor of the magician Merlin.

It may have helped that both the *Aeneid* and the *Iliad* majored on struggle and endurance, producing many verses applicable to these moments of dilemma or uncertainty. But *sortes Virgilianae*, and equivalents using other texts, are dependent on book form as much as book content. Sticking a pin into one edition will not produce the same result as the identical action with a different-format book. Perhaps Abraham Cowley's convenient portable Virgil was the 1542 edition printed in Lyon by the humanist Sébastien Gryphe, or Gryphius. Gryphius published in the small format of sextodecimo—a single sheet of paper folded into sixteen leaves or thirty-two pages, resulting in a book about the size of a modern smartphone. It was pocket-sized, designed specifically to be carried around for consultation. In bibliomancy, the book reads its readers rather than vice versa.

Reading by lottery privileges the book as object rather than the book as text. The particular distribution of the words on the page might seem a random accident of the print shop rather than something purposive. But under the particular close attention of bibliomancy, the book becomes a specific object that offers access to deeper meanings, and those meanings are about format, rather than content. (It's a version of the kind of "found poetry" discovered in Jo Hamill's brilliant *Gutter Words*, which uncovers a spine running through the Penguin edition of Joyce's *Ulysses* by cutting away all but the words adjacent to the gutter, or central fold.) Bibliomancy has some powerful adherents. St. Augustine's account of his conversion is indebted to the power of the material book. Weeping in spiritual despair under a fig tree, Augustine heard a nearby child playing and singing: "Pick it up and read it, pick it up and read it!" He recorded:

> I understood it as nothing short of divine providence that I was being ordered to open the book and read

the first passage I came across ... In great excitement I returned to the place where Alypius was sitting, for when I stood up I had put down a volume of the apostle there. I snatched it up, opened it, and read silently the first chapter that my eyes lit upon: "Not in partying and drunkenness, not in promiscuity and shamelessness, not in fighting and jealousy, but clothe yourself in the Lord Jesus Christ and make no provision for the flesh concerning its physical desires Rom 13:13–14." I neither wanted nor needed to read further. Immediately, the end of the sentence was like a light of sanctuary poured into my heart and every shadow of doubt melted away. Then I put my finger, or some other marker, into the book and closed it.

Augustine's account of spiritual transcendence is appropriately detailed about the physical book and its handling: his epiphany could not have happened except through the specific medium of the book object.

The *sortes* tradition moved on from antiquity and attached itself to different books in different cultures. The *Falnama*, for example, was specially made as an illustrated book of omens for divination, drawing from mythology, folklore, and religion. Surviving examples from Turkey, Syria, and Iran date from the sixteenth and seventeenth centuries, the end of the Islamic millennium, when anxieties about the future were prevalent. The *Falnama* books are large enough that a crowd can gather around outdoor divination sessions in streets and marketplaces. In the Christian tradition, the Bible became the dominant book for bibliomancy. Looking back on his youth in the 1630s, the elderly John Dane of Roxbury, Massachusetts, recalled how he was resolved to leave England for New England, contrary to his parents' wishes:

> I sat close by the table where there lay a Bible. I hastily took up the Bible and told my father if where I opened the Bible there I met with any thing either to encourage or discourage, that should settle me . . . The first I cast my eyes on was "come out from among them, touch no unclean thing, and I will be your god and you shall be my people."

Both he and his parents were convinced: John set sail for the New World, and his parents soon followed him. The modern apotheosis of the *sortes* tradition might be found in the verses identified in copies of the Gideon Bible, produced since 1899 in large quantities for free public distribution on the streets, in hotel rooms, schools, prisons, and the armed forces. Here the book channels the *sortes* impulse, recognizing that readers might turn to the book in times of uncertainty, but neutralizes its randomness, identifying at the beginning of each volume appropriate verses for consultation at different points or emotional states.

Bibliomancy and the other nonreading uses of special books endow these objects with magical powers. It was a condescending trope of colonial ethnography in the nineteenth century that illiterate tribal peoples did not understand learning and treated any book as a fetish. Jack Goody describes a traditional diviner called Oyie in Birifu in the early 1950s, who used an exercise book "as a mode of communication with the supernatural powers." He reports on the use of Protestant Bibles in Ndebele warrior head plumes in late-nineteenth-century Ngamiland, where the local missionary Reverend James Hepburn drew on local beliefs in likening his Bibles to a "powerful charm." In Chapter 8 we saw the explorer Henry Stanley encountering fear among the inhabitants of Mowa that his notebooks were a form of powerful magic (as indeed they were, since his travel accounts were later weaponized by the brutal Belgian colonial regime that sponsored his expedition). Isabel Hofmeyr has traced how John Bunyan's *Pilgrim's Progress*, itself an allegorical narrative of spiritual journeying, was transported globally across the Protestant world, especially into sub-Saharan Africa. Hofmeyr notes that books were discussed as "white man's fetish." But fetishized books were and are, in fact, at the center of modern Western democracies.

Reverence to, or swearing on, the Bible, is still a routine part of court proceedings. Swearing on a holy book is a standard part of legal administration, and in the UK the 1978 Oaths Act allows for an Old or New Testament, or Qur'an, as an alternative for those of different faiths. A debate among the UK Magistrates' Association in 2013 proposed discontinuing the use of religious books, suggesting that they had lost their power to secure truth-telling in court, and that a statement showing that the participants in court understood the serious temporal punishments for perjury would be more effectual. This motion was defeated. Despite census data that suggests almost half the UK population does not identify as religious, the power of the holy book as an object is still enshrined in statute, although witnesses can now "affirm" on their own honor rather than swear on a book if they prefer. Swearing on a book outside the courtroom is also common. Conducting a marriage in Central America without a Bible, one nineteenth-century engineer allegedly married a couple by swearing on the unlikely scriptures of Sterne's *Tristram Shandy*, from which he read a chapter at the service. In Congreve's Restoration comedy *The Way of the World* the maid Mincing reminds Mrs. Marwood that when she found her mistress in a compromising position, "you swore us to secrecy upon Messalinas's poems": it's not quite clear what book she might have in mind, but the licentious associations of Messalina, wife of the Roman emperor Claudius, make the oath deeply comic.

The American presidential oath is traditionally sworn on a book—usually a Bible. George Washington's Bible has been reused by several of his successors in office; John Quincy Adams swore his oath on a law book containing a copy of the Constitution. Harry S. Truman took his on both a facsimile Gutenberg Bible, representing Roman Catholicism, and a small English Bible, for Protestants, to signal his commitment across doctrinal communities. In the confusion and shock after Kennedy's assassination, Lyndon B. Johnson was sworn in aboard Air Force One, using Kennedy's own Catholic missal, as the most convenient book on hand. Donald J. Trump swore his oath on two copies of the Bible, one given to him as a child by his mother, the other borrowed from the Library of Congress, the book that Lincoln used at his inauguration in 1861, and used by Barack Obama in 2007 and 2011. This metal-trimmed, velvet-bound edition was printed by Oxford University Press in 1853: it is a small, thick volume bought for the purpose by a Supreme Court clerk because Lincoln's own books were in transit from Springfield, Illinois. It is an ordinary mass-printed book that has been sacralized by its ceremonial use: a commodity turned into a ritual object.

When, in 2006, Keith Ellison, the first Muslim elected to the US congress, declared he would take his oath of office on the Qur'an, there was considerable outrage from conservatives. "America should not give a hoot what Keith Ellison's favorite book is," Dennis Prager wrote in his political column, "Insofar as a member of Congress taking an oath to serve America and uphold its values is concerned, America is interested in only one book, the Bible." Prager's intervention stoked a controversy: the American Family Association asked its members to email their representatives requesting that swearing on the Bible be made a legal requirement for oaths of office. Ultimately, Congressman Ellison of Minnesota was allowed to take the oath on Thomas Jefferson's copy of the Qur'an, an eighteenth-century edition in two volumes, translated from the Arabic by George Sale. Sale's work, *The Koran, commonly called, the Alcoran of Mohammed* (1734), was credited with bringing Islamic teachings to a Western audience. Sale addressed the reader in a preface: "If the religious and civil Institutions of foreign nations are worth our knowledge, those of Mohammed, the lawgiver of the Arabians, and founder of an empire which in less than a century spread itself over a greater part of the world than the Romans were ever masters of, must needs be so." It was this particular Qur'an that went some way to defuse the tensions revealed and amplified by the furor. The provenance of the volume, owned by one of America's founding fathers and transferred from his personal library to the Library of Congress to replace volumes destroyed by the British in 1812, worked to cancel Prager's insidious charge against Ellison's decision—that it was un-American. Here, as a riposte, is an American Qur'an, the size of an exercise book, bound in red leather with marbled covers, authorized with the presidential initials T. J. in both volumes. It is the Alcoran of Jefferson, as well as of Muhammad. One unarticulated irony of Ellison's choice, however, is that Sale's translation was largely hostile to Islam: presenting his new, "impartial" translation "To the Reader" at the beginning of volume one of his work, he aligns himself with precisely the Protestant triumphalism that was still resonating in the debate over the Bible as the

only fit holy book for American lawmakers: "The Protestants alone are able to attack the Koran with success;
and for them, I trust, Providence has reserved the glory
of its overthrow."

The power and status ascribed to Bibles for bibliomancy, protection, and verification has also made them
obvious objects for historical record-keeping. The British
Library holds a striking autograph manuscript by John
Milton. Not a poem, not a pamphlet, not a letter, but
a copy of a Bible marked up with family history. The
small, thick volume of the 1611 King James, or Authorized, Version, is well used, with worn and torn pages. It
carries Milton's neat script in brown ink on the front flyleaf. From the different shades of ink, it looks as if it was
the birth of his first child, Anne, in 1646, that prompted
his act of memorialization. One single writing session
begins with the retrospective account of Milton's own
birth "half an hour after 6 in the morning" on December 9, 1608, and his brother Christopher, with slightly less
specificity, "on Friday about a month before Christmas
at 5 in the morning 1615." He gives the rough ages of his
two nephews, Edward and John Phillips, who had joined
his household around 1640, and then announces that
"my daughter Anne was born July the 29th." There are
entries for other children, Mary, John, and Deborah, the
account that "my wife her mother died about three days
after. And my son about—6 weeks after his mother."
Somewhere around 1651, when Milton lost his eyesight,
someone else with noticeably curlier writing takes up the

record-keeping, still using the first person: "my daughter." A final entry records the birth and death of two
Katherines, Milton's second wife and his daughter, in
1657. It is a sad, sparse chronicle of life and death, with
its intimate details of the times of the births, its delinea-
tion of a particular household family unit, its inscription
of the poet's blindness, and its unemotional but poignant
ledger of human hope and disappointment.

The tradition of marking family events in a Bible
began in the century before Milton and continued for
centuries afterward. Some Bibles seem to have had additional blank leaves included to make it easier for them
to serve as genealogical repositories; some modern
editions, likewise, have pages with headings to inspire
family record-keeping. Mike Spathaky has written about
his own family Bible online, including revealing that a
later family member seems to have tried retrospectively
to amend a birth date to make it seem as if their ancestor
Devina Roper was born after (1826) rather than before
(1825) her parents' marriage.

Bibles are obvious repositories for family records for
a number of reasons: availability (in many households it
might be the only book), size (its weight and dimensions
mean it is unlikely to be lost or damaged), and content
(genealogies—in the King James translation of Matthew,
chapter 1, "Abraham begat Isaac; and Isaac begat Jacob;
and Jacob begat Judas and his brethren"—are intrinsic
to biblical narratives). This last factor may be the least
important, since there are numerous examples of other,

non-genealogical books being used for a similar purpose. What matters is the reader's apprehension of the
book's significance and durability. Laura Knoppers has
written about how readers recorded their family history
on pages of Charles I's *Eikon Basilike*, responding to the
emphasis on conjugal family and shared humanity at the
heart of this sympathetic royal story. *Eikon Basilike* was
published days after Charles's execution and purported
to be his spiritual autobiography (later editions included
an affidavit confirming his authorship, in response to
ongoing dispute). The book has a full-page-spread
engraved frontispiece showing Charles kneeling before
an open book with the Latin motto *in verbo tuo spes mea*
("In Thy word is my hope"), and accompanying verses
establish him as a Christian martyr: "With joy I take this
crown of thorn." *Eikon Basilike* established the sentimental story of Charles's martyrdom, and even Milton's
powerful riposte, *Eikonoklastes*, could not ultimately challenge the royalist narrative of Charles's execution.

As Knoppers lists, there are numerous extant copies
with manuscript annotations recording births, deaths,
and baptism dates, as well as the sometimes random
or extraneous material that readers write in their books
(for example, "Master Morgan Evans is a very civil man
and behaves himself substantial in company with servile
persons besides gentlemen"). A small-format edition of
this best seller, now in the University of Glasgow, shows
how a royalist family called Couperthwaite living in the
English Lake District in the later seventeenth century

annotated Charles's account with details of their own relations and events. Stanley Couperthwaite has signed the records, including baptisms and burials at Grasmere church. Isabel Hofmeyr has likewise traced annotations and family records in copies of *Pilgrim's Progress*, including the forward-looking family history: "Hannah Williams—the gift to her daughter Jane Froud on her dying bed Aug 21 1852 at her death it is to be given to Emma Froud daughter of the above"; and a Welsh-language edition inscribed, "plece yo give this book to David John Beynon the son of John Phillip Beynon after is father and if David will die be fore Elizabeth his sister plece to give her." Significant books have sometimes been entrusted with commentary beyond the immediately domestic or familial. A copy of Shakespeare's First Folio has the pencil record "August 4th 1914 war declared on Germany" and then, below, "Nov 11th 1918 armistice signed at 5am" on the binder's leaf; perhaps this valuable book was seen as the most appropriate and weighty location to register momentous world events.

The ultimate use of books as talismans is their inclusion in coffins with their owners (perhaps in expectation of this, it is now possible to buy a coffin that serves as a bookcase until it is needed). This may draw on ancient Egyptian traditions of packing the dead off to the underworld with the guiding papyrus scroll of *The Book of the Dead*. The St. Cuthbert Gospel was found inside the seventh-century saint's coffin. The will of the physician Sir William Browne asked that he be buried with his much-loved edition of

Horace, published by the preeminent European book dynasty Elzevir. William Osler had the 1862 edition of *Religio Medici* "handsomely rebound and evidently much read" on his coffin at rest in Christ Church, Oxford; Tennyson was buried with a copy of *Cymbeline*. Perhaps the most cramped coffin was that of Mr. John Underwood of Whittlesea, whose funeral in 1733 was marked by conspicuous eccentricity. *The London Magazine, or Gentleman's Monthly Intelligencer* reported that his

> Coffin was painted Green, according to his Direction, and he was laid in it with all his Cloaths on; under his Head was placed Sanadon's Horace, at his Feet Bentley's Milton; in his right Hand a small Greek Testament, with this Inscription in Golden Letters, εἴ μὴ ἐν τῷ σταυρῷ [from Galatians: "save in the cross"], J. U. in left Hand a little Edition of Horace, with this Inscription, Musis Amicus, J. U. and Bentley's Horace under his Arse.

This indecorous bodily encounter with books punctures ritualistic bibliophilia and returns the book, and its owner, to the material realm. The next chapter explores how far we've pushed these intimate associations between people and books.

13

Skin in the game: bookbinding and African American poetry

A man constructed from books. His shock of white hair is actually a concertina of open pages, the straight line of his right arm is formed of a large orange volume. His ribs, or the folds of his doublet, are suggested by a horizontal stack of end-on smaller, pale vellum-bound books; a flutter of protruding paper bookmarks indicates his delicate fingers; and a floating ribbon bookmark traces the outline of his left ear. His soft, tufted beard is a book duster formed of marten tails; his spectacles are made of the keys to the chests in which books were stored before the widespread adoption of open bookshelves in the eighteenth century.

This painting of a person made of books is part portrait and part still-life: books are both subject and object. It was painted in 1566 by Giuseppe Arcimboldo, an Italian employed at the intellectual, bookish Habsburg court of Maximilian II in Prague. Under the patronage of the emperors in the period 1562–88, Arcimboldo's work encompassed stained-glass windows, tapestries, and costume designs, but his most instantly recognizable works are those surreal portraits composed of assemblages of fruit, flowers, or other natural objects. Attempts by scholars of Renaissance art to identify this book portrait known as "The Librarian" as a satire on a particular learned man in the imperial circle seem a bit overliteral. Recognizing its potentially satiric impulses as "a parody of librarianship and of intellectualism," one recent critic notes drily that "contemporary librarians are reluctant to embrace this image." (If you're looking for a gift for your favorite librarian, then trust me: a 5-inch Nancy Pearl–inspired action figure of the librarian as caped superhero standing against "censorship, anti-intellectualism, and ignorance," with a button on her back to activate the infamous "amazing shushing action!" is more likely to hit the spot.) Arcimboldo's quirky assemblage surely gives us a more general truth: we are all made up of the books we have loved and, more, of the books we have owned, gifted, studied, revered, lived by, lost, thrown aside, dusted, argued over, learned by heart, borrowed and never returned, failed to finish, and used as doorstops or to raise a computer monitor.

Perhaps we really can, sometimes, become book substitutes. I find myself returning to Ray Bradbury's powerful fable of a future without books, *Fahrenheit 451*. Here, since the burnt books can no longer serve as the repository for texts and histories, humans with "photographic memories" have taken up their role. Montag meets these human books—"I am Plato's *Republic* . . . I want you to meet Jonathan Swift, the author of that evil political book *Gulliver's Travels* . . . better to keep it in the old heads, where no-one can see it or suspect it"—but the phrasing makes it clear that it is easier for the people to imagine themselves the author than the book. Like something out of Bradbury's dystopia, the Human Library in Copenhagen hosts "events where readers can borrow human beings serving as open books and have conversations they would not normally have access to. Every human book from our bookshelf represent[s] a group in our society that is often subjected to prejudice, stigmatisation or discrimination." "Want to be a book?" the website asks cheerfully (I realized my answer was no). The motives are laudable—the library's slogan is "unjudge someone," but the human books are disturbingly dehumanized by being classified by type: "Muslim," "polyamorous," "alcoholic." Is that what the Dewey decimal system or Library of Congress classification feels like if you're a book?

The book–human relationship is reciprocal: if we are made up of books, books are made up of us. Books are deeply anthropomorphized. Technical book terminology emphasizes our long kinship by giving books human attributes, including heads and shoulders and spines and backs and jackets and signatures. The technical term for books published in the early period of print, before 1501, is incunabula, deriving from the Latin for swaddling clothes or cradle. They are biblio-babies, infants from Gutenberg's nursery. Books are often discussed in terms of lifespan and, as objects made from biological materials, like us they mature over time. Covers fade, pages yellow and wrinkle, spines become less flexible, and margins become foxed with liver spots.

For centuries, people emphasized this intimate connection by making their books personal. Until the
twentieth century, many books required manual cutting
by their owners to release their folded pages, and early
books were often sold as unbound sheafs of printed
quires so that buyers could customize the binding to
match their library and their means. Soft vellum was
the cheapest, calf on hard boards the most expensive,
and tooling, decoration, or heraldic crests added to the
cost. Completing books in manuscript (Chapter 14), or
engaging in the margins (Chapter 15), folding down corners, highlighting—these are all ways that books become
unique to their reader. These marks of use confer their
own value and authenticity on the book, as the comic
writer Flann O'Brien acknowledged when he proposed
a valuable new service: book-handling.

Having visited "a newly-married friend . . . of great
wealth and vulgarity," the author was shocked to gather
that he had paid "some rascally middleman" to provide
him an appropriate library of new books. Half a century later, the celebrity bibliophile and book curator to
the stars, Thatcher Wine, discussed something similar.
Wine was in the news for buying books for Gwyneth
Paltrow, and he told *Town & Country* magazine about
his philosophy. Personal libraries are far from merely a
collection of the books you've acquired over the years.
Rather, they "are a reflection of where you've been
and where you want to go." Wine's bespoke service
offered custom book jackets in specific Pantone shades

to match interior decor, and he was full of suggestions about current book fashions (Stoic philosophers "are having a moment now"; "gorgeous oversize" art books are very collectible). But his service, like the newlywed's bookshelves, lacked one detail: what O'Brien proposed was "a professional book-handler to go in and suitably maul his library," such that the collection will look convincingly "read."

Warming to his theme, O'Brien imagined different service levels, from the most basic—handling each volume, dog-earing four leaves in each one, and inserting at random a tram ticket or cloakroom docket—to the most deluxe "Traitement Superbe," supervised by a "master-handler." Intermediate service standards would include French-language, or theatrical, high-end bookmarks and memorabilia, and "treatment with old coffee, tea, porter, or whiskey stains." Class-four book-handling, meanwhile, would require underlining "in good-quality red ink" with a smattering of annotations chosen from a list ranging from the bracing "Rubbish!" to the archly academic "Yes, but cf. Homer, Od., iii, 151," the insertion of some old invented letters as apparently forgotten bookmarks and, to cap it all, "forged messages of affection and gratitude from the author of each work." A follow-up column reported on the success of the scheme and revealed, with mock regret, that some handlers failed to undertake their work with the attention to detail clients might expect. "Books have been savagely attacked with knives, daggers, knuckle-dusters, hatchets, rubber-piping, razor-blade-potatoes, and every device of assault ever heard of in the underworld." One novice handler had attempted "to train terriers to worry a book as they would a rat," "not realising that toothmarks on the cover of a book are not accepted as evidence that its owner has read it." As a spoof on book use and the marks it should leave on the book itself, this is a pretty thorough spec.

People do leave their marks on books, even becoming part of their fabric. This is more than the simple traces of prior lives in those uprooted inscriptions in second-hand books (Chapter 3), and even than the whiskey stains offered by O'Brien's operatives, as scientific studies have begun to explore. Art historian Kathryn Rudy has ana-lyzed numerous medieval missals with a densitometer, measuring the darkness of the vellum or paper surface to identify dirt and other signs of handling. She notes that, under a microscope, vellum looks "like a rug, with trapped dirt and grime in its fibers." She has focused in particular on those parts of the book kissed by the priest in worship, "depositing secretions from his lips, nose, and forehead onto the page." Her analyses of books of hours and other compilations of medieval religious texts show that prayers that carried indulgences (time remit-ted from Purgatory) were read much more frequently than those that did not offer similar assurances. Of one prayer book from the early sixteenth century now in The Hague, Rudy deduces from marks of soiling and other use something about the book's early reader: they were interested in earning indulgences, less interested in saints; from another late-fifteenth-century prayer book she deduces that the reader was concerned about plague (because they frequently returned to prayers to St. Sebastian and St. Adrian, who were credited with warding off bubonic plague) and not about toothache (the prayer pages to the relevant saint, Apollinia, are pristine). It's a version of my cookbooks, with spattered pages for favorite recipes, and complicated ones, mostly desserts that I like someone else to make for me, pristine. But the messages of these pages transmit obliquely, perhaps misleadingly, across the centuries: a Rudy of the future looking at my cookery shelf might assume that I subsist on Claudia Roden's lamb mishmishiya and don't like sweet things.

When we read a book, thousands of microscopic particles of our DNA rub off on its pages. The gutters—the channel between facing pages of a book—are full of human material: the book accretes and stores literal traces of its readers. Inside each book there is a minuscule, uncatalogued but carefully preserved library of its human handlers. Analyzing proteins via a mass spectrometer in a technique called proteomic analysis, Pier Giorgio Righetti and Gleb Zilberstein have discovered traces of human sweat and disease from archival book samples. A similar applied technology was able to distinguish so-called endogamous DNA (from the animals providing the skin for the parchment) and exogamous DNA (traces of readers and other handlers) in the York Gospels, a book dating to the tenth century CE. The microbiome residing on the pages reports contact with human skin, mouth, and nose microbes, again showing how the devotional encounter with this holy book has left its trace. Swabbing the gutter of a 1637 Bible, the Folger Shakespeare Library found the DNA of a Northern European individual who suffered from acne, in a project named Operation Dustbunny. Older books are now being examined for their potentially therapeutic supplies of reader DNA that predate modern medical problems such as antibiotic resistance. These scientific techniques applied to books and archives help to recover the invisible residue of historic human contact. Books register us in many different and vital ways, taking life from their readers.

A particularly gruesome variety of book has taken this interconnection and literalized it. Known as anthropodermic bindings, these are books bound in human skin. Their existence has long been rumored and they play a prominent role in the fictional genre of horror/sci-fi associated with H. P. Lovecraft, whose short story "The Hound" includes, alongside his famous Necronomicon, or invented grimoire, a secret portfolio covered in "tanned human skin." While there is an air of Gothic fantasy about this category of book, in fact, some anthropodermic bindings are real, and this has recently been confirmed by DNA analysis. They are chilling objects, in part because they suggest that *Homo sapiens* might not be considered completely ethically distinct from other animals whose skins have provided the leathers traditionally used for bookbindings. Human "leather" seems remarkably similar, visually and practically, to calf, pig, or goat. And further, often the connection between the human skin of the binding and the contents of the book asserts some sort of moral or symbolic significance. A copy of the works of the Marquis de Sade was allegedly bound in the skin from a woman's breast (erotica is one of the genres of book most associated with anthropodermy). A nineteenth-century edition of Holbein's "Dance of Death" series of memento mori engravings was bound by the German binders Zaehnsdorf in human skin described as "rather scanty" and so split in two, producing a "smooth" front cover and a "rough unfinished" back. The Brown University Library catalogue record adds, "This volume is considered human remains and access is restricted in order to treat it with care, respect, and dignity."

Not all such books receive this sensitive curation. A true-crime account telling the story of a violent murder was bound in the skin of the hanged murderer, eighteen-year-old John Horwood of Bristol (there are relatively few English anthropodermic examples). The dark-brown cover of the book was embossed with admonitory skull-and-crossbones motifs and the gilt-lettered inscription *Cutis vera Johannis Horwood* ("the actual skin of John Horwood"). In 2007 a descendent of William Corder, who was hanged almost two centuries previously for the murder of Maria Martin in the infamous "Murder in the Red Barn" case, applied to have an account of the case bound in Corder's skin returned from a Suffolk museum. Her wish to cremate these human remains was a request for a category shift, reallocating the material from objectified "leather" back to subjective "skin." It offered an institutional opportunity to deal respectfully with the material. The museum still holds the book, and a tweet from its account in 2020 claiming it as "our #creepiestobject" suggests that it relishes the Madame Tussaud's Chamber of Horrors appeal. Indeed, most discussions of anthropodermic binding on museum and library blogs adopt a similarly gruesome tone and suggest that these books pull in eager crowds: the kind of debate in the museum sector about the appropriate care and display of human remains has been slow to reach special book collections.

Some associated stories are painful and puzzling. Three gynecological works from the 1890s now in the College of Physicians library in Philadelphia are partly bound in skin from the thigh of Mary Lynch, an immigrant from Ireland who died of consumption, aged twenty-eight, in a paupers' hospital in Philadelphia in 1869. According to immigration records kept by the Ellis Island Museum, more than a dozen Irish Mary Lynches in their twenties came to the US in the 1860s. This could be the story of any one of them, since the dehumanizing practice of making human skin into leather involves, perhaps even requires, erasing the details of the individual life. The bindings were commissioned by Dr. John Stockton-Hough, the doctor who conducted Lynch's postmortem (he wrote about the results for a medical journal). Stockton-Hough was a keen bibliophile who published a catalogue of his substantial collection of fifteenth- and early-sixteenth-century books as *Incunabula Medica* in grandiose faux-medieval style in 1890 with the pseudo-Latinized imprint "Trentonii: Novo-Caesarea." That's to say, he presented himself as a serious book collector, not a ghoul. Nevertheless, his inscription in the front of one of the gynecological books is almost jaunty in tone, effecting a queasy rhetorical back-and-forth between human subject and book object: "The leather with which this book is bound was tanned from the skin of the thigh of Mary L—— ... tanned in a 'pot de chamber' [a chamber pot, presumably because of the use of urine as a tanning agent] ... Mary L was an Irish [inserted "widow"] aged 28 yrs."

These books raise so many questions. Mary Lynch's books, which were first published in the seventeenth and eighteenth centuries, are not included in Stockton-Hough's catalogue: Had they been within the chronological scope of his list, would they have found a place among all the other volumes? Why did he remove some of her skin and keep it for twenty years after her death (where?) before using it for the binding of these medical books in his collection? What's the relationship between female skin and the specific specialism of the books? There are a handful of other examples of women's skin being used for works on virginity and on the soul. As the librarian Megan Rosenbloom, who has made a study of anthropodermic books, points out, most are connected with physicians, as if human leather is a kind of professional trophy. Why does Stockton-Hough not include Mary's full name in the inscription? Is he protecting her, or himself, or the rebound books, or does she simply not matter as a human subject, and what might this say about the acceptability of this range of practices, from reserving cadaver tissue to using human skin in bookbinding, in nineteenth-century Philadelphia? Ultimately, could this have ever been thought the acceptable conduct of a respectable doctor-collector?

There is a disturbing aspect of the broader anthropodermic binding story that deserves further investigation. The human subjects whose skin has been appropriated for book purposes are all vulnerable or disempowered: paupers, felons, patients in asylums. It is not surprising in this context that Black skin should also have been expropriated. A copy of Dale Carnegie's 1932 biography of Abraham Lincoln, *Lincoln the Unknown*, now in Temple University Library, claims in its flyleaf that a small patch of leather on its spine "is the human skin taken from the shin of a negro at Baltimore Hospital and tanned by the Jewell Belting Company." Again, the shift in register, from dehumanizing theft to product placement, is more than uncomfortable, and the book's publication date, 1932, as the earliest date of this binding seems troublingly recent. That Lincoln is popularly associated with the emancipation of enslaved Black people (although his attitude to abolition was morally complex and militarily pragmatic) makes the specificity of the choice sickly resonant. The Wellcome Library in London's catalogue entry for one of its items is skeptical: "A notebook allegedly covered in human skin. The label reads 'The cover of this book is made of Tanned Skin from the Negro whose Execution caused the War of Independence.' *c.* 1770–1850" (this probably refers to Crispus Attucks, an American of mixed-race ethnicity killed by British soldiers in the Boston Massacre of 1770, and often claimed as the first victim of the American Revolution).

Neither the Wellcome nor the Lincoln book at Temple University have been tested by the modern DNA methods recently brought to bear on allegedly anthropodermic books. But two copies of works by the same author, proven to be bound in human skin, amplify the stories of the "Negro" and the Black man from Baltimore: poems by the enslaved writer Phillis Wheatley. These volumes embody, literally, some of the ambivalent and racialized debates about Wheatley's work that have accompanied her poetry since the 1770s.

Wheatley was a literary prodigy who, like 6 million others in the age of slavery, had been taken from Africa in childhood. She was sold in Boston, Massachusetts, in 1761. She became the first person of African descent to publish a book in the English language and the first Black transatlantic celebrity. Her 1773 book of *Poems on Various Subjects, Religious and Moral*, attributed on its title page to "Phillis Wheatley, Negro servant to Mr. John Wheatley, of Boston in New England," was published in London. Her name registers her enslaved status: she took her surname from the name of her new owner, who gave her as a first name that of the slave ship, *Phillis*, that had brought her from Africa to Massachusetts. All trace of her African identity has been lost to the records. According to later accounts (which seek, with hindsight, to obscure the transactional nature of this degraded human trade), Susannah Wheatley "wished to obtain a young negress" as "a faithful domestic": she chose her from among the available stock because of "the humble and modest demeanour and the interesting features of the little stranger." Wheatley's biographer Vincent Carretta suggests that perhaps the Wheatleys were looking, consciously or not, for a substitute daughter: Sarah Wheatley had died earlier the same year, at around the same age of the child Phillis. As an enslaved person in New England, Phillis Wheatley's life was quite different from those taken to the South for plantation work: the word "servant" was, in this context, a euphemism for an owned person, but it did register a slightly more favored position in the household. It seems that the Wheatleys treated their child servant as a kind of pet project, teaching her to read and write and using her to display their own evangelical Christian commitments within the affluent Boston community. Phillis clearly responded with quick intelligence to these opportunities, learning Latin, attending sermons, and writing poetry, at first elegies for the family's network of acquaintances.

In 1772 Phillis was summoned to a panel of redoubtable

Boston intellectuals and citizens who examined her on whether she was the true author of a manuscript collection of twenty-eight poems that Susannah Wheatley was keen to see published. As the foremost scholar of African American literature, Henry Louis Gates Jr., has observed, "this trial was about more than Phillis's authorship of a bundle of odes": confirming her as their creator "would demonstrate that Africans were human beings and should be liberated from slavery . . . Essentially, she was auditioning for the humanity of the entire African people." Whatever the course of this daunting interview, Phillis passed this colonial scrutiny: the printed edition of her works was prefaced with a statement confirming that she was indeed "but a few Years since, brought an uncultivated Barbarian from Africa," and yet "has been examined by some of the best Judges, and is thought qualified to write them." Joseph Rezek has pointed out that many extant copies of Wheatley's poems—as well as the books she herself owned—are signed by her, and suggests that this is her own authoritative riposte to those Boston worthies who presumed to mark her work with their own imprimatur.

The first edition of her poems carries a frontispiece engraved portrait of a dark-skinned woman sitting at a table with a book and an inkwell writing with a quill pen. She looks into the middle distance with her left hand on her chin, thinking: the skin of her right arm contrasts sharply against the white paper on which she is writing. The portrait is the basis of a powerful statue by Meredith

Bergmann in Boston, although Bergmann has cleared the table of these symbols of Phillis's education and creativity. Wheatley's poems are Romantic and often express orthodox evangelical spirituality: this probably explained their acceptability in her own time, but they brought criticism later. In the 1960s she was diagnosed with "Uncle Tom syndrome . . . She is pious, grateful, retiring, and civil"; June Jordan explained her poetic preoccupations as "regular kinds of iniquitous nonsense found in white literature, the literature that Phillis Wheatley assimilated, with no choice in the matter." If, for her early readers, Phillis's poetic authorship was unlikely, for later ones it has been unwelcome: entirely different expectations of a Black woman's voice have, ironically, converged to denigrate her poetic achievement.

"On being brought from Africa to America" begins "'Twas mercy brought me from my Pagan land / Taught my benighted soul to understand / That there's a God," and ends "Remember, Christians, Negros, black as Cain, / May be refined, and join th'angelic train." Gates calls this "the most reviled poem in African-American literature," remarking, "No Angela Davis she!" Another poem recasts the same trauma in slightly less optimistic terms. Addressed to Lord Dartmouth on his arrival as Secretary of State for the Colonies, and published three years before American Independence, it predicts freedom for the country in terms that powerfully recall Black enslavement within America rather than colonial government from Britain: "No longer shall thou dread the iron chain, / Which wanton Tyranny with lawless hand / Had made, and with it meant t'enslave the land." Wheatley explains her own particular commitment to freedom as a product of her experience of forcible capture and trafficking: "I, young in life, by seeming cruel fate / Was snatch'd from Afric's fancy'd happy seat: / What pangs excruciating must molest, / What sorrows labour in my parent's breast? / . . . can I then but pray / Others may never feel tyrannic sway?" Not everyone was impressed. Thomas Jefferson found nothing in Wheatley's poetry to challenge his assertion that Black people did not have creative skills except in music: "In imagination they are dull, tasteless, and anomalous." But a visit to England saw Wheatley greeted as a celebrity, gaining more subscribers to her volume, meeting literary people, and accepting numerous book gifts, including works by Milton and Cervantes. Wheatley's celebrity was intense but brief: she gained her freedom, married a poor man, worked in domestic service, and died, aged just thirty-one, in poverty and obscurity, like so many others.

Two anthropodermic copies of Wheatley's *Poems*, given by the same local bibliophile donor, are now housed in Cincinnati Public Library and the Library of the University of Cincinnati. Megan Rosenbloom rightly reminds us that "we cannot confirm the motives behind skin binding" in the specific case of authors of color and suggests that perhaps the previous owner, Charles Heartman, known as a collector and champion of African American writers, admired Wheatley's poems so much he wanted to create super-special collectors' editions through this choice of the rarest of all bindings. That may be true—but the objects themselves cannot carry this benign intention. We know nothing about the ethnicity of the person whose skin was used on the bindings, but many discussions of the volumes seem unduly reassured by the fact that there is no evidence that the person was Black. More precisely, we do not know that the skin is from a Black person; as we've seen, however, human skin was typically removed and invasive autopsies undertaken for purposes of research, without consent, from people whose status was judged to be inferior in some way; further, Black people's historic experience of the medical profession has been structured by this kind of racist assumption and practice. But the question about ethnicity seems to miss the point. Almost all other human skin bindings elsewhere are on bodily books: medical texts, murder accounts, memento mori. But Phillis Wheatley's poems are religious and spiritual, not physiological. What is bodily about this writer? The only possible answer can be: her race. The human skin bindings of Wheatley's poetry return this pioneering Black writer to the contested, hierarchized, and racialized realm of the body.

One of the anthropodermic Wheatley volumes is full "leather"—the word seems hardly appropriate—and the other half "leather" and parchment. They are tooled with gold decoration. Racialized discourse in the eighteenth century and beyond has been preoccupied by human skin, its coloration, and its meanings, and skin has been the primary site of racist and colorist differentiation. The bindings' focus on human skin thus traps Wheatley's writing—literally *binds* it—forever in the realm of the corporeal rather than the intellectual or spiritual. The racist irony of these volumes is how they materially disregard the poet's own morally urgent call for human dignity and freedom. Composer and abolitionist Ignatius Sancho, himself a former enslaved person and a creative artist, described Wheatley as a "genius in bondage": the phrase serves to categorize these copies of her work, too. Her poem addressed to the revolutionary General David Wooster calls out the failure of patriots to free enslaved peoples: it stands, too, as an ongoing plea to liberate her poems from their literal bondage in skin.

> But how presumptuous shall we hope to find
> Divine acceptance with the Almighty mind
> While yet O deed ungenerous they disgrace
> And hold in bondage Afric's blameless race
> Let virtue reign and then accord our prayers
> Be victory ours and generous freedom theirs.

14

Choose Your Own Adventure: readers' work

From the earliest printed volumes in the West, books were designed for completion by hand. Gutenberg's first Bibles were rubricated—printed, like a manuscript, with contrasting red ink. This required each duochrome page to go through the printing press twice, and it was soon discovered that it was more efficient to pay scribes to add the rubrication. A printed supplement to the Gutenberg Bibles gave a list of headings and guide words for scribes to add in the blank spaces: a how-to instruction booklet for manuscript completion. It was always the plan that illuminators would add decorative initials—and all surviving copies have some decoration added by hand. But by comparison with manuscript Bibles the overall look of the Gutenberg was austere. "What is the use of a book," Lewis Carroll's Alice asks in her perspicacious way at the beginning of her adventures in Wonderland, "without pictures?" Alice responds to new technologies that by the mid-nineteenth century had made illustrations more affordable and widespread, including the John Tenniel pictures in the book about her. Before then, however, underillustrated books were being visually pimped by their readers.

Bibles, such as the 1611 King James or Authorized Version, which were originally published without pictures, were commonly bound with engravings selected by their owners in a practice known as extra-illustration or, after the prominent print-collector James Granger, grangerization. To capitalize on this fashion, an illustrated Bible, including many full-page engravings, was published in serial form in the 1790s by Thomas Macklin, with the encouragement to readers to supply more illustrations. Elizabeth Bull (died 1809) did just that, expanding her copy of Macklin's Bible to a whopping twenty-five volumes by the insertion of several thousand woodcuts and engravings. Another reader went still further. Robert Bowyer employed an agent in Paris to seek out biblical illustrations for his own copy of Macklin. Bowyer's day job as a royal miniaturist seems to have found its necessary balance and supplement in his maximalist work on the Bible. The forty-five volumes are now in their own special bookcase in the municipal library at Bolton. A later report of Bowyer's bibliophile activities describes him as "engaged for upwards of thirty years in rendering it perfect": it was, of course, an unfinishable task. Turning the apparently complete, purchased book into a potentially endlessly expandable receptacle for more and more material created out of a finished book a radically, restlessly incomplete one. The extra-illustrated book restyles an object into a process.

Readers have gone down many other avenues as they filled out, amplified, modified, participated in, or otherwise set out on doomed attempts to complete their books. Errata lists from early printed books instruct readers to make the corrections themselves on the appropriate page: in some copies the list has been ripped out from the book, having done its job. The scholars of the seventeenth century and beyond had their books bound with interleaved blank paper to aid their annotation: the great Shakespearean editor Edmond Malone had his precious Elizabethan play quartos rebound with large margins and spare pages for his editorial commentary and glosses, reframing the throwaway pamphlets of the sixteenth century as significant academic material of the late seventeenth. And many readers made more precise running interventions onto the printed page. As Laurie Maguire has brilliantly shown, early readers of John Donne's bawdy verse filled out, perhaps unnecessarily, their faux-decorous gaps. In Satire II the speaker expresses his contempt for bad poetry and bad law, including "they which use / To out-doe ———" and "to out-sweare the ———." In the 1633 edition of Donne's *Poems* the gap is physical and a heavy line draws attention to the expurgated content. We might recall the objection to a redacted *Lady Chatterley's Lover*: the gaps make the work coarser and more salacious than if the omitted words were to appear (Chapter 10). One early reader of Donne has written in the margin of his copy next to "out-doe" the word "Dildoes." Maybe he got this from metrical and contextual guesswork, maybe from consulting an unredacted manuscript copy of the poem, maybe through

lubricious literary gossip: whatever the means of supplying "Dildoes," that method failed for the second gap. The
reader could not discover or intuit that this gap erases
religious rather than sexual content in a phrase reading
"out-sweare the litany" in later editions. What is significant is that at least some readers understood the printed
gap as a placeholder, signaling something missing that
needed to be supplied by hand if possible.

These book-handlers do to the material object what
theorists of reading have long suggested the reader does
to the immaterial words. The reader-response criticism
of the 1970s and '80s suggested, in the words of its
prominent practitioner Wolfgang Iser, that a text must
"be conceived in such a way that it will engage the reader's imagination in the task of working things out for
himself, for reading is only a pleasure when it is active
and creative": the job of the reader is to "fill in the gaps
left by the text itself." What was new about this theory
was its conceptualization of creativity as shared between
author and reader rather than concentrated in the
inspired literary language of the writer. For Iser, these
necessary literary gaps are understood as conceptual.
They are the silences in prose storytelling, the narrative
equivalent of withholding the name of the murderer in
a detective story, so that the reader has the enjoyment of
assembling and supplementing through conjecture and
guesswork the evidence that has been drip-fed throughout the reading.

Reader-response theorists *avant la lettre*, the authors

and publishers of the eighteenth century developed sophisticated and playful techniques for engaging readers and developing their understanding of their role, particularly in regard to the new form of the age, the long narrative. In *The Life and Opinions of Tristram Shandy*, Laurence Sterne's experimental eighteenth-century romp dubbed by James Boswell "a damn'd clever book," a number of bookish tricks are played on the reader. Sterne exploits typographical jokes that revel in the possibilities, or as media theorists would put it, the affordances, offered by the eighteenth century's dominant literary form: the novel. Wherever you open *Tristram Shandy* you will find dashes of variable length, Sterne's major unit of punctuation, deployed to disrupt the flow of reading and to embody hesitation, silence, what is indecorous or otherwise unsayable within the plot. As Donne's expurgated poems a century previously show, readers were accustomed to trying to fill out such omissions, in literal ways by supplying a missing word, or in more metaphorical ways by piecing together continuous ideas of character and plot. The long dash is the book's cue to its readers to take an active role in the creation of meaning.

Sterne deploys other, physical *jeux d'esprit*. Tristram, who knows fine well that he is in a book, declares that he has torn out "a whole chapter" from volume 4. The "chasm of ten pages" is marked in the original edition by a jump in pagination from 146 to 156. This omission forces the disruption of the numbering convention in which rectos are always odd-numbered (have a look!), to corroborate this fictional act of violence to the book now in the reader's hands. The humor here is based on a shared understanding of book production and the willingness to reframe accidentals of print, such as pagination, into meaningful parts of the novel's imagined world. Shandy lives inside a bookscape: a paper world in which the progress of his life is judged not in years but in pages and chapters. In volume 6, Sterne famously challenges the reader to complete a blank page left for the depiction of the siren Widow Wadman: "Never did thy eyes behold, or thy concupiscence covet anything in this world, more concupiscible than Widow Wadman." Facing a leaf blank except for the page number, [147], the reader is invited "to conceive this right,—call for pen and ink—here's paper ready to your hand.—Sit down, Sir, paint her to your own mind—as like your mistress as you can—as unlike your wife as your conscience will let you—'tis all one to me—please but your own fancy in it." Over the page the implied illustration is praised as "exquisite": "Thrice happy book! thou wilt have one page, at least, within thy covers which Malice will not blacken, and which Ignorance cannot misrepresent."

That readers are encouraged to participate in the creation of the book by completing its blank pages is rhetorically clear. But what is also evident from extensive consultation of extant copies is that readers knew instinctively that this invitation was itself fictional. No one actually had a go at depicting Widow Wadman in the allocated space. It was a joke, a rhetorical flourish, not a requirement. Henry William Bunbury, one of hundreds of illustrators drawn to Tristram Shandy's zany characters and scenes in the eighteenth century, sketched a number of episodes in the endpapers or flyleaves of his copy of the novel, now in Yale University Library. Some of these preliminary cartoons developed into a set of illustrations published separately from Sterne's novel. But Bunbury's page 147, too, remains unmarked. Even the Laurence Sterne Trust, which in 2016 invited 147 artists to complete the portrait of Widow Wadman, could conceive of responding to Sterne's apparent bait only outside the pages of the book. A modern edition of Sterne's novel published in 2010 by the innovative press Visual Editions places a shiny plastic oval on their equivalent page. It is part frame to the missing image of the widow; part mirror, suggesting wryly that the reader's fuzzy reflection should serve; but also part impermeable, proofed against the presumptuous ink or pastel of the artistically inclined reader. Sterne's blank page apparently explicitly invites readers to participate in its creation but somehow simultaneously transmits its own completeness and integrity. The blank page is an inviting lawn with an invisible "keep off the grass sign," a trick for the unwary who do not know that their proper role as readers is not to throw themselves innocently into the book and its wiles but to maintain an ironic distance.

Elsewhere, eighteenth-century readers are less reticent. Samuel Richardson, himself a printer as well as author of the innovative epistolary novels *Pamela, or,*

Virtue Rewarded (1740) and *Clarissa, Or the History of a Young Lady* (1748), engaged in extensive reader consultation over his novels. For his first novel, he facilitated this feedback by producing handwritten drafts interleaved with blank pages and circulating them for comment, particularly from a circle of female readers. As *Clarissa* was then published in seven volumes across 1747–48, the end of the novel could incorporate reactions to its earlier stages. Dorothy, Lady Bradshaigh, read the early volumes of *Clarissa* and tried vigorously to persuade Richardson away from a tragic ending. Bradshaigh was a robust reader who likeably described herself that year as "middle-aged, middle-sized, a degree above plump, brown as an oak wainscot, a good deal of country red in her cheeks." A portrait by Edward Haytley dated 1746 shows Lord and Lady Bradshaigh in full eighteenth-century mode: if they had had more money, it would have been a Gainsborough. She sits in a chair amid fashionably landscaped grounds, a dog at her feet; he stands, hand on a telescope and a feathered hat resting on a table; behind them is the Elizabethan Haigh Hall in Lancaster, with terraced grasslands, a waterside pavilion, and a rowing boat on a lake or moat. Lady Bradshaigh's complexion is indeed rosy as she looks out of the painting, holding, in a pose that suggests display rather than reading, a small, red book that could conceivably be one of the octavo volumes of Richardson's *Pamela*. Later generations of the family would build an extraordinary library collection, including a Gutenberg Bible and extensive collections of Arabic, Persian, Turkish, and Chinese manuscripts, at Haigh Hall: Dorothy's biblio-philia was more modest, topical, and readerly.

Author and reader developed an antagonistic friend-ship. Richardson described Bradshaigh's responses as "the best commentary that cd. be written on the His-tory of Clarissa" and considered publishing them. He gave his fierce correspondent, who had been writing to him under a pseudonym, a presentation copy of *Clarissa* marked "From the Author," which she then over-inscribed "Do. Bradshaigh / 1748." This annotated title page establishes them as collaborators on the text: the novel is a literal partnership between author and reader. Or, rather, it captures Lady Bradshaigh's inscrip-tion of herself on top of the record of the authorial gift, overwriting Richardson's dedication. And in case this looks like a clumsy mistake, she does it again, delib-erately, in each of the six further volumes of the novel.

On reading the published novel with her sister Lady Echlin, Lady Bradshaigh was left deeply distressed by the eventual ending in which (spoiler alert) Clarissa Harlowe dies of the anguish caused by Robert Lovelace's sexual assault and he in turn is killed in a duel by her cousin. The two women readers worked individually on alter-native endings that they felt more morally, aesthetically, or emotionally appropriate to Clarissa's story and her virtuous character. Lady Bradshaigh made her extensive handwritten commentary in the margins of her copy of *Clarissa*; she shared it with Richardson, who added his

own annotations (the marked-up book is now in Princeton University Library). "In the margins of this unique
copy," writes Janine Barchas, "Richardson and Lady
Bradshaigh do battle over the interpretation of the novel,
each trying to impose his or her will upon the other and
claim definitive 'ownership' of Clarissa." The annotations
turn this copy of the book into a tussle between reader
and author, an extraordinary materialization of the reading process, which usually leaves no trace. Readers may
mutter under their breath as they read, decry the ending in conversation, or, now, post their review online, but
they probably rarely commit this adversarial commentary
to the pages of the book, and even less frequently receive
the author's own responses. For example, in volume five
of the original seven-volume *Clarissa*, Lady Bradshaigh
is not impressed by a turn in the plot whereby Clarissa
decides to leave Mrs. Moore's dubious lodging-house
alone. Her marginal comment is scathing, suggesting that
it is either improper behavior for an innocent young
woman or implausible behavior in the fictional heroine
of a novel about coercion: "This was a poor device, for
she must think he wou'd have follow'd her, and perhaps
have forced her into a coach & carry'd her where he had a
mind." Richardson was outraged, adding his own defensive reply: "Device, does your Ladiship call it? Cl[arissa].
was above all Devices! . . . she had nothing in her Head
or Heart but once more to get from him." Bradshaigh's
comments are part proofreading (she corrects typos),
part continuity-checking (she points out an inconsistency

about who has a crucial key), part expert witness (she thinks herself a doyenne of upper-class mores, superior to the artisan Richardson), and part fan-fiction or character defense (she cannot believe that characters would behave in such a way or she wishes they had not). This range of forms of reading makes Lady Bradshaigh's *Clarissa* an exemplar of reader responses of different kinds.

Lady Bradshaigh's preferred ending, written on the novel's blank endpapers, included Lovelace living as "a warning, in linguring out a miserable life . . . becoming a cripple, & a sincere penitent," and Clarissa, remaining single, undefiled (Lovelace's attack having been attempted but not ultimately perpetrated) and reconciled to her family and friends. In a letter to Richardson she asked what he thought of her alternative: "What will you say to the last leaf in Clarissa I wonder? I cou'd not help it, perhaps it may be absur'd, but it pleased me. You know I hate death and destruction." On the face of it, Lady Bradshaigh's petitionings for a happy ending to Clarissa's travails were entirely unsuccessful. But her responses have affected the ongoing evolution of the novel and been incorporated into its life in subsequent editions.

Not only does Richardson incorporate some of Lady Bradshaigh's objections and suggestions by adding passages and reworking some scenes. Later editions of *Clarissa* borrow the mise-en-page of Lady Bradshaigh's annotated copy by including a frame of commentary on the printed page integrating her feedback. Much of this revision works to highlight Lovelace's viciousness and thereby to create more sympathy for Clarissa's plight: Richardson was particularly troubled that, to Lady Bradshaigh, Lovelace was a dashing libertine of a thrilling kind. Numerous of her comments make light of Lovelace's behavior, calling it "comical wickedness," and exclaiming, "I wish I cou'd help laughing at him." When Lady Bradshaigh admits in her correspondence with Richardson that "knowing [Lovelace's] wicked End, how every good thing he says, raises my Indignation against him, a deceitful, practiced vilain," Richardson appends, with evident relief, "Now, Madam, at last you see him." In the later printed text, some of the marginal commentary seems to be directed at the unnamed Lady Bradshaigh as it engages with her critiques, as in the formula "We cannot forbear observing in this place that the Lady has been particularly censured, even by some of her own Sex." One editor notes that Richardson's emendations to the novel in the 1751 edition "seem designed to foreclose interpretive multiplicity"—that's to say, they neutralize the power of a resisting reader like Lady Bradshaigh. Richardson edits his novel to assert the power of the book over that of its consumer (in a novel about consent and power, this is very appropriate), and he does this not just by changing its content but by altering its form. Preemptively occupying the marginal space on the page where a reader might put their own handwritten commentary and deploying printed, directive notes that point out the failings of other readers, Richardson uses the revised book form to change the interpretative authority of his novel. The time for collaboration with his readers was over.

Samuel Richardson's work as author and publisher comes from the period when long-form prose fiction was indeed novel. In negotiating a role for the book recipients in some surprisingly literal ways, the collaborative production of *Clarissa* as a joint effort between author and reader anticipates our later attempts to capture this reciprocity. Lady Bradshaigh's engagement with *Clarissa* combines reading and writing in a way that foreshadows the rise of fan fiction, in which well-informed readers, heavily invested in the lives and possibilities of fictional characters, continue or redirect their stories in unauthorized spin-offs or sequels. The biggest internet platform for fan-fiction compositions is dominated by hundreds of thousands of readerly engagements with and continuations of the Harry Potter books, but it also has space for Sherlock Holmes, *Les Misérables*, and *Pride and Prejudice* fan fictions, too. Readers who become writers extending the fictional world of their heroes and heroines are the most literal versions of those creative and engaged interlocutors imagined by reading theorists. Most famous of all is the best-selling *Fifty Shades of Grey*, which started out as self-published fan fiction based on the *Twilight* series. The material weight of the phenomenal popularity of E. L. James's book was revealed when charity bookshops issued a press release asking donors to please not give any more cast-off erotica: a Welsh Oxfam shop built a fort with the hundreds of copies they were given in 2016. They could have done with an artist like Buzz Spector to help: Spector's *Toward a Theory of Universal Causality* is a stepped block composed of 6,500 used books.

How readers make space for themselves and their own narrative desires in the margins of fiction expresses itself differently in the later twentieth century. But the success of the *Choose Your Own Adventure* series of game books for children riffs on some of the same issues of form and content as Lady Bradshaigh's readerly commentary on Richardson's Clarissa. (A *Choose Your Own Adventure Clarissa* would be a terrific postmodern pastiche.) Initially invented by Edward Packard, the *Choose Your Own Adventure* series sold 250 million copies worldwide during the 1980s and early '90s. The premise is a simple but compelling one. Readers begin with a section of text that establishes the scenario and are then given choices about how the story should proceed. Each option has its own page number, to which the reader then turns. That section, too, offers different routes. The reader skips around the book and there are multiple potential endings.

A warning to the young reader at the beginning of Packard's *The Cave of Time* (1979) sets out the contract:

> Do not read this book straight through from beginning to end! The pages contain many different adventures ... The adventures you take are a result of your choice. You are responsible, because you choose! After you

make your choice, follow the instructions to see what happens to you next. Remember—you cannot go back!

The emphasis on readerly agency here takes on an ethical charge: you are the author of your own destiny. The page numbers are the most important navigational tool in the *CYOA* universe, so they are larger than usual, in the top corner of each page. The other noticeable feature of these small-format, cheaply produced paperbacks is the number of possible endings. *The Cave of Time* has more than thirty, each wrapping up with "The End." This structure makes for a more uncertain and unpredictable reading experience: anyone who enjoys detective fiction will recognize the ways in which an awareness of how many pages are left conditions our response to the plot. Too many pages to go and the current revelation must be a red herring. The codex has taught us to expect that the end of the book and the end of the story will be identical: *CYOA* books joyfully disrupt that equivalence.

Grown-up versions have been attempted, such as *Life's Lottery: A Choose-Your-Own-Adventure Book* in 1999. Kim Newman's picaresque novel consists of three hundred short chapters. The second-person protagonist, "you," whirls through a dance of sex, violence, and betrayal and many of the sections end in a choice: "If you tell her you love her, go to 71. If you apologize for being a bastard, go to 79." Others end with the disobliging "and so on": both the book's form, and its content, toy with the idea of multiple paths through the narrative but instead they succumb to a kind of wearied inevitability. The bound book is well designed for the *Choose Your Own Adventure* story, as it allows its reader-protagonist to flip between story lines. Newman's novel toys cynically with this, finally asserting that our lives are pretty predetermined: they are best read from start to finish. Apparent forks in the road are simply detours on the same journey. B. S. Johnson's experimental novel *The Unfortunates* (1969), a box of twenty-seven sections of text, with a first and last chapter specified and the rest to be read in any order, was even more committed to communicating its central premise of the randomness of human life. Johnson described the genre of realist novel as "an exhausted form." To convey his story about memory, he needed something different from the traditional codex, because the "randomness [of his material] was directly in conflict with the technological fact of the bound book: or the bound book imposes an order, a fixed page order, on the material." The loose sections were "a physical tangible metaphor for randomness," and a "better solution to the problem of conveying the mind's randomness than the imposed order of a bound book."

These examples of formal book innovation nibble at the fixity of the bound codex, but a more significant alternative to the analogue form is the digital book. Many column inches have been devoted over the last quarter-century to the death of the book, and, broadly, it has been Amazon's e-reader, the Kindle, first launched in 2007, that has been fingered with this putative murder (see Chapter 16). In 2010 Amazon's chief executive announced a "tipping point": e-book sales had out-stripped physical book sales in Amazon's store by about a third. However, rumors of the death of the codex, on this and on multiple other occasions, turned out to be premature. The balance has tipped back. And as the *Choose Your Own Adventure* publishing success, and then collapse, suggests, the book's ultimate nemesis may not be its digital avatar the e-book but a different medium entirely: the computer game.

Myst, a graphical adventure puzzle game designed in the 1990s by Robyn and Rand Miller, has been read by media studies scholars as an exemplar of remediation: the historical transition from one form (in this case the codex) to another (the video game). The game becomes an allegory for the book's own apparent obsolescence in the digital age. Players of *Myst* are encouraged to work to re-gather scattered leaves from two books, one red and one blue, from a family library. They come to real-ize that the character Atrus has imprisoned his sons in the books, and if the books are reassembled the prison-ers will escape and the gamer will be trapped in their place. As Jay David Bolter and Richard Grusin argue in an influential reading of *Myst* that brings out its reso-nances for a wider cultural shift, either "the player wins by helping the father destroy the brothers' books" and thereby "transcends the book," or "fails [and] is trapped forever in the book itself—the worst possible fate in the age of graphics." Neither scenario has much truck with the codex. Books function as props and tokens in the plotting of *Myst* as a jeering reminder of the superiority of the video game in creating an immersive, participative fictional world. What would Lady Bradshaigh have thought?

But the victory of the video game over the codex, if such it is, is Pyrrhic. *Myst* was developed for a medium that now seems as antique and unreadable as the scroll: the CD-ROM. It has had numerous formatting updates since its original launch to keep up with the devices and consoles on which players might wish to access its fictional world: user reviews on the smartphone versions are mixed. By contrast, *Clarissa*, in its original seven volumes, is still entirely legible and works as it was intended by Richardson, its author and printer. Books last, and their long lives sometimes have unexpected consequences, as the following chapter will explore. No battery, no updates, no screen to crack: the book's ultimate superiority, and the source of its extraordinary longevity, is its technological simplicity.

15

The empire writes back

Three passengers en route to New England on the *Prudent Mary*, which sailed from Gravesend to Boston in the summer of 1660, are known to history. Two, the fugitive Parliamentarians Edward Whalley and his son-in-law William Goffe, had been signatories to Charles I's death warrant and were evading retribution at the restoration of his son Charles II. They would survive for more than a decade, concealed among the American Puritan communities, despite English government attempts to discover them. Similar ideological forces to those that propelled Whalley and Goffe toward Massachusetts also brought the third significant passenger aboard the *Prudent Mary*: the printer Marmaduke Johnson. New World Puritan communities had a great appetite for printed material, for sermons and spiritual guides and Scriptures, and an experienced printer would not be in want of work in the expanding colony. But in fact Johnson's job was not to produce material for these colonists or, at least, not directly. He was sent to Boston by the Society for the Propagation of the Gospel in New England in response to a request for an "honest young man, who hath skill to compose," that is, to gather type accurately into lines for typesetting "(and the more skill in other parts of the work, the better)." This imported artisan was to work under the College Printer at Harvard "in impressing the Bible in the Indian language." Oh, and "with him send a convenient stock of paper to begin withal." Aged around thirty, Johnson arrived for a three-year posting, but never returned to England. Instead he put down roots and developed his career in colonial Massachusetts.

Johnson had been summoned to America by the remarkable English evangelist John Eliot. Eliot had been working as a missionary in New England for three decades, having arrived in Boston with twenty-three barrels of books in 1631, in the vanguard of the migration that would see 20,000 English emigrants settled in the newly chartered Massachusetts Bay Colony in the 1630s. In 1640 he co-authored, with other elders of the colony, the first book printed in New England, now known as the Bay Psalm Book. That the first printed book should be this translation of the Psalms into English meter for singing speaks to the priorities of these intensely religious colonial communities: the full title is *The Whole Booke of Psalmes Faithfully Translated into English Metre. Whereunto is prefixed a discourse declaring not only the lawfullnes, but also the necessity of the heavenly Ordinance of singing Scripture Psalmes in the Churches of God.* It's estimated that around 1,700 copies were produced, of which around a dozen eye-wateringly expensive copies now survive.

The Bay Psalm Book was cheerfully, wonkily printed on a printing press that had been imported by the

Puritan minister Joseph Glover. Glover died while traveling to America, but his work was continued by his wife, Elizabeth. The type is worn (it is sometimes suggested that, as a separatist Puritan, Glover would have had to acquire the typeface illicitly and secondhand from a sympathetic printer rather than via a licensed type foundry), with few italic letters and, apparently, no apostrophes. The colophon claims credit for America's first printer: Stephen Day. Day was the Glovers' indentured servant, a locksmith by training and now the new colony's pressman, based at Cambridge, Massachusetts. He was soon at work, printing first a copy of the freeman's oath, then an almanac to get his hand in, and then the metrical psalms. The psalter carries a highly selective list of "Faults escaped in printing" at the back, with the permission "The rest, which have escaped through oversight, you may amend, as you find them obvious."

There are a lot of faults: Day's inexperience as a printer is evident. On some pages the lines of type have bent, revealing that they were imperfectly locked into the form from which the impression was taken. There's evidence of clotting ink and some imperfect inking of the lines, producing some pages that are blurrily black and some that are vanishingly faint. Further, a wiser hand would have reformatted the book as an octavo (printing eight leaves to a sheet) rather than quarto (four leaves), making more economical use of the paper, but octavo printing was more complicated to set up, and Day probably knew his limitations. The print run of this small quarto, measuring around 17 centimeters high and comprising about 140 pages, took up 130 reams of imported paper stock. It would be more than a century before a press was made in America; paper manufacture took even longer to develop, and printing ink was also probably imported for much of that period. Early American printing was thus materially dependent on Europe during its own incunabula, or cradle period. The Bay Psalm Book is a poignant souvenir of this era of frontier printing and the first extant book published in colonial America.

John Eliot's main mission, however, was not to his fellow colonists but to the Native population. Oliver Cromwell had established the Corporation for Promoting and Propagating the Gospel of Jesus Christ in New England in 1649, and Eliot worked under its auspices to prepare and publish a translation of the Bible into the language of the Algonquin peoples. He had learned enough Wôpanâak, the language spoken in eastern Massachusetts and Cape Cod, to preach his first sermon in 1646, and, aided by Native members of the so-called Praying Towns in New England, he began a phonetic transcription of the Scriptures. (Praying Towns were settlements established by missionaries for Native converts.) The New Testament was published in 1661, with a complete Bible published in 1663. It was an extraordinary imaginative linguistic feat since, previously, Wôpanâak had had no written form. The combined book is a stout quarto with narrow margins and two printed columns of text.

Linguists distinguish between "naturalized" and "denaturalized" approaches to transcription: the former produces language in a standard form that does not draw attention to itself; the second uses orthographic (writing and spelling conventions) and other means to convey nonstandard linguistic usage. Bristling with "q" and "k" and double "a" forms, Wôpanâak emerged in Eliot's print version through pointedly denaturalized transcriptions. Eliot's invented orthography looked foreign. The title of his Bible was *Mamusse Wunneetupanatamwe Up-biblum God naneeswe Nukkone Testament kah wonk Wusku Testament. Ne quoshkinnumuk nashpe Wuttinneumok Christ not asoowesit John Eliot.* (It might seem unfair to notice that Eliot's own name is in prominent large type—larger than the word "Christ.") This conscious strangeness made his Bible as much a colonial propaganda curio for supporters back in England as it was a tool of his missionary work with Native speakers. A printing press, a new set of type with extra letters "k" and "q" to support the new print language, plus a new character devised by Eliot to represent Wôpanâak pronunciation, and the skills of an experienced journeyman printer, Marmaduke Johnson, were the resources Eliot imported from England on the *Prudent Mary* to bring the project to completion.

The Bible title page has a decorative woodcut border and credits Samuel Green and Marmaduke Johnson as printers. Green, the father of a great American printing dynasty, had arrived in New England in 1630 but does not seem to have begun work as a printer until the 1640s. Less visible in the book but vital to the entire project were Native labor and linguistic competence. Native translators working with Eliot included Job Nesutan and John Sassamon. We know that a Native Nipmuc printer, Wowaus, was apprenticed to Samuel Green at the press in Cambridge and took the anglicized name James Printer on his conversion to Christianity. We can assume that his skills in checking Eliot's translations and setting them correctly in type were invaluable to the project. Writing about translations of *Pilgrim's Progress* in other Protestant evangelical contexts, Isabel Hofmeyr identifies that "the basic working unit [of mission translation] comprised a second-language missionary and first-language convert . . . these 'couples' worked long hours, were locked in tense and often intimate relations of dependence, and produced a style of translation that was co-authored." Eliot does not acknowledge this collaborative authorship, but it probably captures the work behind the scenes. Even when he does mention James Printer's importance, in a letter to the natural philosopher and chemist Robert Boyle, who became the governor of the New England Company in 1662, he does not give him either his Native or his convert name: "We have but one man viz. the Indian printer that is able to compose the sheets, and correct the press, with understanding." Only one book from the Harvard press active over the following decades records Printer as printer: a 1709 psalter.

However much their contribution has been occluded and erased from the printed book, Native translators and artisans were so central to the production of the Bible that it is a cultural object neither wholly colonial nor wholly indigenous. It is, like jazz, Chicago pizza, or the "Last Supper" painting in Cuzco cathedral in Peru, where Christ breaks a roasted guinea pig with his disciples, syncretic: a blend of traditions. Some words from Wôpanâak were loaned into English, including "moccasin," "powwow" (originally meaning a healer), and "moose." Perhaps most prominent was "mugwump." Eliot fluently translated roles including officer, captain, and duke into the Wôpanâak for military leaders: mummugquompaog.

Twenty copies of the Wôpanâak Bible were sent home as presentation curios for important institutions and sponsors. These had a specially printed English title page describing it as "translated into the Indian language and ordered to be printed by the commissioners of the United Colonies in New-England, at the charge and with the consent of the Corporation in England for the Propagation of the Gospel amongst the Indians in New-England." It's easy to see that this title page diplomatically prioritizes the sponsors and the institutions. The edition's alternative title pages symbolize the way this book looks in two directions—to England and to New England, to English and to Wôpanâak—and the ways in which it toggles uncomfortably between colonial imposition and indigenized commodity. Extant copies of this Bible and other texts in Eliot's so-called Indian

Library attest to the connections between New England and English institutions. One, now in Oxford, is a gift from Harvard College to its benefactor Ralph Freke, a subscriber to the Bible publication who had given the Harvard press its first font of type: "By order of the overseers of Harvard College in Cambridg in New Engld, To the Right worshippl Ralph Freke, Esq., a noble benefactor to the aforesayd Colleg. 1667."

In the mid-1660s Charles II sent a presentation copy to the Mohegans in Connecticut—although they didn't speak Wôpanâak—in distinctive blue leather binding, with gold gilding and a clasp. It was received as a sign of political alliance, like the book gifts discussed in Chapter 3. The volume, decorated with fore-edge paintings of flowers and cherubs, is now in Illinois University Library. The majority of the print run of the Eliot Bible, however, was produced for Native reading in Massachusetts. These carried no English script other than some proper names.

A number of extant copies of Eliot's Bible record interactions with those Native readers. One copy now in the Bodleian is inscribed "Samuel ponompam [*sic*] his booke 1662." Ponampam was one of four Native schoolmasters employed by Eliot on a salary of £10 a year, and he appears to have taught in Wamesit on the Merrimack River. Eliot sent a stream of letters and testimonies back to England for publication, and Ponampam's conversion narrative was published in a small quarto titled *A relation of the repentance and conversion of the poor Indians in New-England; shewing the wonderfull work of God in their poor souls*. These tracts were popular: a catalogue of "the most vendible books in England" from 1657 lists this one among other Eliot pamphlets. In his confession, Ponampam cites chapter and verse of the Bible, drawing on Eliot's translation, and reveals his struggles with embracing the Christian faith: "My heart did not desire to pray but to go away to some other place. But remembering the word of God, that all shall pray to God. Then did I not desire to go away, but to pray to God. But if I pray afore the Sachems pray [i.e., before the Native leaders convert to Christianity], I fear they will kill me." His experience as a colonial subject caught between indigenous and colonial cultural systems is heartbreaking, all the more because of his limited English vocabulary. Elsewhere, Ponampam struggles to reconcile Christian and Indian values, hearing a sermon on adultery and admitting "my heart did love the having of two wives." His confession, marked by a struggle that blurs colonial resistance to the settlers with the wayward sinner's resistance to God's grace, ends with his declaration: "I give my heart and my self to Christ."

A range of extant Eliot Bibles captures something similar to Ponampam's struggles with Christianity and colonial rule. Numerous copies of the translated Native Bible record the often ambivalent, painful, and bewildered responses of Native readers, in marginalia in the Wôpanâak language (here translated into English by nineteenth-century ethnographers). These examples range in unruly ways across any blank space in the books—margins top, bottom, and sides, endpapers, blank space between biblical books, sometimes writing sideways or, in reference to the orientation of the book for reading, upside down. They are thus in a kind of dialogue, or shouting match, with the book form, even as they seem to use its spaces without much attention to the design of its printed content. Sometimes the engagement is clearly with the biblical text, sometimes marks are not apparently related to the Scriptures. Often these marginal marks involve assertions of identity, sometimes with Native and sometimes converted forms of names. One copy now in the Congregational Society Library of Boston bears the statement "I, Nathan Francis, this is my writing at this time," next to Ezekiel 2; in the book of Daniel, the commandment "You, Thomas, remember: do not fornicate"; in the New Testament book of Romans, "I Mantooekit This is my hand"; and at Thessalonians 1:1, "I am Anannahdinnoo, you are Conouhonuma." A different copy records "I Francis Ned, my writing at Dapequasit." More detail about the circulation of an Eliot Bible is found in a copy now at the Connecticut Historical Society, Hartford: "I, Elisha, this is my book" (repeated three times); and elsewhere, "I Laben Hossuit own this bible, June 11, 1747. Solomon Pinnion sold it to me. It cost four pounds." (Another copy also records paid acquisition, perhaps because it is a novel concept: "I Nannahdinnoo, this is my book," and again "I, I Nanahdinnoo, own this forever. Because I bought it with my money.")

Some marginalia engage more directly with Christian

doctrine. A Philadelphia copy records a more scattered and fragmentary version of the narratives of despair and self-denigration that are part of the genre of conversion. It begins with "This is Papenau's book. I am looking after it," and urges, "Remember you people, this book is right and you should do good in all your times." The annotations become more plaintive: "I do [n]ot like very much to read many writings, because I am too . . ."; "I am forever a pitiful person in the world. I am not able clearly to read this, this book"; "I am a pitiful person. I do not like very much to read this book for I am too pitiful in this world." Finally, another annotator asserts, "I, Joseph Papenau, this is my book. I say this at this time July 22 1712." Partial, painful narratives of engagement with the book, and with the violent cultural changes it embodied, are fleetingly recorded.

Other annotated Eliot Bibles give dispersed glimpses of life in the Praying Towns. "At this time . . . on February 7, 1715 . . . have already come five great snows"; "I Banjmon Kusseniyeutt caught (?) a Negro man and a white woman"; "Know ye all people there is going to be a new storm"; "I am a man and a sannup [a married Native man]." A copy now in private ownership records a sequence of family deaths in the margins: "Jacob Seiknout's daughter died May 17, 1727, the one called Sareh . . . Ephraim Naquatta died on July 7, 1731. Joshua Seiknouet died January 22, 1716. Peapsippo died August 9th, 1715." The probable annotator signs himself: "I (am) Matthew Seiknout, this is my Bible, clearly."

These vestiges of Native interaction with the Eliot Bible are both troubling and touching. Ethnographers use the word "transculturation" to capture the ways in which subordinated groups respond to and repurpose the materials of a dominant culture, sometimes using them for self-assertion, contrary to the intentions of the colonizer. The critic and theorist Mary Louise Pratt asks how, or if, people on the receiving end of empire are able to talk back to imposed modes of representation, and wonders, "What materials can one study to answer those questions?" Perhaps the Eliot Bibles offer one kind of answer. In the blank spaces of these printed books we can map forms of compromised Native identity, self-assertion, spirituality, and storytelling. The Bibles, and the invasive cultures of literacy they represent, are deeply colonial objects, but their reworking by Native Christians challenges the authoritative voice of the printed text. Pratt's idea of the "contact zone," the place where colonizers and colonized interact, improvise, and interlock, often within radically asymmetrical relations of power, is a suggestive one for thinking about these imperial artifacts of print and manuscript. If ethnography is the writing about Native peoples by colonizers, "auto-ethnographic expression" "involves partly collaborating with and appropriating the idols of the conqueror." Perhaps the relationship between print and manuscript annotation is always a kind of contact zone involving asymmetric power relations; perhaps the book has always offered a space for interaction and transformation that ameliorates the specific imbalances of the colonial encounter recorded in Eliot Bibles. Or, more simply, perhaps the empire writes back.

Eliot's ultimate aim was to eradicate Algonquin culture by transforming it into Anglo-American culture. His "Praying Towns" were conspicuously nonindigenous in style, with stone houses and English orchards and farms, English clothes and patriarchal English families. Fines were imposed for Native customs such as polygamy, Native healing, or wearing long hair. The teacher, convert, and Bible-owner Samuel Ponampam got the message: "I found that all my doings were sins against God . . . I saw that in everything I did, I sinned." God's commandments, and the imposed rules of colonial England, were indistinguishable in this coercive program of reeducation through translation. Eliot's missionary aims were clearly directed toward breaking Native societies through conversion and anglicization. In 1647 he had predicted, ambitiously, that "in forty years more, some Indians would be all one English, and in a hundred years, all Indians here about, would be so." He spoke true. The work of evangelizing he set in place would virtually eradicate the language of his translated Bible within just one century.

The cultural forces embodied by Eliot's translation were apparently unstoppable: Wôpanâak was virtually extinct by the early eighteenth century. The Praying Town of Natick, ten miles west of Boston, stopped using the language in administrative records around

1720; the 1787 tombstone of Silas Paul, a Native minister of religion, is one of the last pieces of linguistic evidence. By the beginning of the twentieth century, an anthropologist from Columbia University could retrieve only some twenty-five remembered Wôpanâak words from the memories of Native elders of the Mashpee community in Cape Cod. Translating the Bible began the process of exterminating the language. But there is a postscript to this narrative of colonial imposition and Native decline, as the ongoing life of the Eliot Bible has taken one striking turn in the twenty-first century.

Wampanoag linguist jessie little doe baird (she does not capitalize) is spearheading efforts to revitalize the Wôpanâak language among Wampanoag communities in Massachusetts, Cape Cod, and Martha's Vineyard, east of the Merrimack River. The Wôpanâak Language Reclamation Project aims at "bringing back to life the tribes' sacred privilege and right—our ancestral language" through language immersion camps, community classes, and self-directed workbooks. An online dictionary, supported by MIT, has almost ten thousand words and definitions. Key to this recovery is Eliot's Indian Library and, in particular, his translated Bible. The website of the project hosts a facsimile copy of the 1663 Bible as a key reference work for contemporary language learning. That Wôpanâak "enjoys the largest corpus of Native written documents on the continent" is now a linguistic strength rather than a catastrophic colonial injury. The imposed English orthography invented by

Eliot is now pragmatically rationalized as an established alphabet useful for teaching the language to English speakers denied their linguistic heritage. In this project of revivifying, Eliot's invention of written Wôpanâak through his translation of the Bible turns out to be an unintended linguistic ark, a resource for the recuperation of the culture that it sought to destroy. The very book that purposed to break Wôpanâak has preserved it for future generations.

16

What is a book?

I thought I would stay away from the existential question "What is a book?" In part this is because the answer is usually either reasonably uncontentious or insufferably pretentious. If we don't know by now what a book is, this book itself is a bit of a dud. But the question of definitions recurs whenever books are discussed, and this seems a good point in *Portable Magic* to address it. On the one hand, administrative attempts to clarify what is and is not a book come up against hard cases: objects that clearly are books but somehow wriggle out of the definition. On the other, creative experimentation with books as sculptural forms, or the fabricated artist's book, bring questions of bookhood and its limits to the playful fore. If there were a third hand, it would be juggling the largely phony debates about the status of e-books compared with their physical counterparts. So which definition should we adopt?

Administrative definitions first, since they seem, on the face of it, least complicated. In 1964, UNESCO defined a book as a "non-periodical publication of at least 49 pages, exclusive of the cover pages, published in the country and made available to the public."

The definitive factors here are interesting: singularity, length, and availability. It was a definition that excluded many children's picture books, self-published works, and imposed an arbitrary length. The original installments of Dickens's novels, published in serial form, would not have counted as books under this designation. The 1964 definition was the first step in identifying books solely as commercially produced codices, while excluding magazines or pamphlets. A second step in the international book bureaucracy allocated every book title a unique number, the International Standard Book Number. "What is a book?" could be answered, in the contemporary world, with the prosaic answer: an item with an ISBN.

Defining "book" for the purposes of identifying what commodities are exempt from VAT or purchase tax (books are again treated as a special case; unlike, say, CDs or audiobooks, they are exempt from the tax in the UK, placing them in a category of essentials alongside food, medical supplies, crash helmets, and children's clothing), the government outlines that the relevant object would "normally consist of text or illustrations, bound in a cover stiffer than their pages. They may be printed in any language or characters (including Braille or shorthand), photocopied, typed, or handwritten, so long as they are found in book or booklet form." A book, here, is form, not content, but it is not a specific length nor is it necessarily commercially produced. The thickness of the cover comes to surprising prominence in the definition. When Google tried to estimate the number of books ever printed, it first had to come up with its own definition:

> One definition of a book we find helpful inside Google when handling book metadata is a "tome," an idealized bound volume. A tome can have millions of copies (e.g., a particular edition of *Angels and Demons* by Dan Brown) or can exist in just one or two copies (such as an obscure master's thesis languishing in a university library).

It is striking to see the outdated word "tome" in this contemporary definition. Derived from the Latin for papyrus, "tome" has a great etymological pedigree, including the regrettably disused "tomecide" for a person who destroys books. It is almost always now a cliché, qualified by "weighty" and used with a slightly disparaging or archaic air. (It's hard to imagine anyone using it seriously: "Can't wait to start reading my new tome"; "My tome club is reading *Cat's Eye* this month"; "Don't panic: I've just picked up a tome about puppy training.")

Scholars have developed these practical working definitions in different directions. Joseph Dane distinguishes between the abstract "book," meaning all the copies of a particular edition (in Google-speak, a "tome"), and the book-copy, or the object on your desk. Stephen Emmel opts for something that emphasizes completeness: a book is a "written work that comes to a conclusive end." Roger Stoddard reminds us that "whatever they may do, authors do not write books," a formulation that redirects the book as the product of materially artisanal, rather than verbally creative, labor. Stoddard's initially counterintuitive formulation is helpful in showing how in conventional book production there is a decisive separation of roles between the author preparing the text and the editor, designers, printers, and so on preparing the book: the book here is absolutely not its words or images but its typesetting, paper, and binding. In an expansive set of questions about what might be included, or not, in the definition of book, James Raven stresses, like Stephen King in my title, portability: what distinguishes a book from an inscribed monument that it might resemble in many other ways is its capacity for movement. Some books, nevertheless, push that to its limit. The unstealable Audubon elephant folio (Chapter 9), or the 34-kilogram *Codex Amiatinus*, an enormous biblical manuscript prepared in Jarrow in Northumbria in the eighth century CE and sent as a gift to Pope Gregory II, or the massive atlas sent to Charles II, now in the British Library, that is almost as tall as the (tall) monarch himself—these are books that would stretch Raven's definition, since they need almost as much oomph to move as a stone tablet but are nevertheless still recognizable *as* books.

One recent academic article suggests that a book is "a linear long-form text that can be read on paper or screen and evokes deep or immersive reading." Here specific use—"deep or immersive reading"—is constitutive of bookhood. A book that no one enjoys, that is rebarbative or encourages skim-reading (one of the codex's technical affordances, as we saw in Chapter 14), by this definition, would not quite be a book. We can all surely think of examples of boring or unread books that are, nevertheless, still unarguably books. This attempt by researchers to sift and establish a working definition of a book in order to inform the publishing trade gathered four necessary criteria: a minimum length; emphasis on textual content; boundaries to its form; book information architecture. They argue that "the artefact that meets all four criteria is the printed book."

Poets, of course, have a different take, but few of the great poems on books are actually concerned with their materiality. We don't find out anything about the book in which Keats reencounters *King Lear*, and Emily Dickinson's striking assertion "There is no Frigate like a Book / To take us Lands away" is similarly about being transported by a book rather than dwelling on or in it. The early American poet Anne Bradstreet addresses her book, published as *The Tenth Muse* without her consent, as a shameful urchin or "rambling brat," "in rags, halting to th' press," and dressed in "homespun cloth." Gertrude Stein writes in a kind of modernist reverie in her puzzling, poetic inventory of objects *Tender Buttons* (1914) that books just *are*: "Book was there, it was there. Book was there." Just there. Stein captures the stubborn particularity of the book object, but in one of those gnomic and self-canceling statements that are asseverations rather than definitions. We wouldn't look to Stein for clarity. As I said at the beginning of this chapter, defining the book is either self-evident or unexpectedly obscure.

Perhaps it might be possible to define the book with reference to its historical development: if we can pinpoint the emergence of the book we will simultaneously have defined its most salient features. The evolution of portable written material from the clay tablets of the Sumerians and the papyrus scrolls developed by the Egyptians went through various stages on the way to the codex. Immediate precursors include wooden tablets fastened together in a single unit as a polyptych, which survive in some wonderful examples. A concertinaed set of such wooden pages report on food supplies at the Roman fort on Hadrian's Wall, Vindolanda, and date from the early second century CE. In 1914 a man cutting peat in County Antrim, Northern Ireland, discovered six yew wood and wax tablets connected with leather. Dating from the seventh century and about the size of a modern paperback, these tablets are inscribed, with a stylus in two columns, with Psalms 31–33 from the Latin Vulgate Bible. These tablets feel like books: they are bound, their pages turn, they contain text, they are portable. Somewhere between the scroll and the modern codex we get objects that work recognizably as books. Here it's the binding of multiple leaves into a format that allows them to function as a singular object that conveys bookhood. A book, here, is defined by turnable pages.

Some of the heat around the definition of a book is because of an often antagonistic or defensive relationship with digital texts. *Portable Magic* is about books as objects, not as works, and therefore I haven't included those immaterial etherized texts for e-readers, or audiobooks. This is a working boundary decision rather than a moral judgment. I am in no way opposed to e-books and often—on holiday, for instance—find them terrifically convenient. I would often like to be able to buy a physical copy of a book and automatically have access to a digital version without additional payment and, in the academic sphere, the increasingly prohibitive cost of e-books is a source of concern, as it replaces the one-off cost of the object with an eternally recurrent charge for access to its content. Like many readers and researchers during lockdown, I have been very reliant on, and grateful for, online materials. Closed libraries had locked away the physical books that have, for centuries, symbolized my university's intellectual ambitions (the crest of the University of Oxford is an open book, with gilt-edged pages, and while the design encourages reading across the opening, its motto reads, book-like, down the verso then down the recto: *Dom inus illu mina tio mea*: "The Lord is my light"). Lots of the wonderful books I discuss here can be viewed up close and in detail via online digital surrogates prepared by their custodians.

E-books, though, are the equivalent of books as content, rather than books as form. In the terms we encountered earlier, they are platonic rather than pragmatic.

In separating that content (the Kindle edition) from the form (the Kindle reader) they suggest that the comparator for the physical book is actually the reading platform, the Nook, Kobo, or Paperwhite. What's striking about these e-readers is how closely they have shadowed the codex form. They want to be books. Amazon's first Kindle was quarto-sized, around 13 by 20 centimeters, and Brian Cummings has noted that e-readers produce a standard ten or so words per line, "in common with many manuscripts in Carolingian minuscule from the tenth century CE, just like many texts from the print shop of Aldus Manutius in Venice in 1500." While e-books are intangible, e-readers have their own physicality and in this are closely correlated with the familiar forms of the Western book. Text is presented in a vertical orientation (an e-reader is portrait, rather than landscape, in format), pages are flipped from right to left to move sequentially through the text, and there is a facility to bookmark or underline particular passages. There is even a progress gauge that serves as a numerical equivalent of the haptic pleasure of how many pages are left, and therefore how much more story there can be. Jane Austen slyly incorporates this physical inevitability—the physical book is nearly finished—with an inexorable generic narrative toward the end of her knowingly meta-fictional novel *Northanger Abbey*: "The anxiety [about marital conclusion] can hardly extend, I fear, to the bosom of my readers, who will see in the tell-tale compression of the pages before them, that we are all hastening together to perfect felicity." I don't yet know of a writer for the e-reader who has made a similar self-reflexive point about that form, although the Kindle version of Ali Smith's novel *How to Be Both* allowed readers to choose with which of the two perspectives, the historical or the contemporary, they wanted to begin. Print readers were randomly allocated one of the two versions of the book, opening either with one of Smith's brilliant, insightful modern teens, George, or with the Renaissance painter Francesco del Cossa.

In fact, for all it has been predicted as the ultimate publishing disruptor, e-book technology seems to have been surprisingly similar to the codex it proposes to supersede. It has frittered its inventive technological energies on creating book simulacra of, for example, page-turning or the gutter and curve of an open physical page, rather than developing a new, post-codex interface. Johanna Drucker, an insightful scholar of book history and book art, points out that e-books and e-readers have, thus far, been keener to mirror what a book looks like than to interrogate how it works. She suggests that the kitsch skeuomorphic interest in reproducing "bookness" is the redundant equivalent of "preserving a coachman's seat on a motorised vehicle." E-readers have tended to preserve page-turning (perhaps, like the Vindolanda tablets, acknowledging that turnable pages are intrinsic to the definition of the book), whereas text-reading software on computers has reverted to scrolling as the means of serial information delivery (although modern electronic scrolling orientation is vertical, rather than, as in the classical world, horizontal). Innovative, enhanced e-books with specific digital features have tended so far to be expensive to produce and relatively unattractive to readers: the convenience of the physical book simply translated into e-reader format seems to be more commercially successful. One consequence of the availability of books in digital form has been to reenergize the market for physical books with higher production values: elegant typography or letterpress printing, fine bindings, and quality design. At the same time, author events in bookshops or literary festivals have made the signed, dedicated book and the personal handover of the object from author to reader a distinct part of the modern book economy. As soon as e-books begin to dematerialize the book as object, we've invented compensatory protocols and habits that reinstate the sensory pleasures of bookhood.

Until e-books develop their own particular communicative rhetoric, design, and features, they seem to be the shadow or supplement of the physical book rather than its opposite. One such innovation might be the Amazon Kindle subscription-fee model, which pays author royalties based not on the book as a unit but on the number of pages read by any individual reader. (If you're still reading—thank you.) Another decisive shift would be the development of distinct editions for e-readers and for conventional print. The novelist Fay Weldon suggested that future novelists should prepare two versions: a contemplative and longer one for traditional immersive reading and a shorter, plot-driven version meeting the needs of commuters reading while strap-hanging on the Tube or waiting in a sandwich queue.

The other kind of book-not-book is the audiobook: you may not be following these words on the page but instead be listening to this chapter as you commute or exercise, and, if so, I'm delighted you're here. Listening to books read aloud has a noble tradition from classical antiquity, and books designed for reading aloud, such as Bibles or choir manuscripts for singers, have been produced in larger type or format since at least the medieval period, allowing them to be consulted by multiple readers simultaneously. The audiobook developed along with new sound technologies, including the gramophone, but it was the cassette tape in the 1970s that made an audiobook possible and portable. Cassettes or CDs tend to offer an audio replica of the printed book, with some of the same organizational features—a printed cover with chapters or other means of navigation, an assumption of serial listening. Their materiality is hinted at, as they borrow branding from the book jacket, but, like e-books, they are content rather than material form. It's precisely that relative immateriality that makes them convenient at the gym or while dog-walking. Audiobooks have expanded their market share substantially in recent years, but largely without the *cris de coeur* that tend to accompany any mention of e-books.

E-books and audiobooks, then, can be differentiated from books in their prioritization of content. The opposite is true of those books that are books only in formal terms. Ben Denzer's *American Cheese: 20 Slices*, for example, is a book made of plastic-wrapped cheese slices. It is pleasingly cheese-slice sized, with a processed-yellow cloth cover and the words "20 slices" on the front and "American Cheese" on the spine. There are twenty slippery slices that can be turned like pages. Or that are pages. That's it. Denzer has also produced books of dollar bills, ketchup packets, sweeteners, lottery tickets, toilet paper, and, best of all, mortadella (pink, with the title "20 slices" picked out in white fat). All are recognizably books: they deploy familiar Western book architecture of left-hand binding, turnable pages, hard cover, title on the front and the spine and seem to anticipate reading across a horizontal axis from first to last page. Their pages may be made of unexpected materials, but they turn from recto to verso just like the earliest codex bindings. If you came across *American Cheese: 20 Slices*, you'd know immediately how to operate it, and so, if processed cheese could time travel, would our medieval book-nerd Richard de Bury. But Denzer's Andy Warhol-y codices completely evacuate from the book any text or narrative. To put it another way, they combine form and content so completely that these are identical. What is the book of mortadella about? Mortadella. What else could it possibly have to say to us?

Actually, the real answer to that is probably that the mortadella book is precisely a three-dimensional version of the same question, "What is a book?" It becomes a metabook, a book testing the limits of bookhood. There are various other book objects that ask something similar. The so-called nonbook is an object that uses the shape of the book and draws on its visual conventions: badges worn by medieval pilgrims, salt cellars, lighters, home safes. All these articles use the book form as disguise or decoration, drawing sly attention to a disjunction between form and expected content. In her book about her collection of modern book-shaped objects, Mindell Dubansky calls them book-looks, or blooks: these include toy spy cameras disguised as books, a ceramic bookshelf of spice jars with their names on their spines and a digital clock radio in the form of a three-volume stack with the humorous title "Time." A Huntley & Palmers biscuit tin reproduces the marbled pages and art nouveau cover designs of 1920s book-collecting, with spines indicating classic content such as *Pilgrim's Progress* and *Robinson Crusoe*. These blooks have a long history in different contexts. Charles Dickens asked for spare book backs from his binders, Eeles, to decorate his study at Tavistock House. These picked up the fashion for comic mock titles, including "Jonah's Account of the Whale," "Hansard's Guide to Refreshing Sleep" and "Kant's Eminent Humbugs." The film cliché of the bookcase that pivots to reveal a secret passage, or the book that houses a weapon (Chapter 12): these, too, riff on books as objects, not words.

Blooks, then, evoke the familiar object through a few indicative architectural features, primarily spine, binding, and title, and disrupt the commonsense assumption that the book is primarily a transmitter of written material.

Because physical books can be used in different ways in different contexts, however, the distinction between books and blooks can become fuzzy. The Huntley & Palmers biscuit tin has relatively little in common with the modern paperback edition of *Robinson Crusoe* on my shelf that I use regularly for teaching, but a valuable *Robinson Crusoe* first edition, in a highly decorated binding, with marbled-edge papers, kept in a locked cabinet and occasionally looked at rather than read, is closer in function and feel to the tin version (except you can't keep biscuits in it: although Cambridge University Library did once find the greasy traces of a fruit bun inside a sixteenth-century copy of the works of Augustine, claiming hastily that it happened before the book came into their care). Perhaps, then, collectors' books are also blooks (see Chapter 16).

A different kind of artifact tests the definition of a book by adapting found books into new sculptural objects. Theorists love this stuff: it's a kind of bibliographic catnip. Garrett Stewart coins the admittedly awkward word "bibliobjets" as a term for the book as artistic object or conceptual sculpture, "taken out of circulation for sheer pondering as objects, reading matter reduced to cubic inches or feet of worked surface, all verbal mediation disappeared into its physical support." For Stewart, these bibliobjets are almost "anti-books," which sounds promising for the oppositional definition of what a book actually is. But we can see that his definition of the anti-book rests on an overly narrow concept of the book itself. Stewart's descriptions are of canceled codices "vacated of reference," but in fact bibliobjets, like the mortadella book, become self-conscious meta-books by default. They are books about books, reflections on bookhood and its limitations. Sometimes they even register books' absence, as in the empty shelves of Micha Ullman's *Memorial to the Nazi Book-Burning* (1995), or the inscription of cultural losses registered by the vacant, book-shaped spaces in Rachel Whiteread's large sculpture of phantom volumes, *Untitled (Paperbacks)* (1997), in MoMA. Phew! This developed quickly from that currant bun in Augustine.

What these apparent limit-cases on the definition of the book seem to demonstrate is that "book" needs to be an expansive and inclusive definition. Johanna Drucker notes that all books, even ordinary ones that we might read, are already sculptural, existing in space and material. Book art that seems to abdicate textual transmission often amplifies it, or communicates text differently. Tom Phillips's famous *A Humument* is an artwork-in-progress built from within a secondhand copy of an obscure Victorian book, *A Human Document*, by W. H. Mallock. Phillips works by painting, cutting, and molding the printed pages, leaving fragments of texts to reassemble themselves into a comic, surreal, bawdy counternarrative. On the face of it, Phillips has destroyed the original book to create his own art piece. But as he explains, he is deeply respectful of the form of the book and commits himself to self-made rules that respect its original identity. These include "Not to change the place of the page. I'm tied to that. I do little variations but they all scrupulously fall in where they fall." *A Humument* has itself been published in book form, and it has inspired other cutout experiments with novels' materiality. (It has, as Adam Smyth points out, also made the original, once obscure book *A Human Document* into a collectors' item with a price to match.) Jonathan Safran Foer's *Tree of Codes* (2010) was produced by cutting out paragraphs and sentences from the text of a preexisting book, Bruno Schulz's *The Street of Crocodiles* (Foer's title is, as you can see, a cutout of Schulz's), and there are other contemporary book objects that play with the conventions of mise-en-page. Interestingly, and somewhat disobligingly, when interviewed by book historians Adam Smyth and Gill Partington, Phillips was particularly beguiled by the digital app of his work. "Don't we lose something with the app?," "Don't you like paper?," "Do you think it is a special kind of book?" the academics press him. "We're not in Harry Potter times. It's not a magic book," replies the artist, apparently disavowing the material charms of his own book art.

A Humument's relation to books and its own host book is paradoxical: it builds on, and cuts away, it supersedes and revivifies its predecessor. It draws on a long history of books as three-dimensional objects with technologies beyond the flat page, of books that encourage readers to interact beyond simple page-turning. Movable discs known as volvelles were incorporated into high-end astronomical, cipher, and mathematical books from the sixteenth century onward. Johann Remellin's 1675 book of anatomy, *A Survey of the Microcosme*, allowed readers to mimic the processes of dissection and investigation by folding back layers of paper representing particular human tissue: skin, muscle, arteries, bone. Similar movable tabs and flaps that could be lifted to reveal alternative pictures became popular in the nineteenth century, and in the early twentieth century flip or flick books that use the technique of thumbing rapidly through the pages in a book bound with a soft spine to create the illusion of movement were developed alongside cinema (the lovely German term is *Daumenkino*, or "thumb-cinema"). Readers have also been encouraged to cut books. A French Franciscan, Christophe Leutbrewer, listed every conceivable sin the miserable (or completist) reader might need to confess in his book *La Confession coupée* (1677). Each sin occupied a cut strip that could be lifted to serve as a reminder—a kind of built-in Post-it note—for ease of record and for communication to the priest in the confessional. It somehow—and no doubt heretically—reminds me of picture books for children in which pages are cut horizontally, producing composite images such as a monstrous animal with the head of an elephant, the body of a cat, and the feet of a duck. It is also the ancestor to high-concept books of self-selection, such as Raymond Queneau's strips of sonnet lines that can be combined to produce an almost infinite number of poetic combinations, *Hundred Thousand Billion Poems* (1961).

So, what is a book? Next contestant Sybil Fawlty from Torquay, special subject the bleeding obvious, as *Fawlty*

Towers might put it. But the answer has turned out to be a bit muddier than it might initially have seemed. Some of these examples of non- or not-quite-books sharpen and complicate the boundaries of the book. They draw on our familiarity with how books look, feel, and operate while subverting our expectations of what they might contain and thus cleverly (perhaps sometimes too cleverly) remind us that bookhood is a balancing act of form and content. These definitions have made me come up with my own: a book becomes a book in the hands of its readers. It is an interactive object. A book that is not handled and read is not really a book at all.

Epilogue:
Books and transformation

Early-twentieth-century etiquette lessons for Western women frequently featured balancing a book on the head to train out slouching and encourage good posture (NB: modern therapists don't seem to advocate this practice). It's an encounter with bookhood that is all form—evenly weighted, flat surface—and no content. But it is a trope that carries with it the promise that is in all books—that the reader will be transformed.

As books became part of human life, they began to change us. They do not simply reflect us, but shape us, turning us into the readers they would like to have. When, for example, books aimed specifically at young readers began to become popular in the mid-eighteenth century in Britain they participated in a cultural reconceptualizing of childhood as a distinctive human life stage. Children were no longer considered small adults; instead, their particular developmental needs were increasingly appreciated and codified. Books both established and met these needs. The extended title of one early book for children first published in 1744 gives a sense that the genre and the readership are mutually constitutive: *A Little Pretty Pocket-Book, Intended for the Instruction and Amusement of Little Master Tommy, and Pretty Miss Polly.*

With Two Letters from Jack the Giant-Killer; as also A Ball and Pincushion; The Use of which will infallibly make Tommy a good Boy, and Polly a good Girl. Children's books help to define the very category of child that they seem in fact to reflect; they work to construct the child who is simultaneously their implied reader. Something similar happens to all of us when we choose a book. Some aspect of it connects with who we already are, otherwise we probably wouldn't pick it from the shelves, but in reading it we will be turned, imperceptibly but inevitably, toward being the reader it imagined before we ever encountered it.

Books with a moral or didactic purpose make this transformation explicit—we will be thinner, or more successful, or saved, by reading them. The early editions of Dale Carnegie's *How to Win Friends and Influence People*, a self-proclaimed manifesto for transformation published in New York by Simon & Schuster in 1936, included unprinted pages at the end for "My experiences in applying the principles taught in this book." It's a nice, material invitation to think about the blank pages that are a standard feature of most books as a space for the reader to reflect on the ways the book has changed them. It's an example of what I've been arguing for throughout: that books as objects convey meanings in excess of their verbal content. Even their blank pages signify. Carnegie harnesses the form of his book explicitly to engage the reader in the kinds of self-improvement the chapters have been expounding. But this same expectation of change is really part of the invisible contract between all books and their readers. In this sense, all books are really self-help books. Where we don't enjoy or connect with a particular book, it is because we are resistant to our part of the bargain.

In fact, books can transform us without our even opening them. They are decorative as well as functional, props as well as properties. When people come into my office, which is stacked with books overflowing from every shelf and surface, they often ask if I have read all of the books. I haven't. There are lots of reasons for this nonreading. I buy some books because other people recommend them or they seem like things I ought to have but I don't have a particular reason to read them right now. I have books for review, and books for research, and books that I have been given or have otherwise acquired. And, I admit, I own many books I have bought as a substitute for reading them, or as a psychological reassurance that I have made a start on a project or begun to get to grips with a topic: buying a book, even if it remains unopened, often lends this entirely unjustified reassurance. The sum of this is an office that is part working library and part—I admit it—a carefully disheveled stage set cueing "bookish academic." My books here have a symbolic value, so that it is not really about what's in them but about how they are "read," without even being opened, by me or others. I'll leave to the reader to decide whether this breaks my own definition of books in the last chapter.

As this book has explored, we have always had different,

complex motives for our relationships with our books. Jorge Luis Borges described a book as "a relationship, an axis of innumerable relationships": *Portable Magic* has argued for two particular kinds of relationships in our long love affair with books. One is the interconnectedness of book form and book content. And the other is the reciprocity and proximity of books and their readers, in relationships that leave both parties changed. This copy of *Portable Magic* now carries traces of your DNA in its gutter, your fingerprints on its cover. If you own it, you can bend its page corners or write your name in it or make satirical comments in the margin. You can lend it, or give it away, or send it to the charity shop, but it will always be somehow yours. Thank you.

Notes

Introduction: Magic books

Joseph Jacobs's *English Fairy Tales* has been extensively reprinted since its first edition in 1890, from which I am quoting here. Stith Thompson's *Motif-Index of Folk Literature* (1955–8) is widely available online. Richard de Bury's *Philobiblon* ("The Love of Books") was written in Latin in the early fourteenth century, spread across Europe in manuscript and then in print, and was published in London at the end of the sixteenth century. I have quoted from the 1960 Shakespeare Head edition. Stephen King's *On Writing: A Memoir of the Craft* was first published in 2000. David Scott Kastan's distinction between platonic and pragmatic writing comes from his book *Shakespeare and the Book* (2001). The historic book odor wheel is discussed in C. Bembibre and M. Strlič, "Smell of heritage: a framework for the identification, analysis and archival of historic odours," *Heritage Science* 5 (2017); thanks to Sarah Wheale for the cat-litter tip. I've quoted Garrett Stewart from his stimulating book *Bookwork: Medium to Object to Concept to Art* (2011). Roger Chartier quotes the anecdote about Borges and *Don Quixote* in the introduction to his *Inscription and Erasure: Literature and Written Culture from the Eleventh to the Eighteenth Century* (2007). Milton's *Areopagitica* is widely available, most conveniently in William Poole's edition for Penguin Classics. The observation that every document of civilization is also a document of barbarism, and much more besides, comes from Walter Benjamin's collected essays *Illuminations*, translated by Harry Zohn and introduced by Hannah Arendt, first published in 1968 and reprinted many times since.

1. Beginnings: East, West, and Gutenberg

Online copies of Gutenberg Bibles are available via the British Library, the Beinecke Library of Yale University, and the Library of Congress in Washington, DC. In this section, I have drawn on Christopher de Hamel's great study *The Book: A History of the Bible* (2001), on Eric Marshall White's *Editio princeps: A History of the Gutenberg Bible* (2017), which gives a brief account of each known copy, and on the essays by Peter Kornicki, J. S. Edgren, Emile G. L. Schrijver, and Hortensia Calvo on global book traditions, including colonial printing, in Simon Eliot and Jonathan Rose (eds.), *The Companion to the History of the Book* (2nd edn., 2020). John Foxe's *Acts and Monuments* is available and searchable online at https://www.dhi.ac.uk/foxe/. The material on print and the Ottomans is indebted to Norman Housley, *Crusading and the Ottoman Threat, 1453–1505* (2012), and my early reports of the Gutenberg Bible are quoted from Martin Davies, "Juan de Carvajal and early printing: the 42-line Bible and the Sweynheym and Pannartz Aquinas," *The Library* s6-XVIII (1996). Louis Lavicomterie is quoted from Gary Kates, *The Cercle Social, the Girondins, and the French Revolution* (1985). The account of the Lenox sale is from the March 15, 1847, issue of *The Times*.

2. Queen Victoria in the trenches

I'm indebted here to Molly Guptill Manning, *When Books Went to War: The Stories that Helped Us Win World War II* (2014), William M. Leary Jr., "Books, Soldiers and Censorship during the Second World War," *American Quarterly* 20 (1968), John Cole (ed.), *Books in Action: The Armed Services Editions* (1984), and to the archives of the Council on Books in Wartime at Princeton University Library. Virginia Woolf's praise of Lytton Strachey is in her essay "The Art of Biography" (1939), included in numerous collections of her work, including *Selected Essays*, edited by David Bradshaw. Some of the history of paperback innovations comes from Kenneth C. Davis, *Two-Bit Culture: The Paperbacking of America* (1984). The aftermath of the Armed Services Editions draws on John B. Hench, *Books as Weapons: Propaganda, Publishing and the Battle for Global Markets in the Era of World War II* (2010) and Frances Stonor Saunders, *Who Paid the Piper? The CIA and the Cultural Cold War* (1999). John Preston's *Fall: The Mystery of Robert Maxwell* was published in 2020.

3. Christmas, gift books, and abolition

Archive.org and the New York Public Library have digitized a number of early-nineteenth-century gift books, from which I have taken the sample inscriptions; Katherine D. Harris's book *Forget Me Not: The Rise of the British Literary Annual 1823–1835* (2015) is their indispensable companion. Vita Sackville-West, with Dorothy Wellesley as editor, introduced a selection called *The Annual: Being a Selection from the Forget-Me-Nots, Keepsakes and Other Annuals of the Nineteenth Century* in 1930. Isabelle Lehuu's chapter on gift books in her *Carnival on the Page: Popular Print Media in Antebellum America* (2000) stresses networked emotion. Stephen Nissenbaum's *The Battle for Christmas: A Social and Cultural History of Our Most Cherished Holiday* (1997) discusses the history of seasonal gift-giving. I was alerted to the abolitionist gift books by Meaghan M. Fritz and Frank E. Fee Jr.'s article "To give the gift of freedom: gift books and the war on slavery," *American Periodicals* 23 (2013). The Royal Collection is searchable online at rct.uk. The story of Emperor Akbar and the Plantin Bible is told by Pierre du Jarric in *Akbar and the Jesuits: An Account of the Jesuit Missions to the Court of Akbar*, edited and translated by C. H. Payne (2004). Marcel Mauss's resonant anthropological study *The Gift* was first published in English in 1954 and has been much reprinted. Natalie Zemon Davis discusses sixteenth-century books as gifts in "Beyond the market: books as gifts in sixteenth-century France," *Transactions of the Royal Historical Society* 33 (1983). Wayne B. Gooderham's website bookdedications.co.uk gathers inscriptions from used books: he has collected some in his own book called *Dedicated to . . . : The Forgotten Friendships, Hidden Stories and Lost Loves Found in Second-Hand Books* (2013).

4. Shelfies: Anne, Marilyn, and Madame de Pompadour

The *Great Picture* can be viewed close up on the artuk.org website. I have drawn here on Graham Parry's "The *Great Picture* of Lady Anne Clifford," in *Art and Patronage in the Caroline Courts*, edited by David Howarth (1993), on Katherine Acheson (ed.), *Anne Clifford: The Memoir of 1603 and the Diary of 1616–19* (2007), and *The Diaries of Lady Anne Clifford*, edited by D. J. H. Clifford (1990). Jessica Malay has recently uncovered a contemporary catalogue of Anne's books, excitingly described in "Reassessing Anne Clifford's Books: the discovery of a new manuscript inventory," *The Papers of the Bibliographical Society of America* 115 (2021). Boucher's portrait of Madame de Pompadour is widely available online, including at wikiart.org. I've benefited from Elise Goodman's *The Portraits of Madame de Pompadour: Celebrating the Femme Savante* (2000) and Nancy Mitford's biography, published in 1954. On the annunciation tradition I'm indebted to Laura Saetveit Miles's essay in *Speculum* 89 (2014), "The origins and development of the Virgin Mary's Book at the Annunciation." Eve Arnold's photograph is on the cover of Declan Kiberd's *Ulysses and Us* (2009), and elsewhere. Jeanette Winterson chose the picture in a feature in the *Guardian* on April 29, 2006. Richard Brown asked Arnold for her recollections for his essay "Marilyn Monroe reading *Ulysses*: Goddess or postcultural cyborg?" in R. B. Kershner (ed.), *Joyce and Popular Culture* (1996). I've drawn here on Griselda Pollock's essay in *Journal of Visual Culture* 15 (2016), "Monroe's Molly: three reflections on Eve Arnold's photograph of Marilyn Monroe reading *Ulysses*," and, more generally, on Sarah Churchwell's *The Many Lives of Marilyn Monroe* (2005). Kevin Birmingham tells the story of *Ulysses*'s publication and censorship in detail in *The Most Dangerous Book: The Battle for James Joyce's "Ulysses"* (2014). Buzz Spector's suggestions about the erotics of reading are taken from "The fetishism of the book object" in *Art on Paper* 14 (2009).

5. Silent Spring *and the making of a classic*

Italo Calvino's "Why read the classics?" is reprinted in his *The Uses of Literature*, translated by Patrick Creagh (1987); Gérard Genette's *Paratexts: Thresholds of Interpretation*, translated by Jane Lewin, was published in 1997. *The New Yorker* published three sections of *Silent Spring* weekly from June 16, 1962. Janice Radway writes about book clubs in her *A Feeling for Books: The Book-of-the-Month Club, Literary Taste and Middle-Class Desire* (1997). There is a terrifically informative online exhibition, "Rachel Carson's *Silent Spring*, a book that changed the world," curated by Mark Stoll, at the Environment & Society Portal: http://www .environmentandsociety.org/exhibitions/rachel-carsons-silent-spring. I quote from baby boomers interviewed by Kenneth Davis in his *Two-Bit Culture: The Paperbacking of America* (1984). I am grateful to the library catalogues and booksellers on abebooks.com, whose descriptions have helped me flesh out the editions of Carson's book.

6. The Titanic *and book traffic*

Russell W. Belk's essay "Collectors and collecting" is included in *Interpreting Objects and Collections*, edited by Susan M. Pearce (1994), and his "Collecting as luxury consumption: effects on individuals and households" is in Stephen Satchell (ed.), *Collectible Investments for the High Net Worth Investor* (2009). Norman D. Weiner's essay on the psychopathology of bibliomania is in *Psychoanalytic Quarterly* 35 (1966). I have drawn on the essays by Leslie A. Morris in the *Harvard Library Bulletin* 6 (1995), "Harry Elkins Widener and A. S. W. Rosenbach: of books and friendship," and by Arthur Freeman in the 1977 edition of *The Book Collector* ("Harry Widener's last books: corrigenda"), and consulted A. S. W. Rosenbach's preface to the posthumous printing of Widener's Robert Louis Stevenson collection (1913). There are a disturbing number of accounts and retellings of the sinking of the *Titanic*. I have relied on the witness accounts gathered as *Voices from the Titanic*, edited by Geoff Tibballs (2012) and on Richard Davenport-Hines's

Titanic Lives: Migrants and Millionaires, Conmen and Crew (2012), which focuses on the social differentiations of the experience on board. The details of passengers on the *Titanic* are drawn from the extraordinary web resource *Encyclopedia Titanica* (www.encyclopedia-titanica.org), which includes a biography of every passenger and crew member; the Ellis Island records can be searched at heritage.statueofliberty.org. A digital version of the Kennicott Bible is available at http://bav.bod leian.ox.ac.uk/news/the-kennicott-bible; the picture of the migrants' Gideon Bibles was reproduced in the *New York Times* of July 2, 2018. Anna Pechurina's "Researching identities through material posses- sions: the case of diaspora objects" is published in *Current sociology* 68 (2020); I have drawn on theories of diaspora from the *Routledge Hand- book of Diaspora Studies*, edited by Robin Cohen and Carolin Fischer (2018). Carolyne Larrington's *Poetic Edda* was published in 2014. Jean- ette Greenfield discusses the Icelandic manuscripts in her *The Return of Cultural Treasures* (2nd edn., 1996); Dan Hicks's *The Brutish Museums: The Benin Bronzes, Colonial Violence and Cultural Restitution* was published in 2020.

7. Religions of the book

On the history of book adoption and development, I have drawn on work in the *Oxford Companion to the Book*, edited by Michael F. Suarez and H. R. Woudhuysen. The pioneering scholarship on the associa- tion of Christianity and the codex was by Colin Roberts and T. C. Skeat in *The Birth of the Codex*, first published in 1954. My quotation from Martial comes from the Loeb Classical Library translation by D. R. Shackleton Bailey. Christopher de Hamel's *The Book: A His- tory of the Bible* (2001), D. C. Parker's *Codex Sinaiticus: The Story of the World's Oldest Bible* (2010) and the website codexsinaiticus.org, which carries an account, carefully agreed between the monastery and the three holding libraries, of the history of the manuscript, have been invaluable. Richard de Bury's *Philobiblon* is widely available: I've used the 1960 Shakespeare Head Press edition because it is dedicated to our local bookseller, Basil Blackwell. Marshall McLuhan elaborates his celebrated dictum in *Understanding Media* (1964). I'm not an expert on neuroscience by any means, but I enjoyed reading Anne-Dominique Gindrat, Magali Chytiris, Myriam Balerna, Eric M. Rouiller, and Arko Ghosh, "Use-dependent cortical processing from fingertips in touch-screen phone users" in *Current Biology* 25 (2015). My information on books from different religious traditions comes from Johannes Pedersen, *The Arabic Book* (1984) and Emile G. L. Schrijver on the Hebrew book in Simon Eliot and Jonathan Rose (eds.), *A Companion to the History of the Book,* 2nd edn. (2020). There is more information about the Jedi religion than you could ever need at the official site starwars.com and the expansive fan site starwars.fandom.com.

8. May 10, 1933: burning books

Pepys's *Diary* is available online at pepysdiary.com, or in numerous editions, including the abridgement by Robert Latham, *The Diaries of Samuel Pepys* (2003). Carl S. Meyer's account, "Henry VIII burns Luther's books, 12 May 1521," was published in the *Journal of Ecclesiastical History* 9 (1958). Dirk Rohmann's *Christianity, Book-Burning and Censorship in Late Antiquity* (2017) is helpful on the early antecedents; Matthew Fishburn's *Burning Books* (2008) brings out the paradoxical ineffectuality of this practice. The difference between protocol and biographical objects, and much more about how to think about things as having lives and itineraries and personalities, comes from the anthropologist Janet Hoskins's *Biographical Objects: How Things Tell the Stories of People's Lives* (1998). The anecdote about Stanley came via Stephen Greenblatt, *Shakespearean Negotiations* (1988), and is detailed in H. M. Stanley, *Through the Dark Continent* (1878): this book coined the now-infamous term for Africa. Foxe's *Book of Martyrs* or, more properly, *Acts and Monuments*, is available online (https://www.dhi.ac.uk/foxe/). I quote Heine's *Almansor* from the English translation by Hal Draper. The United States Holocaust Memorial Museum has an important online exhibit about book burnings and the American response. I have drawn on contemporary news reports in *Newsweek, The New York Times,* and *The Times* of London. I quote from Ray Bradbury's "Afterword" to the

1993 HarperCollins edition of *Fahrenheit 451*; Mumford Jones's address is in the *Bulletin of the American Library Association* 27 (1933). Richard Ovenden's brilliant book *Burning the Books: A History of Knowledge under Attack* (2020) offers a powerful counterview to the argument in this chapter.

9. Library books, camp, and malicious damage

Ilsa Colsell's *Malicious Damage* (2013) tells the story of Orton and Halliwell's library découpage and does a brilliant detective job in tracing the source of the images used in the designs. The material related to the case is all held by Islington Local History Centre Special Collections: some of it is online at www.joeorton.org. The trial is covered in *The Times*, May 16, 1962. I've benefited from analyses by Melissa Hardie in *Angelaki: Journal of the Theoretical Humanities* 23 (2018), Emma Parker in *Studies in Theatre and Performance* 37 (2017), and Matt Cook in *History Workshop Journal* 66 (2008). Susan Sontag's indispensable "Notes on Camp" is available as a cute Penguin Modern paperback (2018), which is my go-to birthday card for everyone I know; it's also included in her *Against Interpretation and Other Essays* (lots of editions). The history of the Bodleian Library oath is told by W. H. Clennell in the *Bodleian Library Record* 20 (2007). On libraries I've drawn in particular on Thomas Kelly's *History of Public Libraries in Great Britain 1845–1965* (1973). The essays on object biography—attempts to understand things and their lives—are published as *The Social Life of Things: Commodities in Cultural Perspective*, edited by Arjun Appadurai (1986). The information about disinfection and disease comes from Leah Price's wonderful book *How to Do Things with Books in Victorian Britain* (2012).

10. Censored books: "237 goddams, 58 bastards, 31 Chrissakes, and 1 fart"

The censored Valladolid Shakespeare is online via luna.folger.edu and discussed in David Scott Kastan's *A Will to Believe: Shakespeare and Religion* (2014). Joseph Mendham produced an edition of the *Index of*

Prohibited Books—subtitle: "being the latest specimen of the literary policy of the Church of Rome" in 1840: it is available at archive.org. The transcripts of the trial of Lawrence's novel are published as *The Trial of Lady Chatterley: Regina v. Penguin Books Limited* by C. H. Rolph. Nick Thomas's essay on popular responses to the trial in *Cultural and Social History* 10 (2013) is recommended, and Elisabeth Ladenson's *Dirt for Art's Sake: Books on Trial from "Madame Bovary" to "Lolita"* (2012) gives wonderful longer context on book censorship; Paul S. Boyer's *Purity in Print: Book Censorship in America from the Gilded Age to the Computer Age* (2002) is also indispensable on the long twentieth century. On Salinger I have drawn on Jack Salzman (ed.), *New Essays on "The Catcher in the Rye"* (1991), Stephen J. Whitfield, "Cherished and cursed: toward a social history of *The Catcher in the Rye*," *New England Quarterly* 70 (1997), and Pamela Hunt Steinle's *In Cold Fear: "The Catcher in the Rye" Censorship Controversies and Postwar American Character* (2000): the title of this chapter comes from Steinle's compilation of complaints. On the American schoolroom I've drawn on the American Library Association website ala.org and on Herbert Foerstel's *Banned in the USA: A Reference Guide to Book Censorship in Schools and Public Libraries* (2002).

11. Mein Kampf: *freedom to publish?*

Guenter Lewy's book *Harmful and Undesirable: Book Censorship in Nazi Germany* (2016) traces the regime's attitude to print. On typography, especially Fraktur, see Robin Kinross, *Modern Typography: An Essay in Critical History* (2008). On the history of *Mein Kampf* in the US and the UK, see James Barnes and Patience Barnes, *Hitler's "Mein Kampf" in Britain and America: A Publishing History 1930–39* (1980). A fuller account of all the editions is provided in the bibliography compiled by Stephen R. Pastore, Andreas Stanik, and Steven M. Brewster in 2016. Numerous articles were prompted by the end of copyright restrictions on *Mein Kampf*, including in the *Atlantic* (Steven Luckert, December 31, 2015) and the *Guardian* (Kate Connolly, January 1, 2016). I have drawn on the review of the critical edition published as "Struggles with 'Mein Kampf'" by Anson Rabinbach in the *Times Literary*

Supplement (September 16, 2016). I have also made use of the excellent website of the Wiener Holocaust Library (wienerholocaustlibrary .org). George Orwell's review is reproduced in volume 2 of *The Collected Essays, Journalism and Letters of George Orwell*, edited by Sonia Orwell and Ian Angus (1968). Suman Gupta's chapter "The Indian readers of Hitler's *Mein Kampf*" in his *Consumable Texts in Contemporary India* (2015) is recommended.

12. Talismanic books

Edward Brooke-Hitching's *The Madman's Library: The Greatest Curiosities of Literature* (2020) alerted me to Morosini's gun-book. Rosenbach's nightmarish bullet-scarred regiments come from his *Books and Bidders: The Adventures of a Bibliophile* (1927). The Library of Congress discusses its copy of *Kim* online at https://www.loc.gov/item/myloc12/; Christina Mitrentse's website is christinamitrentse.com. David Cressy's article "Books as totems in seventeenth-century England and New England" is in the *Journal of Library History* 21 (1986); Rowan Watson's "Some non-textual uses of books," in *A Companion to the History of the Book*, edited by Simon Eliot and Jonathan Rose (2020), has some wonderful examples; I've gained much, again, from Christopher de Hamel's *The Book: A History of the Bible* (2001). "Mite Qur'ans for Indian markets: David Bryce in the late nineteenth and early twentieth century" by Kristina Myrvold (*Postscripts* 9 [2019]) helped me to see some of the orientalist work the amulet Qur'an is doing in Lawrence's and other accounts: I'm especially grateful to its author for sending me a copy during lockdown. On *sortes*, I have drawn on Penelope Meyers Usher's "'Pricking in Virgil': early modern prophetic *phronesis* and the *Sortes Virgilianae*," *Journal of Medieval and Early Modern Studies* 45 (2015); Aubrey's account is in his *Remains of Gentilism and Judaism*, collected and published in 1881. Augustine's account of his bibliomantic conversion is found in volume 1, book 8, of his *Confessions*, here translated for the Loeb Classical Library by Carolyn J.-B. Hammond. Dennis Prager's column about the oath of US senators was published on November 28, 2006, at townhall.com. Jack Goody's ethnographic work is taken from his edited volume *Literacy in Traditional Societies* (1968); other examples, including Henry Festing Jones on *Tristram Shandy*, are drawn from Holbrook Jackson's *Anatomy of Bibliomania* (1930). Laura Lunger Knoppers's work on copies of *Eikon Basilike* is published in her *Politicising Domesticity from Henrietta Maria to Milton's Eve* (2011); Isabel Hofmeyr's fascinating "transnational history" of *Pilgrim's Progress* in colonial and other contexts is *The Portable Bunyan* (2004). The British Library has digitized Milton's Bible inscriptions at https://www.bl.uk/collection-items/john-miltons-family-bible; Mike Spathaky's genealogical website is at www.spathaky.name. I found out about John Underwood's funerary arrangements in Elizabeth Barry's fascinating essay "From epitaph to obituary" in the *International Journal of Cultural Studies* 11 (2008).

13. Skin in the game: bookbinding and African American poetry

On Arcimboldo, I have drawn on Eugene Muench's *Arcimboldo's "Librarian": A Biblioportrait* (1990) and Sven Alfons's essay "The museum as image of the world," in *The Arcimboldo Effect: Transformations of the Face from the 16th to the 20th Century* (1987). K. C. Elhard notes that librarians are none too keen on this professional image in "Reopening the book on Arcimboldo's *Librarian*," *Libraries & Culture* 40 (2005). The Human Library is at humanlibrary.org. Flann O'Brien riffs on book-handling in the *Irish Times*, gathered in *The Best of Myles* (2007). Kathryn M. Rudy's "Dirty books: quantifying patterns of use in medieval manuscripts using a densitometer" is in the *Journal of Historians of Netherlandish Art* 2 (jhna.org). Work by Righetti and Zilberstein was reported by Sam Knight in "Do proteins hold the key to the past?" in *The New Yorker*, November 26, 2018. Lovecraft's "The Hound" is out of copyright and thus widely available online and also in *The Complete Fiction of H. P. Lovecraft* (2016). Megan Rosenbloom's *Dark Archives: A Librarian's Investigation into the Science and History of Books Bound in Human Skin* (2020) is an unsensational and clear account building on the scientific project documented at anthropomorphicbooks.org: it was reviewed by Mike

Jay in *The New York Review of Books* on November 5, 2020, and Paul Needham, author of a 2014 blog about the ethics of human skin bindings at https://www.princeton.edu/~needham/Bouland.pdf, wrote a follow-up letter to the paper on December 3, 2020. I have gained from the discussion about appropriate treatment and curation of human material from *Regarding the Dead: Human Remains in the British Museum*, edited by Alexandra Fletcher, Daniel Antoine, and J. D. Hill (2014), available online at britishmuseum.org. On Phillis Wheatley, I have drawn on Joseph Rezek's essay "Transatlantic traffic: Phillis Wheatley and her books" in *The Unfinished Book*, edited by Alexandra Gillespie and Deidre Lynch (2020), Henry Louis Gates Jr.'s *The Trials of Phillis Wheatley: America's First Black Poet and Her Encounters with the Founding Fathers* (2003), which also discusses the late reception of Wheatley in canons of Black writing and experience, and Vincent Carretta, *Phillis Wheatley: Biography of a Genius in Bondage* (2011).

14. Choose Your Own Adventure: readers' work

Grangerized books are discussed by Lucy Peltz, *Facing the Text: Extra-Illustration, Print Culture and Society in Britain, 1769–1840* (2017), and some examples are drawn from Holbrook Jackson's expansive, fascinating, and frustratingly under-referenced *The Anatomy of Bibliomania* (1930). Laurie Maguire's *The Rhetoric of the Page* (2020) provided the Donne examples and a model for the larger inquiry. Wolfgang Iser's work is available in English translation most readily in "The reading process: a phenomenological approach," *New Literary History* 3 (1972). I found out about Lady Bradshaigh from Peter Sabor's article "Rewriting *Clarissa*: alternative endings by Lady Echlin, Lady Bradshaigh and Samuel Richardson," *Eighteenth-Century Fiction* 29 (2016–17), and Janine Barchas, with Gordon D. Fulton, *The Annotations in Lady Bradshaigh's Copy of "Clarissa"* (1998): Princeton University Library has put her annotated copy of the novel online at https://dpul.princeton.edu /pudl0058/catalog/dz010s704. B. S. Johnson describes his aims for *The Unfortunates* in his memoir *Aren't You Rather Young to Be Writing Your Memoirs?* (1967). Jay David Bolter and Richard Grusin discuss *Myst* in their important work on digital media, *Remediation: Understanding New Media* (2000); Adam Hammond reviews that intervention in his "Books in videogames," in Alexandra Gillespie and Deidre Lynch (eds.), *The Unfinished Book* (2020).

15. The empire writes back

Works I've drawn from on the early colonial settlement and John Eliot include Kathryn N. Gray's *John Eliot and the Praying Indians of Massachusetts Bay* (2015); Linford D. Fisher's "America's first Bible: native uses, abuses, and reuses of the Indian Bible of 1663," in *The Bible in American Life*, edited by Philip Goff, Arthur E. Farnsley II, and Peter J. Thuesen (2017); and *Writing Indians: Literacy, Christianity, and Native Community in Early America* (2000) by Hilary E. Wyss. On the early colonial press, see Hugh Amory, *Bibliography and the Book Trades: Studies in the Print Culture of Early New England* (2005). Samuel Ponampam's confession is included in *Early Native Literacies in New England: A Documentary and Critical Anthology*, edited by Kristina Bross and Hilary E. Wyss (2008). The Bible marginalia are transcribed in Ives Goddard and Kathleen J. Bragdon's *Native Writings in Massachusett* (1988). Mary Louise Pratt's concept of the contact zone comes from *Imperial Eyes: Travel Writing and Transculturation* (1992). On marginalia more generally, see H. L. Jackson's *Marginalia: Readers Writing in Books* (2001) and Katherine Acheson's edited collection, *Early Modern English Marginalia* (2019); if you are more a Facebook than a rare-book person, you might enjoy, as I do, the group Oxford University Marginalia, which ranges from finely crafted medieval examples to cheerfully puerile graffiti in contemporary library books. The inspirational Wôpanâak Language Reclamation Project is at www.wlrp.org; please support it if you can.

16. What is a book?

UNESCO's definitions of a book are developed in Robert Escarpit's *The Book Revolution* (English translation 1966). Anne Welsh discusses Google's definitions in her "Historical bibliography in the digital world," in *Digital Humanities in Practice*, edited by Claire Warwick, Melissa Terras, and Julianne Nyhan (2012). I've quoted Joseph Dane from his *What Is a Book? The Study of Early Printed Books* (2012), Stephen Emmel from Andrew Piper's brilliant *Book Was There: Reading in Electronic Times* (2012), and Roger E. Stoddard from his "Morphology and the book from an American perspective," *Printing History* 9 (1987). James Raven's *What Is the History of the Book?* (2018) is recommended: I've quoted from his piece for *LitHub* on https://lithub.com/what-exactly-do-we-mean-by-a-book/. The academic article about immersive reading is Miha Kovač, Angus Phillips, Adriaan van der Weel, and Ruediger Wischenbart, "What is a book?," *Publishing Research Quarterly* 35 (2019). Brian Cummings's observation of parallels between early print and e-readers comes from his own version of "What is a book?" in Alexandra Gillespie and Deidre Lynch (eds.), *The Unfinished Book* (2020). Johanna Drucker discusses e-books and e-readers in her "The virtual codex: from page space to e-space," in Ray Siemans and Susan Schriebman's *A Companion to Digital Literary Studies* (2007). Mindell Dubansky's collection of blooks is documented in the catalogue *Blooks: The Art of Books that Aren't*, which accompanied a 2016 exhibition at the Grolier Club of the same name. I found Garrett Stewart's book *Book, Text, Medium: Cross-Sectional Reading for a Digital Age* (2021) and Keith A. Smith and Fred Jordan's *Bookbinding for Book Artists* (1998) stimulating. Tom Phillips's *A Humament* has a website that includes interviews and articles about the project: https://www.tomphillips.co.uk/humument.

Acknowledgments

Throughout this book, completed during lockdown and library closures, I have made extensive use of online library resources, particularly digitization projects at the Morgan Library New York, the New York Public Library, the British Library, and the Bodleian Library. I want to give a shout-out in particular to the Bodleian's indispensable Scan and Deliver Team via their captain, James Shaw. I have also used the fabulous collective might of abebooks.co.uk to trace editions (and sometimes to buy examples). In the process, I have enjoyed the bookish company of #booktwitter, especially the accounts of @wynkenhimself aka Sarah Werner, author of the wonderful guide *Studying Early Printed Books 1450–1800*; @aarontpratt aka Aaron T. Pratt, curator at the incredible library of the Ransom Center in Austin, Texas; @liamsims aka Liam Sims, posting gems from the Cambridge University Library; my Oxford colleague Adam Smyth @adamSmy36314691, who also blogs on quirky book-related topics, and Martine van Elke @martinevanelk, whose work on women writers and readers is highly recommended. Follow these if you want regular updates from the coalface of bookhood.

I have ranged far beyond my own specialisms in this book and gathered lots of debts along the way. To Charlotte Brewer, David Dwan, Ayoush Lazikani, and Namratha Rao, and our students at Hertford: thank you. To Madeline Slaven, Sallyanne Gilchrist, Jo Maddocks, and Sarah Wheale of the Bodleian Libraries, and to Kate Rudy, for all the work on the delayed "Sensational Books" exhibition, thank you. To Catherine Clarke, Zoë Pagnamenta, Chloe Currens, Sarah Day, Erroll McDonald, Rebecca Lee, Stephen Ryan, and your colleagues for turning this into a book, thank you. And to Abi Adams-Prassl, Jeremias Adams-Prassl, Annie Ashworth, Emily Bartels, Judy Beckett, Julia Bray, Philip Bullock, Ben Cartlidge, Thea Crapper, Charlotte Davies, Stefano

ACKNOWLEDGMENTS

Evangelista, Mitzi Feller, Tom Fletcher, Beatrice Groves, Lucy Gwynne, Carol McNeil Hagan, Jo Hamill, James Hawes, Jeri Johnson, Hester Lees-Jeffries, James Macfarlane, Nan Macfarlane, O. V. Macfarlane, Phil Macfarlane, Laurie Maguire, Hilary Mantel, Val McDermid, Kathryn Murphy, Kristina Myrvold, Paul Needham, Esther Osorio Whewell, Gill Partington, Amanda Robson, Shef Rogers, Alice Roques, Brett Rosenberg, Renée Roux, Beaty Rubens, Paul Salzman, Charlotte Scott, Jason Scott-Warren, Adam Smyth, Hugo Thurston, Christopher Tyerman, Abigail Williams, and Henry Woudhuysen: thank you, for help on books, encouragement, and much else besides. I wish my mum had been here to help: she made books magic. Dearest Rosie Brougham: thank you for stepping into her place on so many occasions, and for those formative childhood visits to Walker's bookshop in Headingley. This book is for Elizabeth Macfarlane, with such love.

Index

Abraham, Joseph and Sophie, 113

Ackermann, Rudolph, *Forget-Me-Not*, 55–6, 58, 59, 60, 62–3

Adams, John Quincey, 216

advertisements, 11, 62

Africa: apartheid in South Africa, 65–6; enslaved peoples of, 35, 64, 235–42; and European colonialism, 34, 141–2, 215; Mowa people, 141–2, 215; printed books in, 133

African National Congress, 65–6

Ai Weiwei, 169–70

Akbar, Mughal emperor, 67–9

Albatross (Hamburg-based firm), 49–50, 52

Albers, Josef, 169

Alchandreus (philosopher), 66

Alexandria, Library of, 121, 156

Algonquin peoples, 264–75

Allen, Woody, 188

Alte Pinakothek, Munich, 79

Amazon (company), 136, 164, 202–3, 258–9, 283, 285

Ambrose, 81

American Animals (Bart Layton crime docudrama, 2018), 159

American Family Association, 187, 217

American Library Association (ALA), 186, 187

American Revolution, 236, 239–40, 242

Andreasson, Pal, 113

annuals, literary, 55–9; blank, illustrated presentation plates, 59–60; literary content, 56, 58, 62–4; luxury bindings, 60–1, 63; marketing techniques, 62

Anselm of Laeon, 200

anthropodermic bindings, 15, 231–5, 240–2

Antiquarian Booksellers' Association of America, 97

antiquity, classical, 123, 124, 125–6, 138, 210–13

Antrim, County, 281

Antwerp, 67–8

Arcimboldo, Giuseppe, 224–5

Arendt, Hannah, 194